AF323456

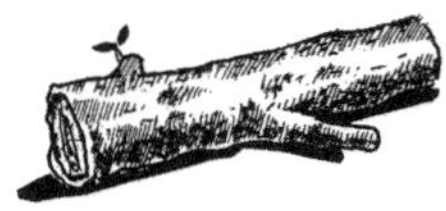

Editor
Cynthia Davidson

Managing Editor
Patrick Templeton

Editorial Interns
Osvaldo Delbrey Ortiz
Anna Renken

Protagonists
Thomas Daniell
Todd Gannon
Catherine Ingraham
Sanford Kwinter
Manuel Orazi
Bryony Roberts
Julie Rose
Sarah Whiting

www.anycorp.com

In late June, when the Gagosian Gallery in New York opened "Social Works," an exhibition of work by Black artists curated by Antwaun Sargent, the gallery also published a glossy compendium of the artists' projects and ideas, often presented through conversations. One of those conversations is between Rick Lowe, a painter in the show, and Walter Hood, a landscape architect whose proposed towers for Oakland were in the Museum of Modern Art's spring exhibition, "Reconstructions: Architecture and Blackness in America." They spoke about many things, including how they feel socially and culturally boxed in because of the way the public perceives the work of Black artists and designers. What follows here is a brief and, I believe, important excerpt from their conversation:

RL: So this exhibition that Antwaun is doing at Gagosian is called "Social Works," and I think it's very interesting that this conversation [on Black social practice] is happening in that kind of space. Also with you and the whole group having that conversation at MoMA about architecture. It's an amazing moment in time – but I don't know if it's the beginning of something, the opening up of something, or if it's just a moment.

WH: Sorry, it's a moment.

RL: Oh, Walter, man, you're too much like me. I'm looking for that person who's going to be like, *No, this is going to open up the world.*

WH: It's a moment because the conversations are still set in these narrow contexts. Going back to our conversation about getting out of a box, I think when more of us break out of this box, that's going to be the moment when shit starts to happen. Because we'll have multiple voices then, right?

RL: Absolutely. We've talked about this before: what's missing in the current movements is any kind of infrastructure that develops institutions that can carry things broader and longer than we as individuals can. How can we build something that's broader than me, broader than you? Because otherwise it's just a moment.

Two pieces in this issue of *Log* seize on this moment: a conversation on Black social practice with Thelma Golden, David Adjaye, and Lowe, and a review of the MoMA exhibition by Charles L. Davis II. Both of these extend the moment with probing insights and questions about the history of Black modernism and Black space and place that warrant thoughtful and actionable responses. A third, a group reporting on the Africatown neighborhood in Mobile, Alabama, attempts to build on the moment so that over time, the revitalization of a historic 19th-century African American settlement has the possibility to become a thriving 21st-century Black space. In other words, the moment that Lowe and Hood discuss cannot be squandered. This moment must be seen as an opportunity to undertake a quest for change, not just in art galleries and museums, but outside their walls, in society at large. – *CD*

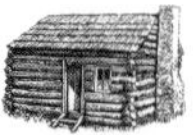

Log 52 Copyright © 2021 Anyone Corporation. All Rights Reserved. ISSN: 1547-4690. ISBN: 978-1-7365007-0-5. Printed in USA. *Log* is published three times a year by Anyone Corporation, a nonprofit corporation in the State of New York with editorial and business offices at 41 West 25th Street, 11th floor, New York, NY 10010. Subscription for 3 issues: $45 US; $49 CAN/MEX; $69 International. Distributed by Idea Books and Motto. Single issues are $18 plus shipping. The opinions expressed herein are not necessarily those of the protagonists or of the board of the Anyone Corporation. Send inquiries, letters, and submissions to log@anycorp.com.

Log

SUMMER 2021 · Observations on architecture and the contemporary city

General Observation:

Mitchell Rue Carson on Living with Other People's Stuff 38 . . .
Osvaldo Delbrey Ortiz on *Ghost Forest* 88 . . .
Ned Dodington on "Nature" 8 . . .
Kate Heath on Vanderbilt Avenue 78 . . .
Anna Renken on a Highway 26 . . .

Cover Story:

Greenwood, Tulsa, Oklahoma
Postcard: Rick Lowe, *Black Wall Street Journey #7*, 2021.
© Rick Lowe Studio. Photo: Thomas Dubrock. Courtesy the artist and Gagosian.

52

An exploration of architecture's ability (or lack of) to evolve in dialogue with society.

Catching Up with Life

Family, love, friendship, work, labour, governance, ownership, debt, consumerism, fertility, death, time, retirement, automation, and digital omnipresence.

Architecture

From 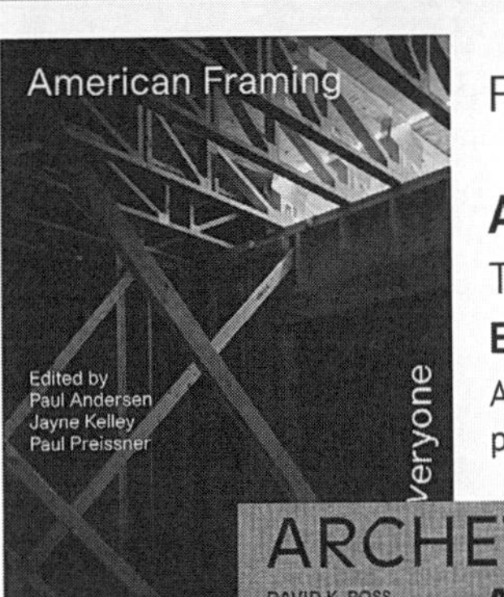 PARK BOOKS

American Framing
The Same Something for Everyone
Edited by Paul Andersen, Jayne Kelley, and Paul Preissner
Archival drawings and historical images, along with newly commissioned photographs by Linda Robbennolt, Daniel Shea, and Chris Strong, in addition to plans and drawings, shed new light on this quintessentially American method of construction.
Paper $40.00

Archetypes
David K. Ross
Edited by Reto Geiser
Archetypes features a recent series by David K. Ross. His images of architectural mock-ups, staged at night with dramatic lighting that isolates structures from their surroundings, demonstrate how these objects have become a charged form of proto-architecture.
Standpunkte
Cloth $49.00

Architecture and Micropolitics
Four Projects by Farshid Moussavi Architecture, 2010–2020
Farshid Moussavi
Moussavi shows how the specific character of contemporary architecture involves enriching the pragmatic aspect of creating architecture with random elements and subjective factors. Thus, the micropolitics of our everyday lives becomes the basis for our built architecture.
Paper $65.00

From *gta Verlag* publishers

Grand Gestures
Edited by Adam Jasper and Stefan Neuner
A grand, symbolic project may shape city identity and serve its needs, but a grand gesture is a performance in which the intention fails to line up with the result. The contributors focus on urban history and architectural historiography that are characterized by this irony.
gta papers
Paper $25.00

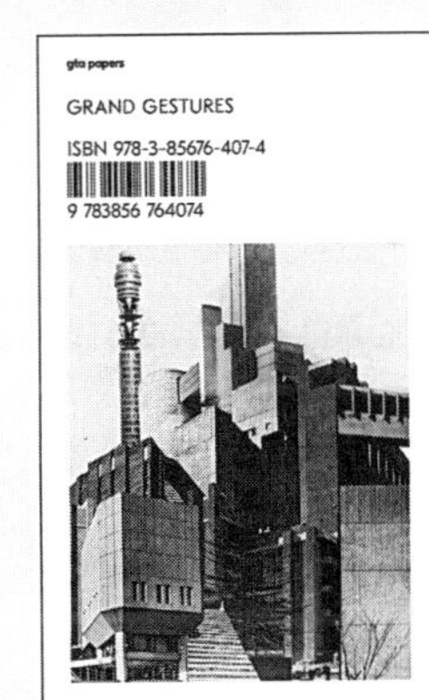

Distributed by the University of Chicago Press www.press.uchicago.edu

Architecture

From **HIRMER** Publishers

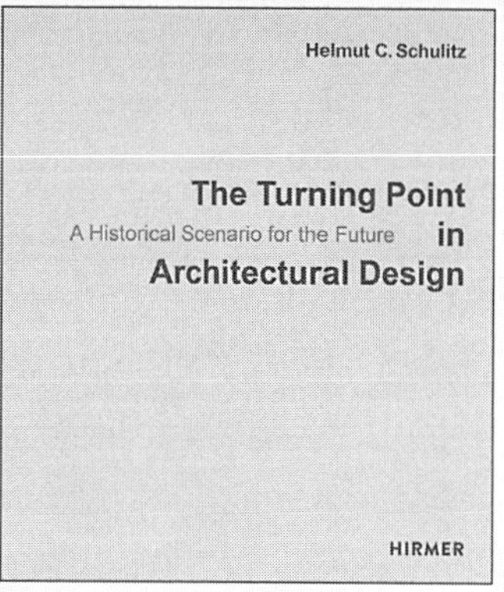

The Turning Point in Architectural Design
A Historical Scenario for the Future
Helmut C. Schulitz

Over the past five hundred years, a rift has grown between the design and construction of buildings. This volume does not lament this rift, but rather sees it as an opportunity to explore new horizons in building design in the era of climate change.

Cloth $45.00

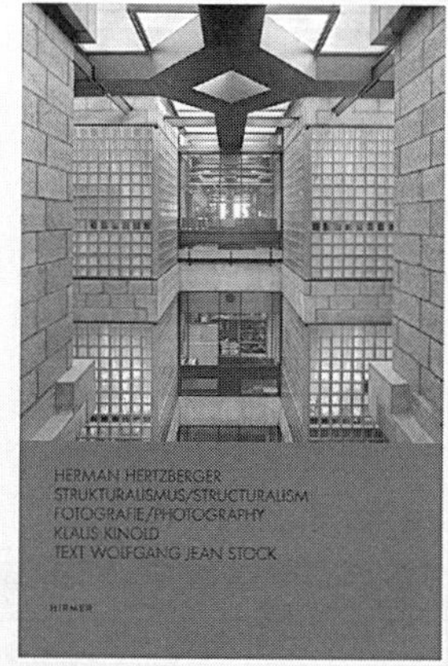

Hermann Hertzberger
Structuralism
Wolfgang Jean Stock
With Photography by Klaus Kinold

The architect Herman Hertzberger is one of the most important representatives of Dutch Structuralism. This movement, which emerged in 1960, takes as its starting point the idea that architecture should value the archetypal behaviors of humankind.

Cloth $45.00

From **REAKTION BOOKS**

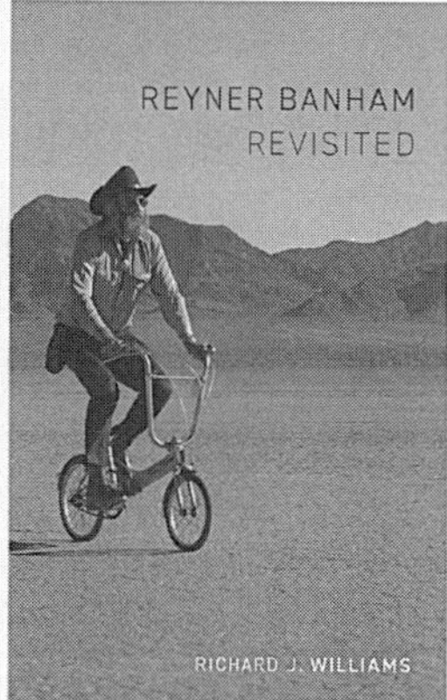

Reyner Banham Revisited
Richard J. Williams

"A truly ambitious task. . . . This book invites readers into the universe of one of the most brilliant and uncategorizable critics of modern architecture, cities, and mass culture."—*Domus*

Cloth $35.00

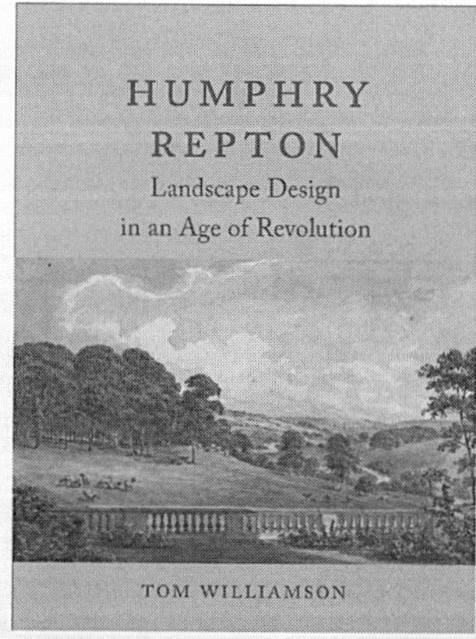

Humphry Repton
Landscape Design in an Age of Revolution
Tom Williamson

"Displays a wealth of new research which has been marshalled with thoughtfulness, curiosity, and intellectual dexterity to produce a forensic analysis of a complex man and his landscape aesthetic."—*Garden History*

Cloth $50.00

SCI-Arc

EDGE
Center for Advanced Studies in Architecture

MS Design Theory and Pedagogy
MS Architectural Technologies
MS Design of Cities
MS Fiction and Entertainment
MS Synthetic Landscapes

sciarc.edu

Hello *Log* Team,

Just a quick note to say that while I very much appreciate the attention to and inclusion of nonhuman and "natural" actors in a broader design conversation I found the segment The Return of Nature in *Log* 49 and the corresponding virtual panel discussion to be surprisingly disappointing.

Despite Gökhan Kodalak's insightful and well-crafted review of Spinoza's treatise and its suggested application to Architecture, I found the subsequent essays and online forum to almost uniformly disregard its lessons (to wit the continued references to "nature" and "city" in the online discussion and the technocentrism in Jenny E. Sabin's work which simply continue to entrench anthropocentrism). But moreover, *Log* 49 seems to have missed or intentionally excluded the work of dozens of currently practicing architects, designers, and artists who are working, while perhaps not explicitly, in all respects in the spirit of Spinoza (and Jakob von Uexküll, Jacques Derrida, Donna Haraway, etc.). Practitioners like Joyce Hwang, Natalie Jeremijenko, Kate Orff, Simone Ferracina, Amy Haigh, to name a few, have significant bodies of work that indeed transcend the nature-culture divide and posit a world where there is no longer an architecture-environment division (see more at expandedenvironment.org).

Finally, with all due respect to Professor Sanford Kwinter, I have to disagree with the reprisal of *nature*. There's good reason why such a word has been relegated to the past. Along with Derrida's *animal*, *nature* is a word that we have given ourselves the right to impose upon others. Not only that, but as Paul Rabinow has famously said, nature has not been "natural" for centuries if ever.

To perpetuate its use in common parlance is at our extreme risk. I believe Spinoza would agree, any concept of "the natural" or "nature," when not tied to an ontological qualifier (God), continues to drive a wedge between "culture," and by extension, "human." If we are to take Spinoza seriously, there never was or has been nature as such but only life and the environment and webs of enmeshment. Humans are part of this enmeshment; our homes, cities and worlds are a part of this enmeshment. Our only hope of avoiding our current existential crisis requires the erasure of such false binaries. Not their revival.

My two cents: *nature* should be buried in the past along with other *n* words not mentioned in polite company.

Sincerely,
Ned Dodington, AIA, LEED Green Associate
Houston, Texas

Fonna Forman
& Teddy Cruz

On Propinquity: Return the Body To Democracy

Editor's note: On March 26, 2021, Fonna Forman and Teddy Cruz presented an earlier version of this text in an online event called Ninety Minutes with Michael, a celebration of the life and work of architect and urbanist Michael Sorkin, who died from COVID-19 on March 26, 2020.

1. All quotations are from Michael Sorkin, *1997 Raoul Wallenberg Lecture*, ed. Kent Kleinman (Ann Arbor: University of Michigan College of Architecture + Urban Planning, 1997).

American society has been divided between those who wear masks and those who don't, between those eager to be vaccinated and those who refuse. The dissolution of social reciprocity, the collision between collective commitment and rugged individualism, between public and private, remains the single greatest obstacle to healing our society and building more equitable and inclusive cities as we slowly emerge from this pandemic. And climate change is accelerating. COVID-19 was the canary in the coal mine, like the universe warning us to get our priorities straight.

We hear every day about viral mutations, and we wonder: Can the virus – this virus that took Michael Sorkin – mutate into an unexpected antidote for selfishness? Can this moment expose the collective costs of austerity, of eroding the social safety net, of neglecting public challenges like racism, deepening inequality, and surging nationalism everywhere?

In 1997, Michael was invited to deliver the Raoul Wallenberg Lecture at the University of Michigan. Wallenberg was a Swedish diplomat and architect who saved thousands of Jews in German-occupied Hungary during the later stages of World War II. Honoring this humanitarian trafficker of people, Michael called his talk "Traffic in Democracy." A powerful reflection on the afflictions of urban democracy, the piece transcends decades, Michael's voice lampooning the idiocy and injustices of rapidly ascending neoliberal life in late 20th-century America – and yet it is astonishingly germane to this moment.

Michael's narrative centers on the idea of propinquity, a concept that he and Joan Copjec explored further in their 1999 collection *Giving Ground: The Politics of Propinquity*. For Michael, physically "being together," bodies in space, was essential to the practice of deliberative democracy – and it was radically opposed to the American version of democracy, born on the frontier and understood as the right to be left alone.[1] Michael valued an urbanity of propinquity – equitable

linkages, connections, flows, and exchanges, where freedom
is a collective and civic concept, active, positive, participatory.
At bottom, propinquity summarized Michael's determination
to coexist with others in urban space. We cannot possibly
imagine freedom "outside of a structure of interaction with
others." *City air makes people free.*

Propinquity was an illuminating concept to us back then,
and we wondered how we had ever lived without it. Now,
with Michael gone, as we convene in our Zoom boxes, we feel
we have never in our lives needed this concept more.

Democracy demands cities designed for propinquity.
Michael loved the Athenian Agora, a "funky" urban space that
"supported both efficient passage and organized encounters
while simultaneously offering innumerable routes and hence
innumerable circumstances for chance, unstructured, acciden-
tal, and serendipitous encounters . . . intrinsic to the working of
democracy." He might as well have been describing his beloved
New York City – a perpetually unstable "juxtaposition engine,"
as he called it.

But Michael worried that propinquity was under attack
by a variety of forces, some remarkably relevant to our
moment. One was the systematic dismantling of the public,
a function of both fashionable communitarian erosion from
within and privatization from without. He worried that iden-
titarian entrenchment fragmented the public into multiple
publics vying for recognition, which undermined collective
resistance to the forces of privatization encroaching into our
public spaces. Communitarianism also unwittingly fueled
strategies to market architecture as a bridge to fixed identities
that typically ends up dispossessing vulnerable people and gen-
trifying urban neighborhoods.

He never imagined the virtual world we now inhabit. But
even in its nascence, Michael saw the internet as a menacing
threat to democracy. While proponents were heralding "the
possibility of instantaneous and free global communication"
– and there were emancipatory examples around the world,
no doubt – Michael worried about reinventing proximity
through virtual encounter and saw little value, for example,
in virtual town halls, which he described as a passive "spectacle of *someone else* being heard."

For Michael, democracy demands participation reliably
"in the open." He asked: "What happens when neither wealth
nor information nor happiness is exchanged face-to-face,
when communication increasingly takes place by dissolving
the space of action?"

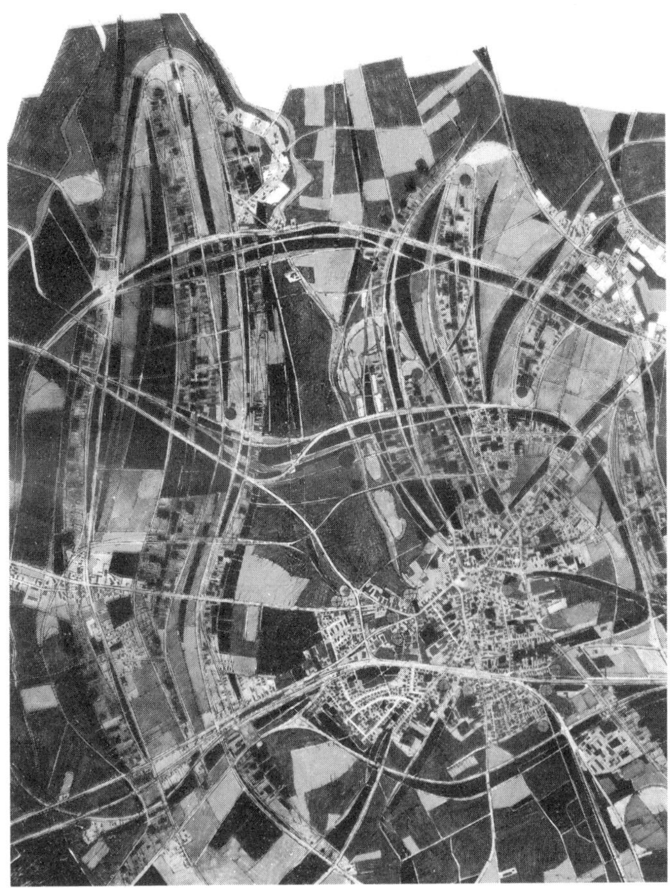

Michael's was an urbanity of the body. "If the body ceases to be the privileged means of participation in and enjoyment of urban life," he said, "urban life is at an end." For him the answer to a bodiless body politic, to antipublic, anticollective, consumerized idiocy, was always *to return the body to democracy*. This is the driving theme of his Wallenberg Lecture, and we have no doubt this would be his response today. *Return the body to democracy*. In Michael's view, the neighborhood is always the urban increment. A space of face-to-face deliberation among bodies in real time, neighborhoods are the logical scale for local democracy and environmental accountability. Neighborhoods harmonize the "speed of the market and slowness of the civic," the private and the public, and they challenge the frontier mentality of growth understood as "an unlimited horizon to manipulate value at the edges." Michael's radicalization of urban ecology was like Jane Jacobs on green steroids, but stained with a little bit of red, reminding us that greening the city without social priorities is just decoration, and a feel-good response to environmental crisis.

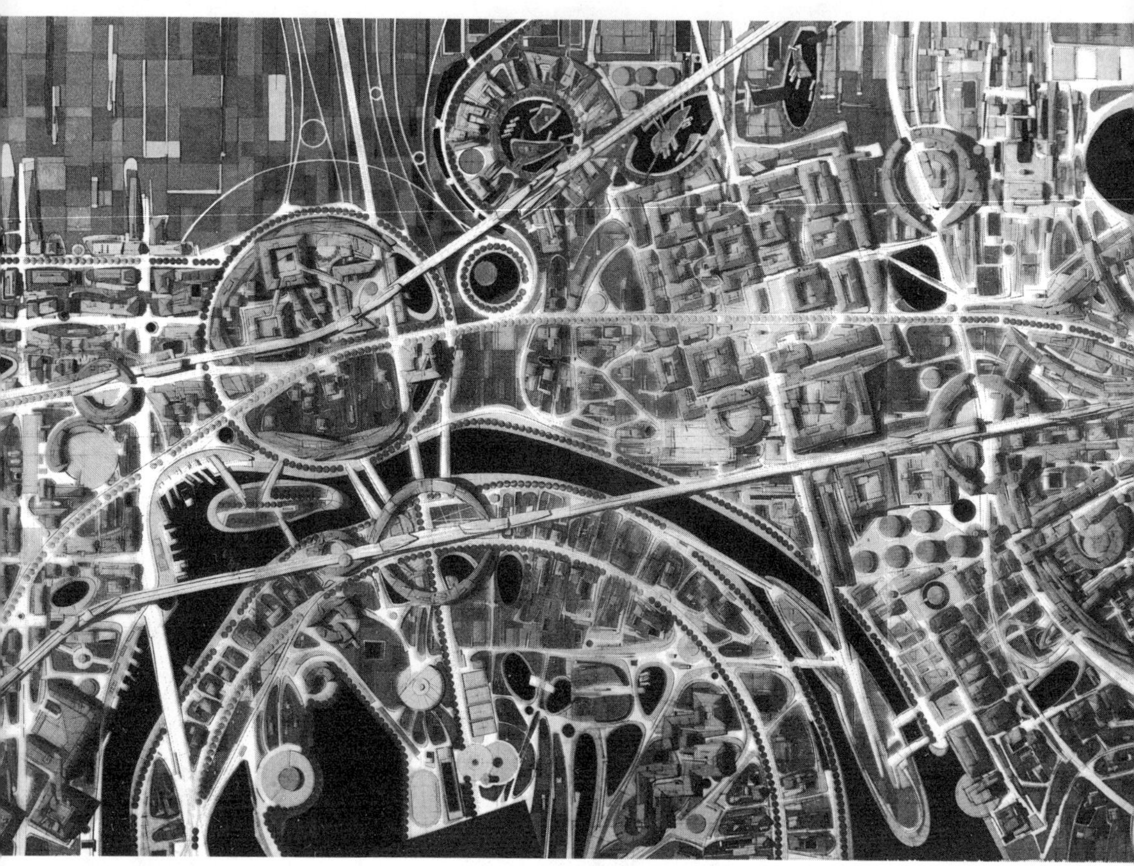

Michael Sorkin Studio, Neurasia, South Asia, 1995.

What a moment he left us in. He might tell us now that the virus that took him could also be the strange harbinger of something better, exposing the stupidity of selfishness during a collective crisis, the catastrophe of freedom thinking, of isolationism, of disinvestment from public goods, and the eroding of public commitment.

Maybe this moment can instigate a paradigm shift in our public priorities as we bodily reunite. Can we envision the end of capitalist greed? The reemergence of a progressive welfare state? A commitment to more equitable and sustainable cities? The reorganization of institutions to confront racial injustice?

Our entrance into the third decade of the 21st century has been a wake-up call to recognize our radical interdependence, our need for truth, transparency, social trust, and planetary coordination. Perhaps from all this, a renewed public consciousness might be born, reminding us that the survival of the individual depends on the health of the collective.

But Michael worried that architects were dropping the ball. He believed we need to engage this reconstruction of common ground. He closed "Traffic in Democracy" with a bucket of cold water, as if to say: If you like what I am saying here, why in practice are you all so damned complicit? Why have you embraced a "politics of disengagement, abandoning the field to . . . the avatars of bigness and smallness who have in common the production of sameness? We've become phobic," he said, "about thinking of cities as physical as well as social constructions. And we suffer from a tremendous poverty of both vision and will in the making of cities. Dominant models for innovation are unsatisfactory, consisting of go-with-the-flow neo-suburbanism, fingers-crossed laissez-faire, tepid riffs on the garden city, retreaded modernism, and Disneyland."

He insisted we scrutinize our clichés and platitudes as urbanists and architects, our banal ways of practicing. He inspired an entire generation, us included, to reflect critically on our own practices. *Why* do we do *what* we do? For *whom*? *Where*? *When*? And *how*? He taught, wrote, and practiced by example.

Michael's urban fantasies over decades, made of strange organic architectural shapes unfolding seamlessly in social and ecological systems and threading public space, mobility, and housing into integrated social scaffolds, were both anarchic and unyieldingly civic. They manifested a commitment to progressive governance and the agency of bottom-up self-organization and civic participation. Michael's writings, sketches, and the echo of his words will always remind us of our radical interdependence.

It's difficult to put into a few words the weight of a legacy. Michael will remain the social and political consciousness of the architectural field. He believed architects can be political agents, taking a position against what is morally and ethically wrong. His memory is rich with the traces he left us. So let's carry forward his infectious optimism for a better world, his childish energy and wicked humor lifting up the potential of everything from the rubble of conflict, injustice, alienation, and pandemic.

Fonna Forman is professor of political theory at the University of California, San Diego and founding director of the Center on Global Justice. Teddy Cruz is professor of public culture and urbanism in the Department of Visual Arts at the University of California, San Diego. They are principals in Estudio Teddy Cruz + Fonna Forman.

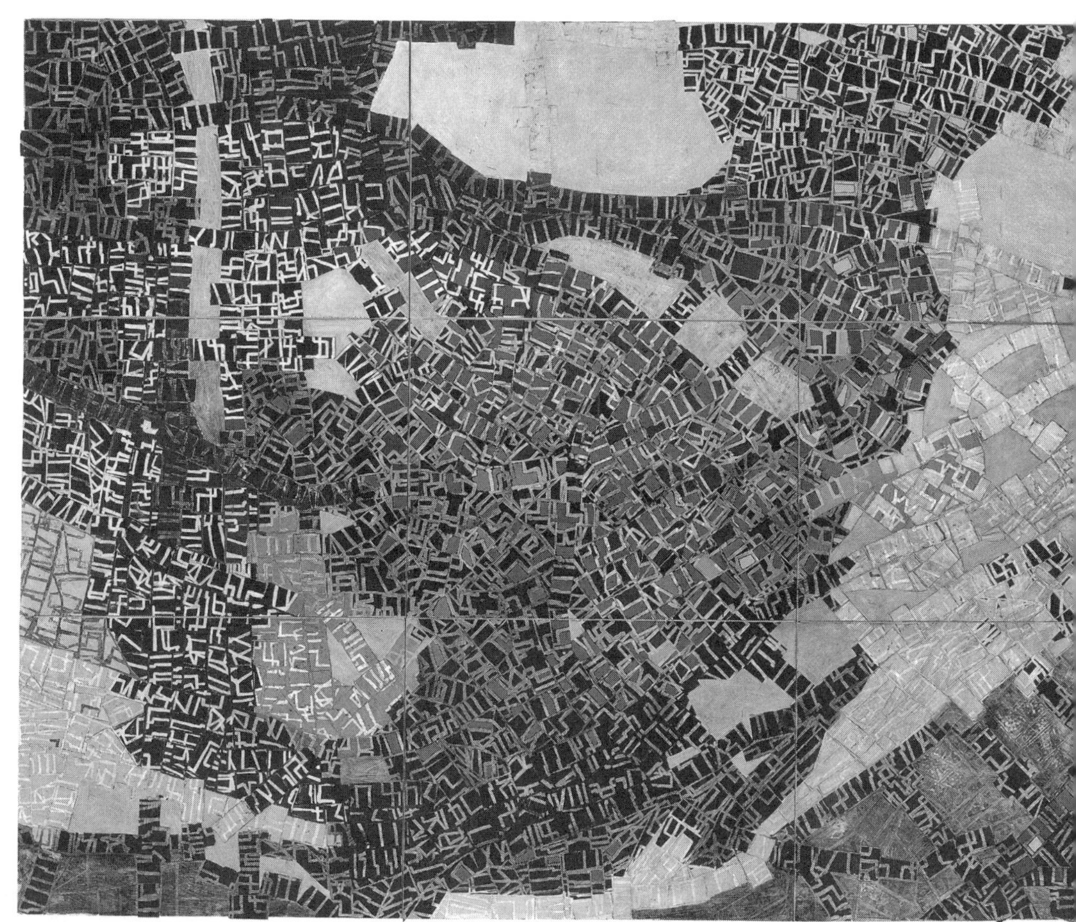

Rick Lowe, *Black Wall Street Journey #5*, 2021. Acrylic and paper collage on canvas, 108 by 192 inches. © Rick Lowe Studio. Photo: Thomas Dubrock. Courtesy the artist and Gagosian.

Thelma Golden, David Adjaye
& Rick Lowe

Space, Place, and Black Social Practice

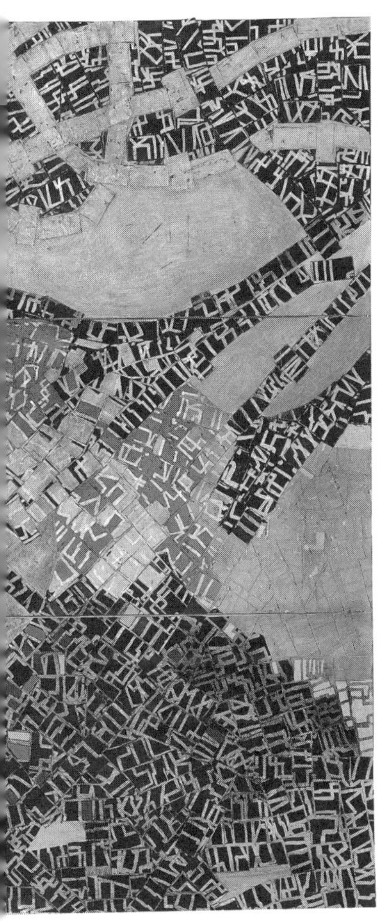

On June 23, 2021, Antwaun Sargent, director of Gagosian Gallery in New York, brought David Adjaye, Rick Lowe, and Thelma Golden together for a conversation about "Social Works," the group exhibition he curated on the relationship between space and Black social practice. David Adjaye, a Ghanaian British architect, founded Adjaye Associates in 2000, which now operates globally with studios in Accra, London, and New York. His most well-known project to date is the National Museum of African American History and Culture in Washington, DC, which opened in 2016 (see Log 40). He was awarded the 2021 RIBA Royal Gold Medal and is the architect of the new Studio Museum in Harlem.

Rick Lowe is an artist and teaches at the University of Houston. His work has appeared at the Contemporary Arts Museum Houston, The Museum of Contemporary Art, Los Angeles, the Gwangju Biennale in South Korea, the Venice Architecture Biennale, and documenta 14 in Kassel, Germany. In 1993, he founded Project Row Houses, a community-based art project in Houston. Additional community projects include Watts House Project in Los Angeles and the Borough Project in Charleston, South Carolina. President Obama appointed Lowe to the National Council on the Arts in 2013, and in 2014, Lowe was named a MacArthur Fellow.

Thelma Golden moderated the conversation. She is the director and chief curator of The Studio Museum in Harlem, where she began her career in 1987 before joining the Whitney Museum of American Art. She returned to the Studio Museum in 2000 as the deputy director for exhibitions and programs and was named director and chief curator in 2005. Golden was appointed to the Committee for the Preservation of the White House by President Obama, and in 2015 she joined the Barack Obama Foundation board of directors.

THELMA GOLDEN: I'm so excited to talk with you about your work, the context of the work in this exhibition, and the many ways that I think your practices are in dialogue. I want to congratulate Antwaun on this fantastic exhibition and celebrate this incredible constellation of artists conversing across media and the generations who are thinking deeply about the concept of Black space and Black practice. Rick, as we are sitting in the midst of your spectacular paintings, can you tell us about this body of work and the context from which it comes?

RICK LOWE: A little over three years ago, I was invited to Tulsa to work with the 1921 Tulsa Massacre Commission to bring in a cultural component to the centennial of the massacre. I visited for the first time with an awareness of this massacre that happened in Greenwood, the neighborhood they called Black Wall Street. And so, I left thinking, wow, Black Wall Street. That speaks to something relevant to Black people in America since emancipation, figuring out how to solidify or gain some footing in terms of a stable economy in America. That took me on this journey of trying to figure it out and think about it. On the one hand, I was working on a community-based project in Tulsa for the centennial, but on the other, the paintings were an opportunity for me to be reflective and to be a little bit critical in some ways, to imagine this idea of Black Wall Street and what that space looked like.

TG: How did you make these paintings? Can you talk a bit about your process?

RL: I was trained as a painter early on. I got away from it for many years and then came back to it through this very odd way of playing dominoes and watching the patterns of what happens when you play. I started to draw them, game after game, and if you layer them, they start looking like maps. And then, when you cut them up, they start looking like a language. These paintings are basically collaged from drawings of domino games that I've produced in the studio. I cut them up and start reorganizing them and making the forms.

TG: David, this exhibition includes your first stand-alone sculpture. Can you talk about the path to making sculpture and about the references for the work and even its title?

DAVID ADJAYE: It's called *Asaase*. It's a reflection of the past two years. But it's about my entire career, probably my entire life, because the last two years have caused deep introspection. When Antwaun reached out to me, the first thing I wanted to do was to make a work, and so the timing seemed perfect. I started at an art school. I didn't finish. I dropped out of art school because I was scared. Then I chose architecture because it was a profession I felt I could be in. And I love it, architecture is my soul, but I've always been fascinated by sculpture. In a weird way, this pause has allowed me to reflect on why I'm not doing sculpture and why it's not part of the practice.

Especially in the last five years, I've become very interested in our relationship to the earth. Of course, there are issues to do with the climate emergency and sustainability, but it's not only that. It's much more anthropological, and it's biographical in a way. It's really about the architecture of the continent and this idea of an extraordinary monolithic architecture that really comes from the earth. It was about raising the earth and creating a symbiotic relationship with earth matter and then with the plant life, the biophilic life. Somehow, that has always been Black life, the roots of all of our ancestors, the one thing they can commonly touch. Until the Industrial Revolution and colonial products, we lived with the earth. So, I feel like that's a deep memory in Black psyche somehow, a deep love.

For me, there are two inventions in architecture: there are cylinders and there are rectangles and squares. It's courts and chambers, and they mutate into many forms. I wanted to deal with cylinders. When I did my show in Venice, I made these negative cylinders that were made from Ghanian soil,

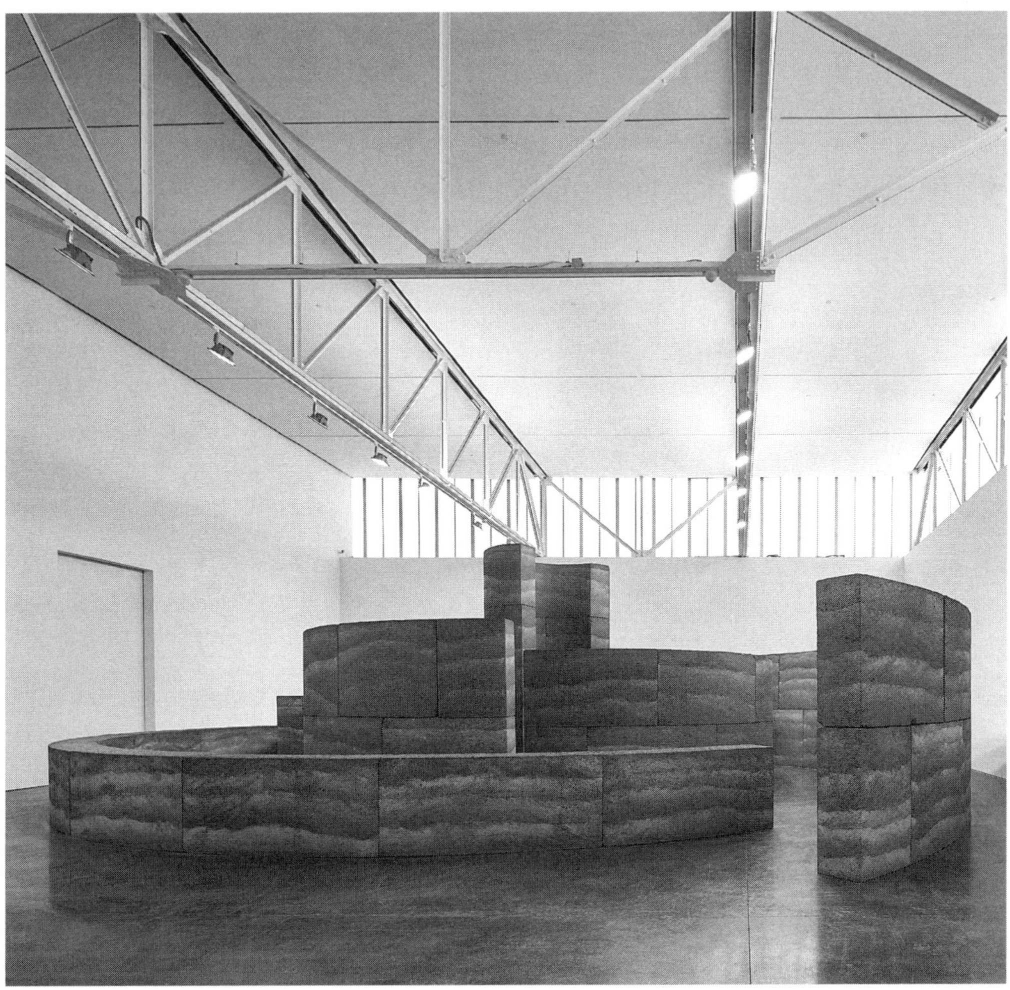

David Adjaye, *Asaase*, Gagosian, New York, 2021. Rammed earth. © David Adjaye. Photo: Dror Baldinger. Courtesy the architect.

which I brought from Ghana to Venice. It was talking about being back to the earth. For this show, which is not an exhibition space but a piece of work, I wanted to make the positive, in a way. These are fragments of different-scale chambers that refer to a chieftain's house, a king's house, a residence of a queen or a mother, a sculpture porch, a granary silo. It's a series of fragments that are randomly thrown together – almost like dominoes, if you could scale it – and then adjusted so you can meander through them. The idea is that you are meandering through walls that are about the relationship we have to what earth walls are, in terms of conversations,

whispers, etc. But this is not made from soil from the continent because suddenly I wanted to think about the soil of the entire planet. This is made from New York rock because there's not much soil here. It's lime-stone and schist. I became fascinated with this and decided just to crush the limestone and ram it, the same way that Black architects did it. And that's what we did.

RL: David and I spent time in Tulsa talking about how he could be involved there. One of the things he talked about was that they need to go into the dirt there. I was blown away to see this piece because this is what that means.

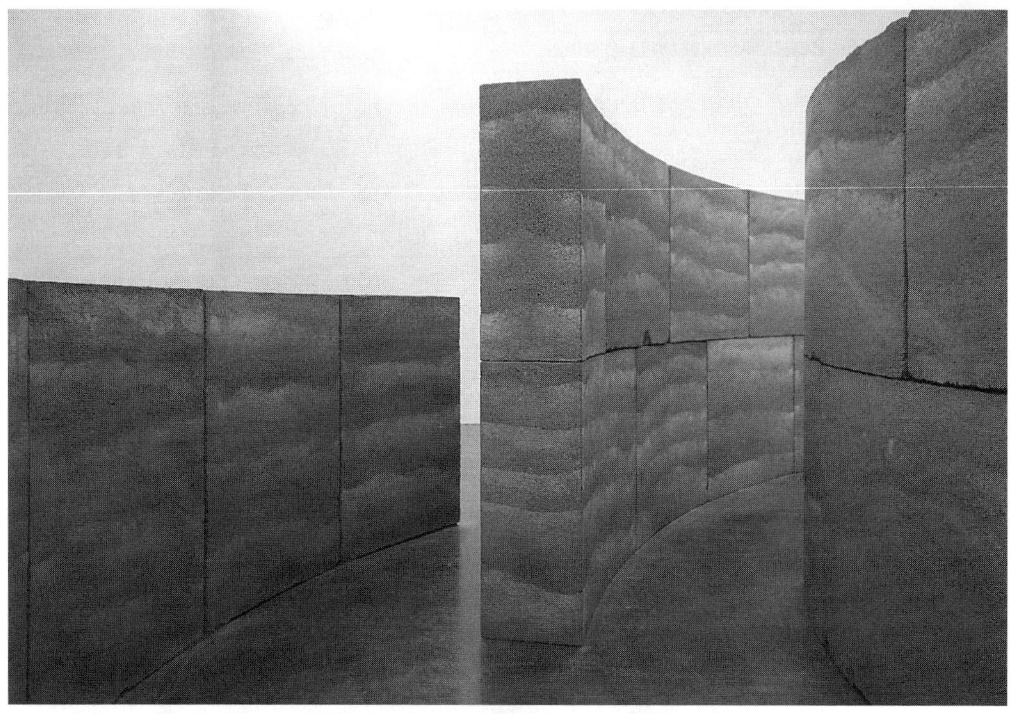

Above and opposite page: David Adjaye, detail of *Asaase*, Gagosian, New York, 2021. Photo: Patrick Templeton.

You went into the earth and brought it up and gave us form. That's one of the things I think Tulsa… well, we're gonna get him around to it.

DA: Rick and I have been trying to do a project together for I think nearly two decades. And I think it's coming to that point where we…

RL: It's gonna happen.

TG: It will happen because, as I said, you share so much between your practices. It seems that both of your works in this exhibition are about mapping. If we think about mapping against an idea of space, it's a way of creating a logic. A visual, perhaps an intellectual logic, even a political logic, to understand place and space. Rick, can you talk about the relationship of your work to place and space?

RL: That's one of the big challenges we have as Black people, I mean, space is very important to us. We came out of a place, particularly here in North America, of not having space or place we could call our own. We've been on this journey forever, from the days of the promise of 40 acres and a mule to now. There are always these things kind of blocking our efforts to find space where we can have some kind of stability. When I'm working on these kinds of works, I'm trying to play around with all the knowledge I've gained over the last 20-plus years of working within space, trying to identify how we build space that supports Black communities and Black culture, and also wrestling with the difficulties of it and trying to find the language to describe it.

With this work, some of it, I'm just exploring. I didn't know that if I do these domino paintings and cut them up that they would look like letters or some kind of language. I've started to approach it in the same way that I'm struggling to understand what's behind gentrification, how we fit within it,

and how we respond to it. As I'm making
these paintings, I'm trying to figure out how
this language speaks about this. I find this
notion of space is something we have to start
generating more information about so we can
gain deeper understandings of it.

TG: David, as an architect, your work has
always been about the creation of space but
also very much about a definition of place.
Can you talk about that collision between
place and space as it informs your architectural practice and perhaps informed the creating of the sculpture?

DA: Place and space. I feel like I'm in a Sun
Ra movie.

TG: *Space Is the Place*. Of course, in thinking
about the Studio Museum, we have talked a
lot about space because we are building a space.
But we also talk about place because, as I've
often said, it's there in our name: The Studio
Museum in Harlem. So, place and space. I see
this exhibition as the place where you and Rick
converge on a set of ideas that, as Rick has so
beautifully said, stand at the core of our thinking about a kind of Black experience. It's reckoning with both of those things, the longing
for, nostalgia, the lack of, the ways both place
and space are invested with ideas of value.

DA: I love the way you are putting the two
bodies of work together. It's powerful. When
I came here and first saw the paintings, I
was gripped by this nebulous mapping of
a Black world. It's as though it exists, with
these coordinates you're creating of different
junctions and different spaces of the sacred,
the collisions, the public. My mind goes off
whenever I'm looking at them.

But going back to what Thelma was saying. Space and, for me, the cataloguing of
space, cataloguing and mapping, are so fundamentally important to the Black experience

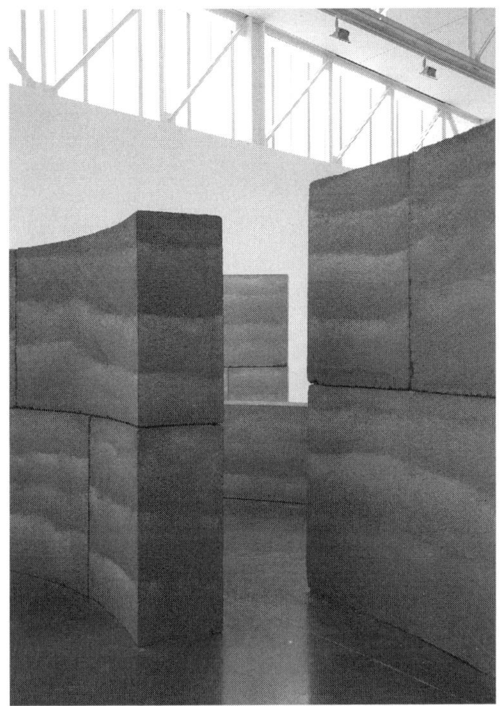

because colonization was about erasure of
the space, and when you erase the history
of the space, you erase the sense of continuity of the community with the earth. In
my work, we are continually searching for
spaces not necessarily built by the Black community but inhabited and hybridized by the
Black community as spaces of ownership that
become part of the catalogued knowledge of
spatial Black experience.

I see myself in the work I produce as an
architect. That's why I'm interested in architecture. Because for me, it stands against a
void of erasure that's so loud and vast, so
absolutely enormous, that it depresses me
when I reflect on it. But we must redress this
erasure. I'm always talking to young Black
architects because it's profoundly important
to have more architects of color in the world
now, to remake the body of knowledge. We
need to make the cartography of knowledge
and the models of knowledge so future generations don't have this nonsense that we're
dealing with because it's a distracting trauma.

When I had the opportunity to work around the world, this idea of a Black spatial formmaker being able to work across the planet was, for me, conceptually what I felt it had to be. I didn't want it to be that you only find my work in Black neighborhoods. The work is a planetary project that's about understanding a world filled with a multitude of peoples and perspectives. The extraction of Black life is also the extraction of Black knowledge, so it's about creating spaces based upon this forgotten knowledge. It's about working away from a world based in singularity and toward a world based in multiplicity and diversity, and through that, you can see how the many spaces can become places we connect to and see ourselves in.

TG: It's the guiding principle of all of our work, right? Space and place. It's about making both, exemplifying both, existing within both, understanding the relationship to both. It's space and it's place.

RL: There's knowledge and language and information about both of those that make them really rich. For the most part, we can kind of *do* space, it's a more physiological thing, but place is sociological. It gets into webs of things we don't quite know how to handle. As I said earlier about gentrification, there are so many things about place that confuse that, right? Take Harlem, for instance. It's changing, but are there wealthier Black people moving into Harlem as well? I remember thinking this in my neighborhood in the Third Ward, oh, gentrification is happening. But then I started meeting – *Wow, you just moved here?* – African Americans, right? So things change, but we don't have the language to be able to talk about what it means when things transform. When spaces transform, we don't understand the broadness of the place of that. Does it mean that Black space has to be space that

is impoverished? Can it mean we can exist within this duality of Black Wall Street, someplace like Greenwood in Tulsa? It was a place of hardworking, honest people who had an understanding of prosperity, and they desired that, Black people wanted that. That's why they went there.

DA: Well, this is the problem when you don't have a body of knowledge of that idea of space and place. You start to work within the limits of what you see as the only possibility of ownership, and you start to clasp onto things that are sometimes actually not things about the expansion of knowledge. That's why, for me, what you're doing at the Studio Museum, Thelma, is this idea of entropy of Black spaces within the context of our environments. And no matter how they evolve and shift, that we are actually contributing to their production creates a kind of extraordinary deepening of memory and also the uprightness of a citizen within the place, so they too feel they are part of something, not just part of a background or part of the system that's being used to prop up another place, to be blunt about it. We're not just the immigrants sitting around waiting to be used. We are the citizens.

RL: When you started out by thanking Antwaun for putting this together, and the meaning of this, I mean, think about this, right? Here we are, sitting in Gagosian, in the context of an exhibition that's called "Social Works." What does that say about this space and the place that we exist in and the sense of culture in the art world? What does that say? I think it's gonna have significant value as we try to understand the fluidity of how things transform.

TG: Rick, can you talk a little bit more about that? Because in the formation of this exhibition, there's also an examination of ideas of social practice. When we think of social

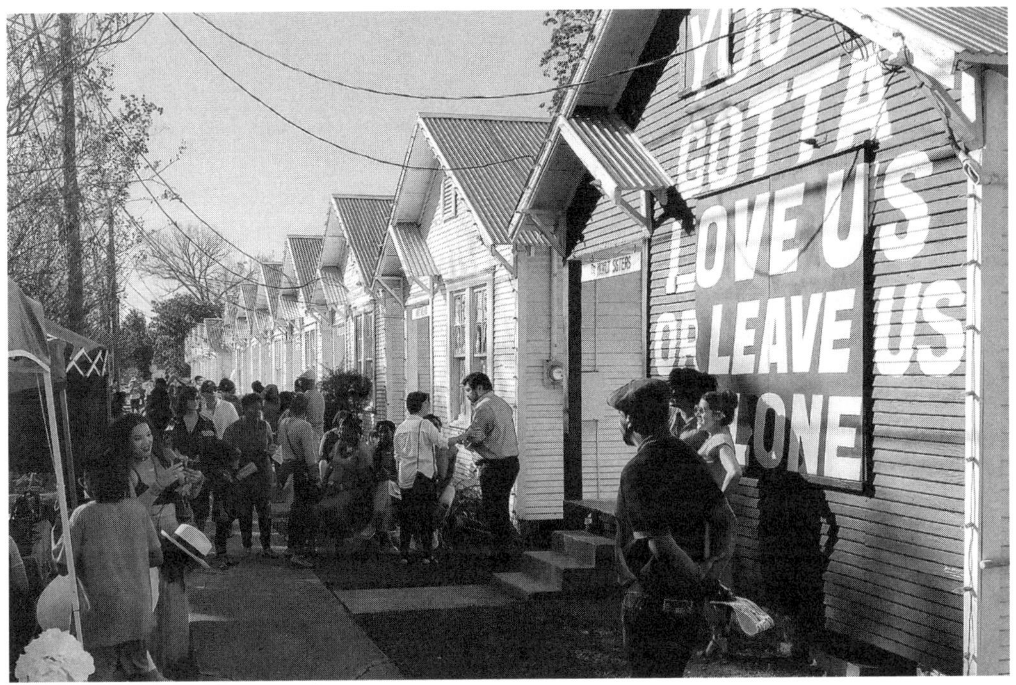

Project Row Houses, Houston, Texas, 1993–ongoing. Opening of Round 46: Black Women Artists for Black Lives Matter, 2017. Photo courtesy Project Row Houses.

practice in its conceptual art definition, it is sometimes divested from civic social practice. Your work has stood as a real example of what social practice means when the lens of the conceptual art practice hits up against true economic development, community reengagement, reinvestment. Can you talk about your path to a social practice and how you defined that?

RL: I have to say it's been a growing process for me. I was more informed by Joseph Beuys's idea of social sculpture, but the whole idea was to figure out how you can merge the symbolic and poetic meaning with practical things in the world. One of the things I find with social practice work is that the practical application is so rigorous, it's hard stuff. Gentrification has been happening forever, so how do you push back in that context? It's really hard.

TG: Can you describe your original idea for Project Row Houses?

RL: Well, the question, back in 1993, was if we have communities that are struggling, and we're artists and we're creative, can we apply our skills in some way? Can we apply our creativity to that context and elevate it in a way that addresses the practical needs and the poetic things as art? Back in the day, the thing about social practice was that you had to brush up against people who were not coming at it from the poetic side but from the practical side, right? I remember very clearly there was a woman, she was 87 years old, and her name was Miss Courtney. She lived in the back of these old run-down houses. We were poking around, doing stuff, and one day she came out with a gun to run us off because she thought we were doing something mischievous. Later, when she had accepted us, she came back and said, *Well, you wanna do something? Just clean this shit up.* And it's like, okay, you get smacked with the kinds of practical things that are valuable to people. And I fully embrace that. But from the art side, it's like, oh, now you have this practical stuff, how do you layer in something that is poetic and symbolic? A lot of what I've found that to be is finding the histories of things and telling that history. There's so much poetry in the experience of Black people. There's so much. These little shotgun houses that are falling down are talked about as the worst places in the neighborhood. But if you can, like Miss Courtney said, clean this shit up, then you can start telling the story of how the architectural type moved from West Africa to the US. Then, all of a sudden, you've got a higher level of meaning in something that was basically a throwaway.

DA: I remember when I first saw Project Row Houses and how profoundly influential it was because it affirmed a value separate from the systemic value given to ideas of rich or poor, or more valuable or less valued places. It was like a magic trick or something. Here was this thing, which any developer would wanna tear down, any city would say clear away, and you had elevated it into social sculpture. The houses became social sculptures, and suddenly they had an aura that meant you couldn't touch them. I remember as a young architect thinking, I don't know how you did this, but it was deeply influential for me. It made me realize the power of being able to make Black space conscious. You made it come into consciousness.

RL: Thank you for that. That's kind of the point about social practice. A lot of it is just merging the creative resources we have with these practical, crazy, messy things that are happening. Layering it and making those things much more than the spatial ways we experience them, and more in a *place* way, which incorporates its history and all the social aspects that go into it. To me, that's where social practice gets its value and its meaning.

TG: I appreciate that as a way to think about what you have done. Your work has also shifted institution making. Before beginning this conversation, I saw you standing next to Linda Goode Bryant and realized that her Just Above Midtown and your Project Row Houses basically have the same DNA – they have created so many of the institutions and organizations that some of us have the privilege to now run or that are represented in "Social Works." Lauren Halsey's Summaeverythang Community Center, Titus Kaphar's NXTHVN, Theaster Gates's Rebuild Foundation. But Project Row Houses and Just Above Midtown proposed complete reevaluations of what it means to create autonomous institutions with values both deeply rooted and expansive.

RL: I've known of Linda's work but had never had a chance to speak with her. It's so great to see how people are doing these incredible things all over. It's like you were saying about magic. How is she doing these gardens here in New York City? It's impossible…

TG: Project EATS, which has farms in four out of the five New York City boroughs, is yet another example. In thinking about the work in this exhibition, it all sits within this concept of what space, Black space, social practice, and social works can be. There also seems to be a way all of these works touch on ideas of memory. In this moment, when I think of memory, I also think of memorials. Rick, what you've created is something about memory but also about memorial. And David, it seems memory informs the space you work from. Can you talk about the ideas of memory and memorial?

RL: Well, because social practice works are ephemeral, or are always moving, you have to think about how you archive them, how you create some longevity for those works. Because some projects are not intended to go

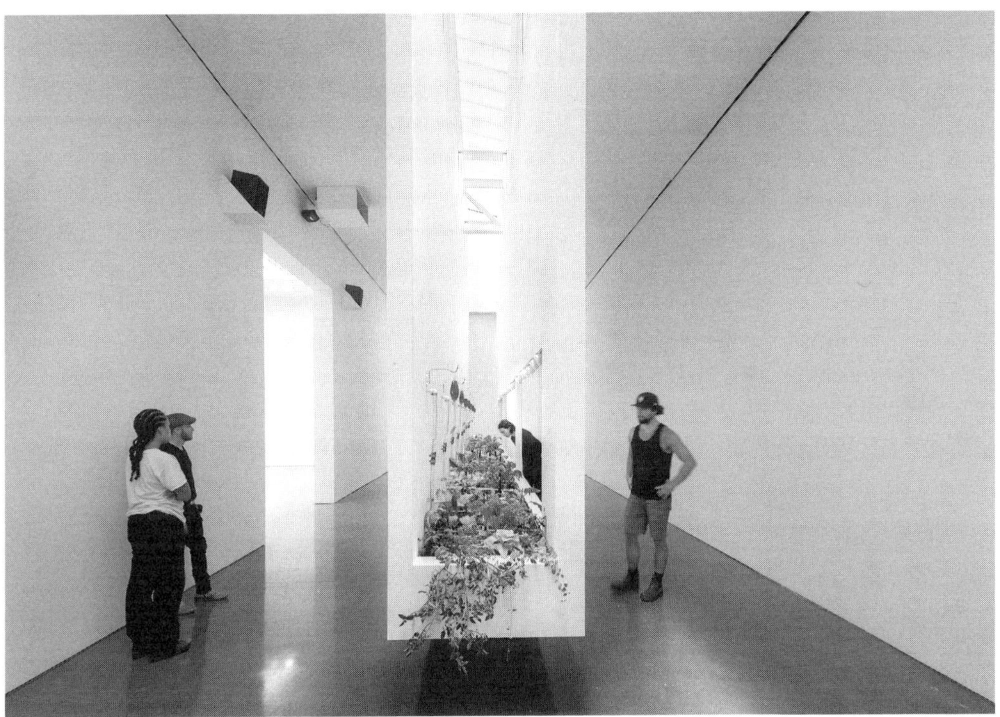

Linda Goode Bryant with Diller Scofidio + Renfro, *Are we really that different?*, 2021, Gagosian, New York. Photo: Brett Beyer. Courtesy Diller Scofidio + Renfro.

on forever. So what happens when they are not there? How do you maintain them? The idea of doing the *Black Wall Street Journey* paintings was a way of asking, how do I take this moment in time, of the centennial, and build some work around this idea that will be lasting? It'll be in collections or exhibitions that will allow that work to live, playing a part in getting beyond the centennial to the bicentennial. Because this is a part of history that shouldn't be forgotten. It is memorial making, in a sense, and of course, with David's sculpture, I'm thinking about that Southern earth too, the red dirt. In fact, one painting started out with the notion of this red clay; that's where that color came from, because I was thinking about our conversation about Tulsa and that dirt down there.

DA: You've just given your work a whole other meaning. For me, in my work, memory and memorials are inseparable twins.

TG: It feels like memory and memorial were embedded in your sense of the architecture of the National Museum of African American History and Culture.

DA: The brief was to make a museum, but in my mind, it was to create a trigger of memory, to pull you back into a deeper history, and to create a space that would honor our ancestors and future generations at the same time. So it's a memorial for the future and a memorial of the past at the same time. I've found a huge amount of confidence in my practice as a creative person because I finally understand these two elements are really the core of what drives my creativity. I find resolution in the way I make work, like the moment when I can stop, when I sense duality or tension somehow being brought into play. It's amazing to hear Rick talk about it in terms of painting because I've never heard it talked about in painting. To use the centennial as a way to make a body of paintings is kind of profound. Actually, this should be a work in one space, like a chamber; it should be like a temple. That's another discussion.

RL: Yeah, that's another one. We'll continue.

DA: For me, the issue at the heart of the project is that I have never felt I was free to just make because I felt a sort of gaze upon everything I was making that was so loaded with issues to deal with. Every time I constructed I had to confront all these issues, not just from the outside but also within myself, thinking each act might be the last. Who knows if I will get another opportunity? And so, what does each act mean? In a way, that has been the foundation of the work. Sometimes people have misunderstood my intentionality with a certain kind of rigor, of wanting to be absolute with every single thing. People are like, *What the hell is he – it's just this.* And I'm like, *No, this little thing hasn't finished yet. We need to focus.* In a way, that's also the thing I call the fear, in a positive way, which is constantly driving my creativity. The fear allows for a focus on and recognition of the preciousness in the opportunity to make things that are dealing with Black space and Black lives, or to make a catalogue for a Black creative to finally say, *I have a relational kind of agency with this work even though it's not my own work. I can confidently mine it, even though it's not what I'm interested in, because, finally, there's a body of work that exists out there.*

At the same time, the making of the memorial is also the making of the archive. The practice isn't simply a practice. It's three things at the same time – memorial, archive, and memory. And, more specifically, memory operating as an alternative. I'm totally fine with Black fantasy, it's profoundly fabulous. In a way, memory is about that – since there's not much memory, fantasy is

operative. But memory is also a dive into history. The memorial is an entropy within this moment, now, and the archive is a projection of the future.

RL: I love that projection of the future. I'm concerned about how we do that. What kind of information do we have to project into the future? Part of the *Black Wall Street Journey* project is associated with a project I'm doing in Chicago exploring this notion of Black wealth. I've been researching this for the last two years. Once a week or so I'll google "black wealth" or "black prosperity." I try to use different ways of searching it, and I never come up with anything other than how much wealth we don't have. It's about the wealth gap, right? Recently, though, something hit me. The problem we have when we're trying to explore this is everybody looks at Black wealth in comparison to White wealth. We don't look at it relative to where we are, or how much have we moved, or how much have we lost. So we don't have opportunities to celebrate who we are because we're looking at it in relation to something impossible.

TG: We're often existing in a corrective to the way these narratives have been written. For me, art is important because it provides us with those possibilities for reimagining narratives. Often people say our history is lost. But it's not lost; our history is held within us. It's one of the reasons I am so obsessed with this idea of place, because Black people hold place deeply.

I live and work in Harlem now, in the very same neighborhood my father was born in, in 1926, and had a relationship with his whole life, until his passing. The Harlem he held with him all through my childhood was one that was 30 years old, but still profound. When I think about gentrification, I often say it's why I love Harlem, because people always talk about what it *was* and what it *will be*. That is the power of this exhibition – to talk about the future and the possibility through art making, place or space making, to imagine a future of Black life, of Black space, and the ways we understand that intellectually, emotionally, psychically, spiritually, politically.

RL: I can't help but go back to what I was just saying about the future. We have to really think about how we imagine Black space and place from a perspective that's relative to who we are, where we are, and where we want to go, as opposed to comparing it to other places. I don't know how that's gonna play out, but I will say this, being an artist has always been an exciting thing. Society is always dealing with these kinds of issues but particularly at this point in time. The Black Lives Matter movement and the circumstances of COVID and George Floyd's murder opened up opportunities for us to create meaningful conversations and reshape how we talk about what the Black experience is and what Black space and place are. Artists are in a great position to lead that conversation. I'm hopeful about that.

TG: What would you say to emerging artists now about their potential or possibility?

RL: I guess I would start by looking back at what I would have said to myself 30 years ago. What I would have done differently is been a bit freer in my thinking, in my capacity to engage. I mean, I understand what I was doing required a certain kind of focus and intensity, and it produced, I think, some interesting work. But I also think I unnecessarily restrained myself. I would say to younger artists, find the thing you're passionate about and really push it because that's where we're going to get movement. Don't restrain yourself from being the full creative being that you are.

TG: David, future thoughts.

DA: Future. Good gosh. I think of it like jazz entering the music world and it never, ever being the same again. What I would call Black architecture, or architecture from a Black lens, is like that moment for the cities of the world. The Black perspective is so profoundly different. The more I research it, and I'm doing a lot of research into it, I find that the built environment is a much more ritualistic, symbolic, powerful space, it's not representational space. I can see in my mind's eye how that will beautifully proliferate and pollinate the world, moving architecture from a commodity and rationale, and from a language, into a kind of spirituality, an essence of itself. We talked about the social reconstruction that's happening right now, that's happening all over the world. It's this idea of searching for something. Are we just stuff? Why are we on this planet? I think the architecture of the Black experience has an answer. I deeply believe it. I think it's an incredible time to understand this. If what we're saying is maybe true, it'd be an incredible future.

RL: Absolutely, and I believe it too.

TG: I do too. I believe, David, you've just framed this: Black art, we could say Black culture as a whole, has the answers, and that's what we have the possibility to unlock. In this exhibition, all of these practices allow us the chance to see possibility and power through the different voices, not only in your work but in all of the works. Thank you both for the opportunity to have this conversation about your work and to do it in the context of so many other artists who are creating for us new worlds and new visions.

To view the original conversation, see In Conversation: David Adjaye and Rick Lowe, moderated by Thelma Golden: https://www.youtube.com/watch?v=hfZSeHZrKpc. "Social Works," an exhibition at Gagosian, 555 W 24th Street, New York, New York. June 24–September 11, 2021.

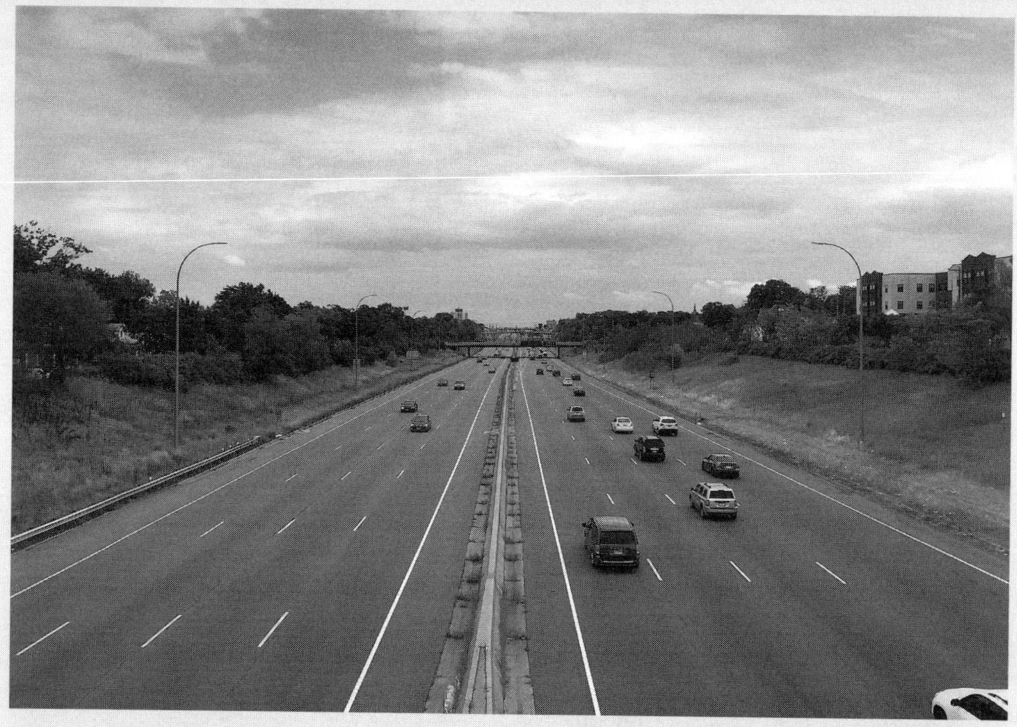

The proposed site of a land bridge over I-94, looking toward downtown Saint Paul, Minnesota, 2021. Photo: Anna Renken.

The construction of the US Interstate Highway System, starting in 1956, facilitated transportation on a new scale, but it also did socioeconomic and environmental damage, particularly in communities of color. To make way for asphalt, homes and businesses were demolished and residents were displaced. When the roads were finished, the ensuing air pollution created unhealthy living conditions in nearby neighborhoods.

In Saint Paul, Minnesota, I-94 cut through the historic Black neighborhood of Rondo in the 1960s, destroying over a dozen city blocks. Today, local organizers are trying to regain lost ground. In July 2021, ReConnect Rondo, a non-profit led by current and former residents of the neighborhood, was awarded state government funds for the master planning of a mixed-use land bridge that would span several blocks, or up to a half mile, of I-94. This strategy of decking over freeways has been employed throughout the US for decades — Seattle's 1976 Freeway Park is an early example — but the Rondo proposal stands out in its ambition to involve community members in the planning of a new center for the neighborhood.

The new ground would host neighborhood fixtures that were lost and are needed today, including housing, retail, institutions like schools and clinics, and open green space. To enable community members to visualize possible configurations, ReConnect Rondo developed augmented reality tools with the Minneapolis architecture firm HGA. Acknowledging the concern that a land bridge might lead to further displacement through gentrification, the organization is advocating for protections such as districting for affordable housing and a community land trust. As Americans rethink US infrastructure following this year's federal legislation, efforts like the Rondo project are potential models for addressing the interconnected issues at stake. — Anna Renken

Charles L. Davis II

Inside the Museum, Outside the Discourse

The espousal of the doctrine of Negro inferiority by the South was primarily because of economic motives and the inter-connected political urge necessary to support slave industry; but to the watching world it sounded like the carefully thought out result of experience and reason; and because of this it was singularly disastrous for modern civilization in science and religion, in art and government, as well as in industry. The South could say that the Negro, even when brought into modern civilization, could not be civilized, and that, therefore, he and the other colored peoples of the world were so far inferior to the whites that the white world had a right to rule mankind for their own selfish interests.
— W.E.B. Du Bois, *Black Reconstruction in America*

If the Department of Architecture and Design at the Museum of Modern Art began as an institution in search of the formal limits of contemporary architecture, then it is now in the uncomfortable position of needing to move beyond its own mythical foundations in order to imagine its future in an increasingly diverse field. This is to say that the general definitions for modern architecture that its first curators established as a historical origin point of a progressive history of design have proven to be not only outdated but almost entirely based on a set of Eurocentric norms and assumptions for art and art appreciation that are made embarrassingly obvious by the exhibition "Reconstructions: Architecture and Blackness in America." Despite the running time of this show (February 27–May 31, 2021) being criminally brief during the first relaxations of pandemic restrictions, this is a historic undertaking that is potentially transformative for the ways curators will discuss the national and global legacies of modern architecture. The work created by the 11 artists and architects of "Reconstructions" – Emanuel Admassu, Germane Barnes, Sekou Cooke, J. Yolande Daniels, Felecia Davis, Mario Gooden, Walter Hood, Olalekan Jeyifous, V. Mitch McEwen, Amanda Williams, and David Hartt – excels most when it employs the fragments of modern architectural formalism to reveal the countercultural projects of African American modernity that have been continuously at work in the United

States, from Reconstruction (1865–1877) to the present. This projective historiography reframes the aesthetic criteria that are necessary to round out the archives of the Department of Architecture and Design by exceeding the European and Enlightenment pedigree of its founding. In a similar fashion to Houston Baker's explanation of the unrecognized modernity of African American literature during the Harlem Renaissance, cocurators Sean Anderson and Mabel O. Wilson, with Arièle Dionne-Krosnick, have crafted an exhibit that reimagines the built environment by paying homage to historical modes of Black creativity.[1] If nothing else, this exhibit provides a curatorial model of intervention at institutions like MoMA that can be applied to recover the historical contributions of other communities of color when they have found themselves written out of the canon of modern architectural production.

The formal premise of "Reconstructions" is that it is an exhibit about the "centuries of disenfranchisement and race-based violence [that] have led to a built environment" in the United States that is constituted by its "segregated neighborhoods, compromised infrastructures, environmental toxins, and unequal access to financial and educational institutions."[2] However, this is surreptitious cover for the exhibition's deeper reckoning with the inequities that were precipitated by a racially biased conception of modern architecture culture in the United States. It is a vocalization of the need for a deeper historical accounting of the discipline's broad role, and the museum's specific role, in dismissing, erasing, and appropriating Black talent for the hegemonic cultural projects of a Pan-European avant-garde dressed up as a universal style of building. The cultural stakes of this exhibit are made clear by the racial politics surrounding its location in the museum, the Philip Johnson Galleries.[3] In a process that inverts the colonial politics of erasure that Ariella Azoulay attributes to the political function of "transcendental imperial art" and museological knowledge, the participants of the show formed the Black Reconstruction Collective and printed their Manifesting Statement on a tarp placed over the wall sign outside the gallery, effectively making it a gallery with no name.[4] In doing so, they made it possible for visitors to specifically place the crime of Black omission from MoMA squarely at the feet of a founding curator while acknowledging the placelessness that Black artists and architects have endured as a result of this very crime.

Does "Reconstructions" solve the problems raised by the historical erasure of Black artists at MoMA? Is it an effective form of repair to the international branding that has given

1. See Houston A. Baker, Jr., *Modernism and the Harlem Renaissance* (Chicago: University of Chicago Press, 1987).

2. "Reconstructions: Architecture and Blackness in America," The Museum of Modern Art, https://www.moma.org/calendar/exhibitions/5219.

3. See Sarah Bahr, "Artists Ask MoMA to Remove Philip Johnson's Name, Citing Racist Views," *New York Times*, December 3, 2020, https://www.nytimes.com/2020/12/03/arts/design/philip-johnson-moma.html.

4. See Ariella Aïsha Azoulay, *Potential History: Unlearning Imperialism* (London: Verso, 2019), 58–63.

5. See James Johnson Sweeney, ed., *African Negro Art* (New York: Museum of Modern Art, 1935).

6. See Frederick Douglass, *My Bondage and My Freedom: Part I – Life as a Slave, Part II – Life as a Freeman* (New York: Miller, Orton & Mulligan, 1855), 441–45.

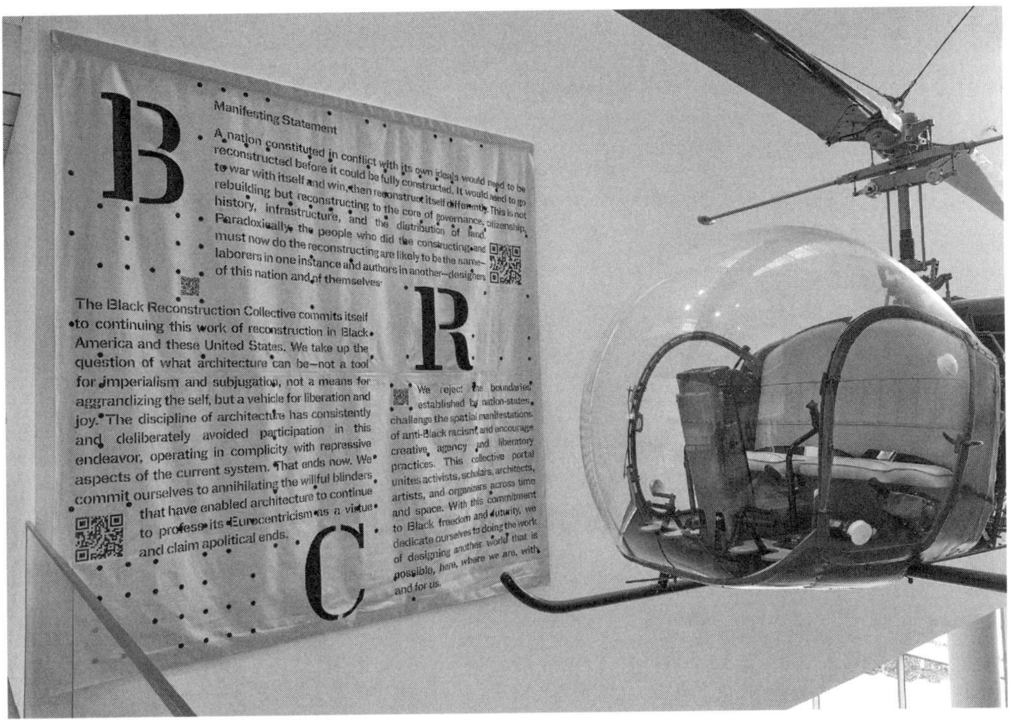

The Black Reconstruction Collective, Manifesting Textile, 2020. Installation view of "Reconstructions: Architecture and Blackness in America," The Museum of Modern Art, New York City, February 27–May 31, 2021. Photo: Robert Gerhardt. © The Museum of Modern Art, 2021.

the museum such pride of place in the past? I believe such questions are beside the point. Repairing MoMA's reputation is not the focus of this exhibit, nor should it be the job of any Black artist or architect operating at MoMA. More important, it is a powerful reclamation of the *intellectual* acumen that was required of the generations of African diasporic artists that found creative ways of existing in the modern world. These modalities are a rebuke of early exhibits on "African Negro Art" that categorized Black genius to be the result of a mere intuitive mindset that was common, if "pure," in the primitive cultures stuck at a premodern level of industrial development.[5] The presumed importance of industrialization and abstraction in the forward march of American modernism is greatly complicated by the inclusion of Black radical talent that is long overdue.

What to the "Primitive" is the Museum of Modern Art?

In 1852, Frederick Douglass asked a largely White audience of Independence Day revelers the rhetorical question, "What to the Slave is the Fourth of July?"[6] He asked this question to give his listeners, and every listener thereafter, an opportunity to contemplate the aporias of American liberalism that went unresolved due to the very existence of slavery. I think this quote is often misunderstood because too many believe they were finally resolved after the abolition of slavery. However, the barbs of his question persist, even to this day, because of the very *possibility* of categorizing a subject of the United States as a "slave" within a liberal democracy. The deeper lessons of Douglass's question provide us with an insightful parallel to the work undertaken by the "Reconstructions" show at MoMA.

When Douglass uses the word *slave* to describe members of the African diaspora living in the United States, he is not offering an empirical description of his community, as there were already Black people living outside of the institution of slavery, even if only provisionally. He himself was a runaway slave who touted his status as a freeman to demonstrate the human potential of Black Americans during his lifetime. Instead of being empirically descriptive, then, his use of *slave* is analytic as it lays bare the poverty of imagination haunting an American liberal consciousness that fails to identify and expunge its anti-Blackness to find a proper place for Black subjects on its shores. We must remember that American liberty was based on rhetorical claims on universal freedoms and suffrage for all, yet existed within a proslavery and settler-colonial state. A slave is a nonentity in the ontological sense; it has no legal recourse to being an individual but only operates for the purpose of counting one's property or things. In this vein, Douglass's question was no mere contemplation of the impracticalities of an enslaved person celebrating the principles of universal freedom, because a slave was not even considered to be a person under the law. Slaves were merely chattel. Instead, Douglass was asking his White audience to locate the racial biases of American liberalism by posing the more complicated question of what inherent limits are contained within a democratic system that was incapable of properly defining a Black person as anything more than a slave. He was asking his audience to imagine slaves, perhaps even their own slaves, as real people with their own modern projects. He was asking his audience to confront an internalized system of racism that was the result of an inherent hypocrisy embodied by a nation of freed White men standing on the necks of the Black laborers who brought them their current wealth and liberty.

Pairing the labels of "Architecture" and "Blackness," the "Reconstructions" exhibit poses a similar question to the founding myths of modern architecture. Of what value are the historical definitions, labels, and principles of a modern architecture that are still too commonly understood to be the universal exponents of the European avant-garde culture that have now become globalized? Like the slave of the antebellum world, the discipline of architecture has been unable to properly define the African and African-diasporic modernities that were created by the Black communities that have lived in the United States. Instead of acknowledging the Whiteness that was essential to the Pan-European conception of modern architecture birthed at MoMA – a Whiteness that seemed capable of switching its support from American democracy to Nazism or fascism if this better enabled the creation of beautiful architectural forms – its founders invented the category of the "primitive" to contain the seemingly aberrant modern subjectivities that endangered the cultural and political hegemony of a sublimated European conception of architectural form that promised to colonize the world anew. The cocurators of "Reconstructions" invite MoMA to make itself anew.

"Reconstructions" asks MoMA's curators, past and present, and any architect who employs its avant-garde legacies to support their own creative activities, the simple question, "What to the 'Primitive' is the Museum of Modern Art?"

The problem with viewing Black artists and architects as something more than the "primitive" subject of modern architecture theory is not one that emerged from within the Black community. It is a problem of the colonial and imperial museum apparatus that fails to identify and authentically express the creativity of these cultural agents.

Of what true value is an artistic worldview that tacitly suspects all forms of Black modernity to be an act of mere intuition, or a chance operation of premodern thinking? What else would describe the historical omission of Black architects in MoMA's archive? We currently lack the conceptual language to even describe the broad range of modern cultural projects that emerged to sustain the diverse forms of life that have existed in the United States. So many of our inherited frameworks only operate at the level of a presumed universality that must be achieved by all subjects, regardless of their actual needs or desires. Within this restricted intellectual context, Blackness has only operated as a symbol of lack, absence, and want. It is the permanent underbelly of a rationalist system of design that requires modernist cultures to renew themselves with the premodern sentiments of so-called primitive subjects. The very act of staging "Reconstructions" is still critically necessary because it begins to provide us with the appropriate lenses to properly see the racial aporias of architectural modernity that we have inherited. However, we are left with the difficult task of critiquing, deconstructing, and reconstructing these founding values so that they

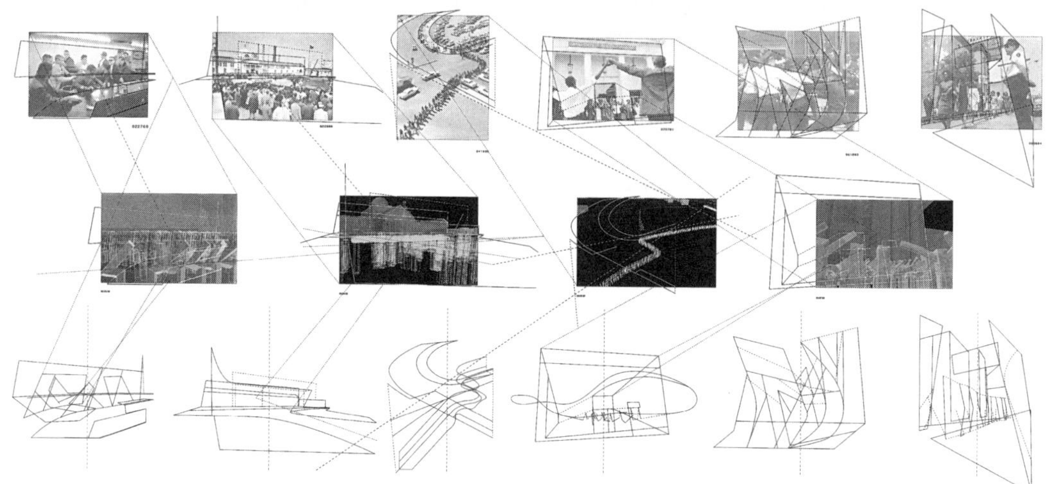

Mario Gooden, The Refusal of Space: BNA Transcripts, 2020. 70 by 29 inches. BNA Transcripts is a mapping of the spatial choreographies, body movements, positions, and postures demonstrating the agility, transformability, and fluidity of the ways in which Black people moved through space, negotiating the barriers of social, political, and economic landscapes during the civil rights era in Nashville, Tennessee. Drawing courtesy the architect.

operate more inclusively. As pioneering as this exhibit is, it does not delineate a prescriptive list of new vocabulary words and design principles for its main audience. The value of "Reconstructions," for better or worse, is not spent formulating a didactic revision of MoMA's institutional culture, but is to be found in a powerful display of the mastery of its practitioners. I, for one, welcome this new list of master architects as I eagerly await the internal reconstruction of the museum's holdings that is inevitable in the wake of this effort.

The Reconstruction of Architectural Formalism at MoMA

The curatorial strategy for "Reconstructions" is purposefully site based, both in terms of the viewer's experience and in terms of the geographic forms of Blackness that are investigated throughout the exhibit. One walks into the gallery space viewing three main orientation elements within: the aforementioned manifesto by the Black Reconstruction Collective; a large wall of text providing a summary of the exhibit's intention to "take up the unfinished project of Reconstruction"; and a wall-sized map of the United States orienting viewers to the 10 cities that the participants reimagine in their work. This spine then splits into a series of perpendicular axes that take the viewer on a virtual tour of what could have been if America had dedicated itself fully to the historical mission of Reconstruction.

At least two pieces reconceptualize the potential meaning of architecture as a discipline from an object-based practice that is primarily concerned with the generation and aesthetic contemplation of static form to a discipline focused on interpreting the building's role in delineating the broader spatial experiences of the built environment. As Gooden notes in his

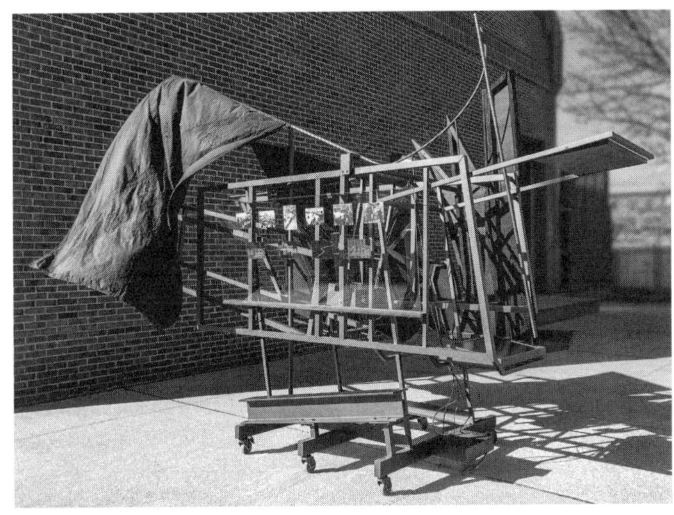

7. "To be really free is to be spatially free |
Ep 9 | REIMAGINING BLACKNESS &
ARCHITECTURE," YouTube video, 6:02,
posted by "The Museum of Modern Art,"
April 29, 2021, https://www.youtube.com/
watch?v=e3qkcuNXRwM.

explanation of the piece The Refusal of Space, "Architecture
is about making space."[7] Moving beyond the presumed uni-
versalism of both postmodern architectural autonomy and
phenomenology, Gooden introduces the possibility of understanding architectural form through the physical and intellectual emulation of Black spatial practices. Hood's contribution,
Black Towers/Black Power, equally reimagines the formal
qualities of the freestanding object by infusing the meaning of
minimalist form with a complex and layered spatial program.
The architectural section drawings of each tower enable us to
concentrate on the structural power that subtends these forms
but is all too often ignored for a superficial and apolitical formalist discussion of a building's exterior form.

Gooden's contribution is a self-described "protest
machine" that encapsulates the Black struggle for spatial
inclusion in Nashville, Tennessee, during the 1960s and '70s.
He specifically chose Nashville for his work because it was the
location of several important moments in American history:
its trolley-car protests predated the Montgomery bus boycott
by nearly 50 years and gave birth to the Union Transportation
Company, a privately owned Black trolley line that better enabled minorities to navigate the city on equal terms.
Nashville was also the location of an early lunch-counter protest that emulated the Greensboro sit-ins of early 1960 to end
racial segregation in private commercial spaces in the South.
The theme of spatial liberation is timely not only in light of
recent Black Lives Matter protests around the nation, but also
in relation to the political strategy of refusal that Gooden references in the title of his piece, as Black Americans have had
to reject the dehumanizing labels that are a structural part

of White supremacy. In disciplinary terms, Gooden stages
his protest machine as a stationary trolley that makes clever
use of the notational systems of architecture, both literal
and representational, to index the spatial dramas of 1960s
Nashville. As a stationary piece, it recalls the permanence
expected of architecture, but as a formal registration of the
Union Transportation trolley line, it subverts our expectation of such fixity with a tableau of projective orientations.
It remains in place only so we can rethink space through
circumambulatory practices. In framing multiple views of
the Black body in the urban landscape, The Refusal of Space
demonstrates the ways that architecture as an object in the
landscape is completely dependent upon the social meanings
it accumulates. Yet Gooden's findings are framed by a careful historical study of Black space, which refuses to make
generalist claims toward what these spaces might have meant
to the White segregationists or new generations of refugees,
Latinx, or Asian migrants living in the area. Even the black-
ened Confederate flag denotes the Blackness of this historical
struggle. The only transferable property of Gooden's work is
its stripped-down aesthetic, which employs the assemblage
of standardized pieces of architectural structure to suggest a
series of open lines of action and projection. While these elements help us to understand the potentialities of space, the
piece does not resolve into a static object as might be expected
of a permanent work of architecture.

Black Towers/Black Power consists of 10 scaled totems
that represent a series of new skyscrapers designed for
Oakland, California, a city that provided an opportunity to
reimagine the contemporary materialization of the revolutionary principles of self-governance and Black ownership
outlined in the Black Panther Party's 1966 Ten-Point Program.
Hood's experience growing up in the area led him to realize the
physical importance of San Pablo Avenue as a material document of the race-based policies of containment that were used
to control Black space, as well as a living record of the rem-
nants of the Black Panther Party's program in the social institutions of the area. On an aesthetic level, the eye is drawn to
Hood's 10 black towers, which stand on axis as discrete mono-
liths in the gallery. At first glance, they seem to exist as pure
formal objects of contemplation. Yet Hood's statuary transforms
the apolitical reading of these abstract elements into an activ-
ist tool. This is only made apparent when one spends some
time with the section drawings of each tower, which imagine Black control of everything, from a community-managed

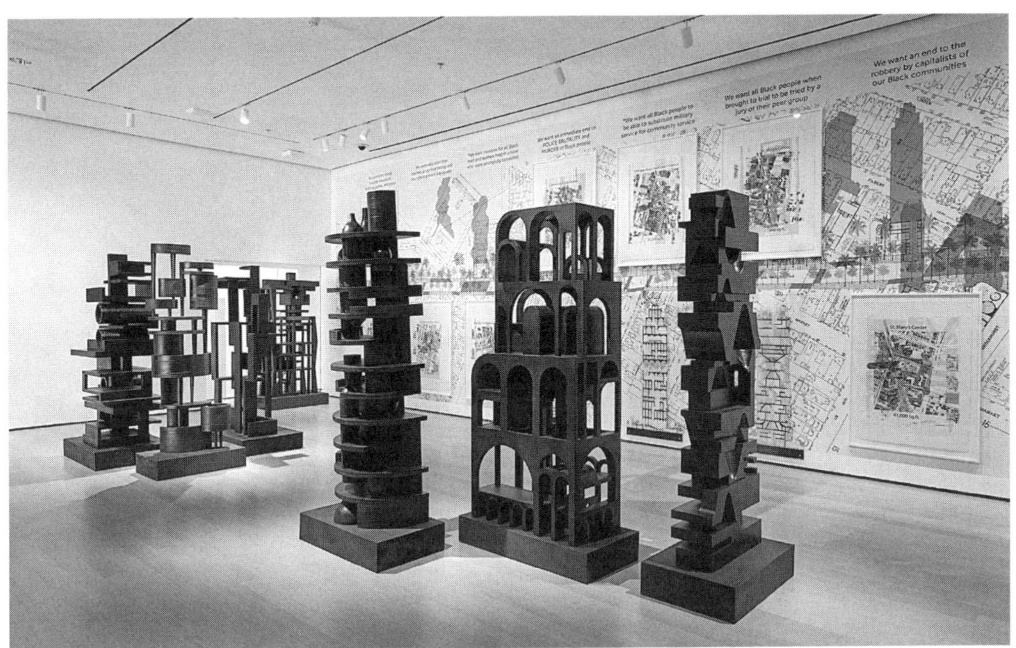

Walter J. Hood, Black Towers/Black Power, 2020. Installation view of "Reconstructions: Architecture and Blackness in America," The Museum of Modern Art, New York City. Photo: Robert Gerhardt. © The Museum of Modern Art, 2021.

8. See James Clifford's "Quai Branly in Process," *October* 120 (Spring 2007): 3–23.

police force to communal housing and a "Hall of Justice." Black Towers/Black Power establishes a material analogue to the revolutionary outline that is often provided by the leaders of Black social movements. On an aesthetic level that extends the Black traditions found within MoMA itself, Hood's pairing of evocative architectural section drawings with the visual traditions of minimalist modern sculpture recodes the potential social meaning of these objects in the museum, enriching pure form in a way that parallels what was achieved by Louise Nevelson's social imbrication of the pictorial practices of the abstract expressionists of the 1940s and '50s. I find it to be a clever way of smuggling the social content of architecture into museum contexts that may be too conservative to entertain the practical realities of "Reconstructions." It is not hard to imagine the display of Hood's sculptures without any social contextualization, much like the recontextualization of literal ethnographical objects as works of art within the formalist interiors of Ateliers Jean Nouvel's Musée du Quai Branly, which was enclosed by a primitive forest that rehearses the sad tropes of the aesthetic principles of Oceanic art so well trod in early modernist circles.[8]

Cooke's We Outchea: Hip-Hop Fabrications and Public Space formalizes the memory of Black public spaces erased by multiple phases of neoliberal development in Syracuse, New York. His methodology recalls Felecia Davis's Walking Tours of Manhattan, which recovers the lost Black sites of the

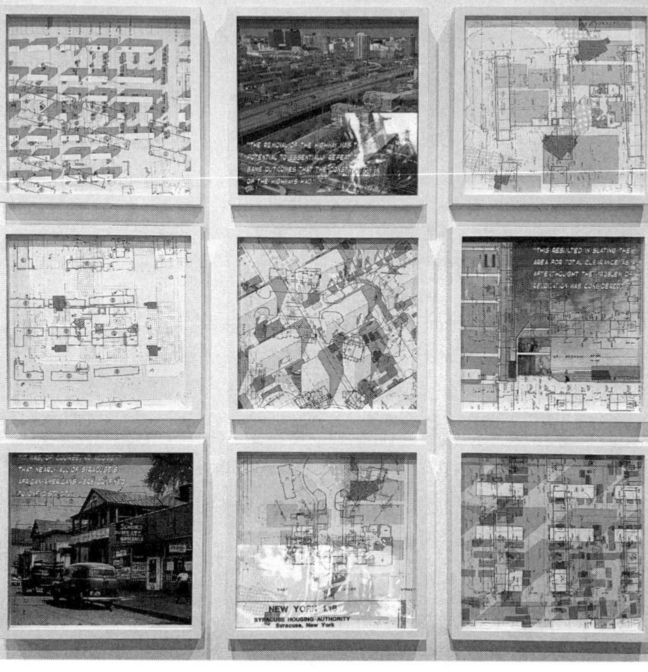

9. See Felecia Davis, "Uncovering Places of Memory: Walking Tours of Manhattan," in *Sites of Memory: Perspectives on Architecture and Race*, ed. Craig E. Barton (New York: Princeton Architectural Press, 2001), 27–36; Sekou Cooke, *Hip-Hop Architecture* (London: Bloomsbury, 2021).
10. See Cheryl J. Fish, "Place, Emotion, and Environmental Justice in Harlem: June Jordan and Buckminster Fuller's 1965 'Architextual' Collaboration," *Discourse* 29, no. 2/3: Race, Environment, and Representation (Spring & Fall 2007): 330–45.
11. See Charles L. Davis II, "Toward a Theory of Pan-African Architecture" in *Sub-Saharan Africa: Architectural Guide*, ed. Philipp Meuser and Adil Dalbai, vol. 1, *Introduction to the History and Theory of Sub-Saharan African Architecture* (Berlin: DOM Publishers, 2021), 136–37; "Improvised Shanty-Megastructures," *ASAP/J*, July 30, 2018, https://asapjournal.com/b-o-s-5-1-improvised-shanty-megastructures-charles-davis/.

island, but Cooke primarily uses the language of hip-hop – sampling, break, freestyle, and remix, to name just a few – to think through architectural form that simultaneously indexes these historical fragments in the present.[9] Despite the formal similarities to other layered architectural schemes, we know that we are working with a palimpsest of memory because of the superimposition of historical images of residents on the facades of the site's original low-rise buildings. In my mind, this work operates as a visual form of oral history that animates the site through the layered presentation of local stories of everyday life. If Cooke's piece is firmly rooted in a visual archaeology of ground, then Williams launches us into a utopian version of Black space that looks a lot like Sun Ra's outer space or a cognitive frontier that is placeless yet ubiquitous in the minority subject's imagination. At the level of notation, her piece, We're Not Down There, We're Over Here, revises illustrations of patents of intellectual labor to index Black creative genius. It physically consists of a video and a series of representations of patented materials. It begins with a cataloguing of the free towns that Black Americans founded from Reconstruction onward to develop their potential in the United States. The constant interruption of White terror and racial suppression, however, necessitated a search for physical territory that lay further and further removed from such negative forces. The beautiful supergraphic of a multicolored

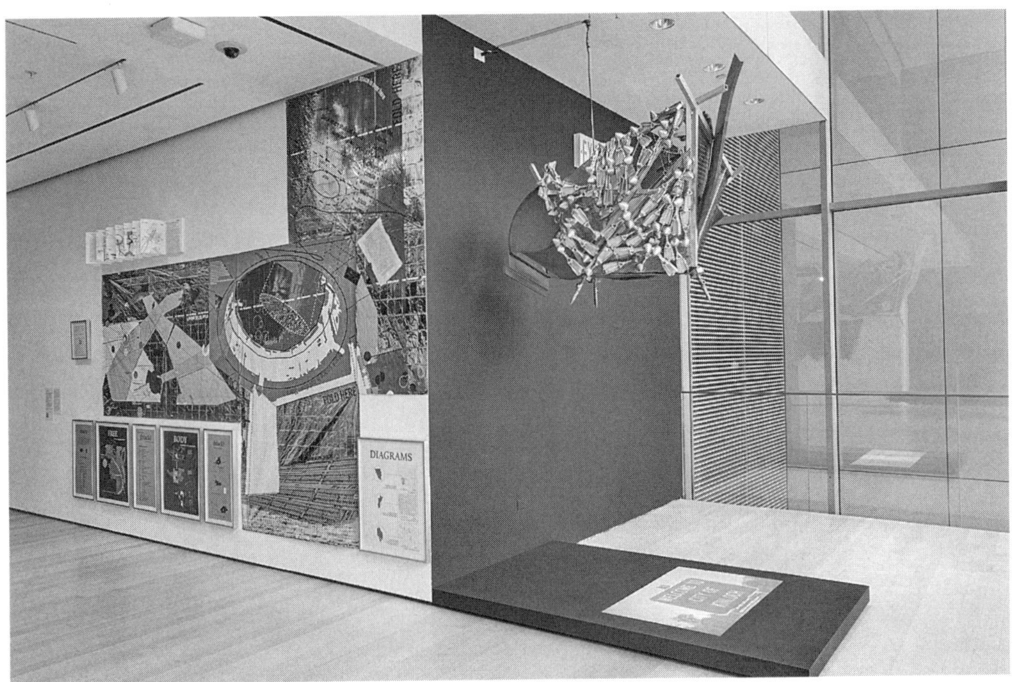

Amanda Williams, We're Not Down There, We're Over Here, 2020. Installation view of "Reconstructions: Architecture and Blackness in America," The Museum of Modern Art, New York City. Photo: Robert Gerhardt. © The Museum of Modern Art, 2021.

Jacob's ladder stretching up into a metal superstructure that hovers above the vernacular housing below should remind us of the visual aesthetic of postwar utopian projects such as June Jordan and Buckminster Fuller's Skyrise for Harlem. Like its predecessor, We're Not Down There, We're Over Here is also deeply infused by the specific memories and cultural projects of the midrise community of Kinloch, Missouri.[10]

Of course, these are only some of the ways that "Reconstructions" challenges the norms of architectural formalism. The connections that are drawn between the fine arts and architecture expand the content of architectural formalism to include the content of new conversations on the visualization and oral performance of Blackness in these fields. I have written on another occasion of the deep reformation of Blackness that Olalekan Jeyifous introduces to the architectural canon as a member of the African diaspora, and the inclusion of visual artists and architects such as Germane Barnes and David Hartt connects the innovations of the fine arts to those of architecture.[11] One can only hope that "Reconstructions" is an opening salvo that inspires others to contribute to the reformulation of contemporary architectural discourse. That would be an effective form of reparations if ever there was one.

Charles L. Davis II is associate professor of architectural history and criticism at the University at Buffalo. He is the author of *Building Character: The Racial Politics of Modern Architectural Style.*

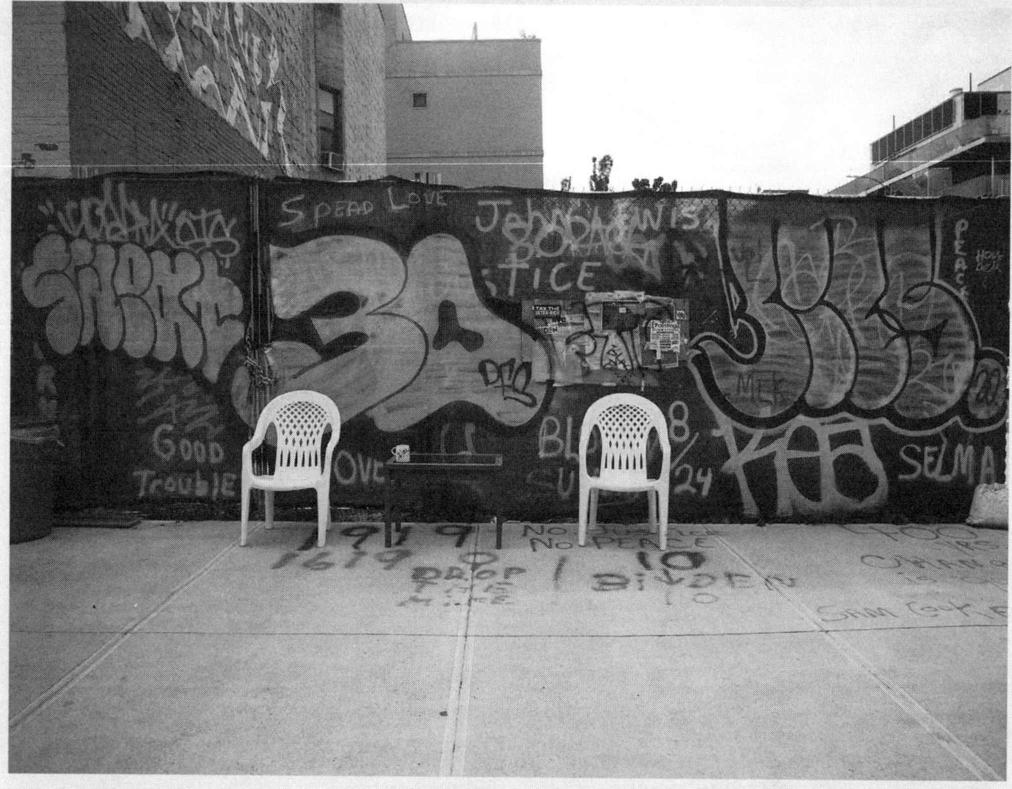

Clinton Hill, Brooklyn, May 2021.
Photo: Mitchell Rue Carson.

I'm a subletter, living in someone else's space with someone else's stuff. I moved to New York City during the height of the pandemic, when there were 1.4 million rooms for rent. I came on a fast-moving train of subletters, just like me, to take care of the plants of those fleeing upstate and across the country to be with family or to get away from crowds. I sleep on a white IKEA Murphy bed framed with dangling vines. On one wall is a large tapestry of Jesus Christ, rendered in reds and blues. Ornate skeletal figures and painted calaveras are nailed to the surrounding walls. In the closet are empty suitcases, plastic-wrapped suits, dress shoes,

a white crate of folded laundry, and a long, leather-encased rod labeled Chuck's cue. Under the bed are shallow containers filled with keepsakes. In many ways, this stuff has been my experience in New York; in describing it, I fear I am giving someone else's version of it.

Now, with summer approaching, the city stirs and bristles with life reclaimed. New Yorkers like Chuck are returning in unmasked droves and subletters like me are searching for new rooms. The sidewalks are free marketplaces and passersby stop and gather things, filling backpacks with books and clothes, carrying furniture on their heads, bringing the stuff

to other places where it will reshape other rooms. A friend and I use the free chairs stacked beneath a pin oak to sit and enjoy a coffee. We talk about the next phase of our lives and the years it might take to feel a sense of belonging or ownership in the city. When we get up, a couple beelines for the chairs and carries them away before we're halfway down the block. New York is a wonderland of rooms, indoors and out, filled with other people's stuff. It is all of ours and it is nobody's, all at once.

— Mitchell Rue Carson

*Vickii Howell
with Joycelyn Davis,
Darron Patterson
& Joe Womack*

Africatown: The Quest for Spatial Justice

History moves in cycles, it is said.

The year that Black architects and designers met in Washington, DC, to ponder what progress their profession had made in the five decades since Whitney M. Young Jr.'s famous 1968 speech to a nearly all White male audience of architects about their role in spatial justice; the year that archaeologists searched a portion of the Mobile River in Alabama, seeking conclusive proof that the last known slave ship, the *Clotilda*, was there; was the same year that I asked my master urban planner friend Renee Kemp-Rotan to imagine a museum honoring the Africans who had been illegally shipped aboard the *Clotilda* and who, after emancipation, came together to build Africatown in Mobile. I challenged her design studio to look to Africatown's incredible past while also proffering a peek into its potential future as a prosperous Black space where Black lives and Black history would be not only memorialized but celebrated, revitalized, and sustained by the growing interest in African American cultural heritage tourism. That year was 2018.

In 2019, the Alabama Historical Commission confirmed the *Clotilda* discovery, bolstering generational stories that the *Clotilda* descendants have handed down from ancestors who told them how they had been kidnapped by the king of Dahomey (in present-day Benin) and pirated in the ship's belly to cross the Atlantic from the beach in Quidah to Mobile. It was the last known shipment of enslaved Africans to North America. In the summer of 2020, despite a global pandemic, millions of Americans of every race, creed, and color flooded streets across the country, protesting the senseless murder-by-cop of George Floyd and the scores of other unnecessary extrajudicial killings of unarmed Black people by police and White vigilantes since Trayvon Martin's murder in 2012. The large protests were among the most sustained movements of civil unrest over the mistreatment of Black people in US history. And finally, this year, on January 6, 2021, a violent mob of mostly angry White people stormed the US Capitol to subvert the outcome of the presidential election, presumably convinced by the losing candidate that massive voter fraud had stolen his right to another four-year reign over America's affairs. Many righteously outraged citizens condemned the acts, saying, "This is not who America is," and "This is not my country."

But this *is* America.

African Americans can wearily recount how angry mobs overturned and prevented democratically elected Black and fair-minded White officials through murder and mayhem – in Wilmington, North Carolina, in 1898, in Colfax, Louisiana, in 1873 and New Orleans in 1874, and in Hamburg, South Carolina, in 1876. In these places, arithmetic was a problem for outnumbered White supremacists, for if free and fair elections meant that they could not win, they would resort to stoking White fear of Black political power in order to foment violence, terrorism, and suppression.

Today, America is at another tipping point in its history, forced again to grapple with its "Negro problem." And yet the still largely White design community is facing questions similar to those Young posed 50 years ago about its relevance, its complicity in designing buildings and spaces that perpetuate the mythos of America's greatness, its democracy and equality in the built environment in ways that dull the memories of very ugly and inconvenient truths.

It feels like we've been here before.

As in past iterations of this cycle, anguished Black voices today cry out in town squares, in streets, in corporate boardrooms, in state capitols, and in museums. The Museum of Modern Art in New York this year gave Black designers and architects a space not just to grieve but to imagine a better world, much like our ancestors did after emancipation and during America's post–Civil War Reconstruction period, only to see their dreams become real-life nightmares. The exhibition, "Reconstructions: Architecture and Blackness in America," investigated the intersections of architecture, Blackness, and anti-Black racism in the American context. The curators commissioned 11 projects by contemporary architects and designers to explore how Black cultural spaces, forms, and practices could be mobilized as sites of imagination, liberation, resistance, and refusal in the face of ongoing abuse and disenfranchisement of African Americans and African diaspora communities. The projects used photographs, drawings, digital renderings, constructions, videos,

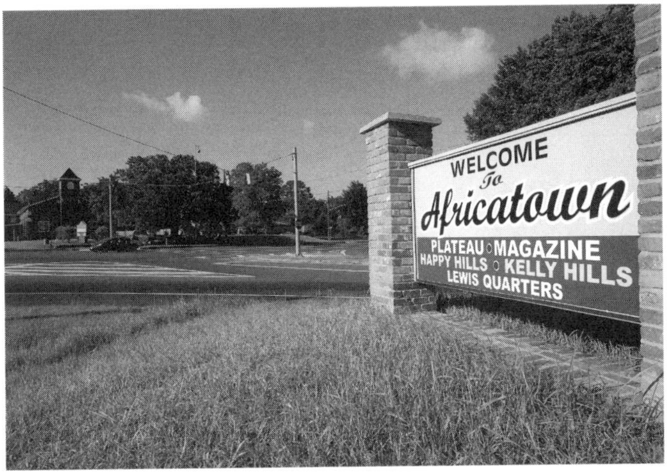

The welcome to Africatown sign acknowledges historical features of the area, and Union Missionary Baptist Church stands across the intersection, Mobile, Alabama, 2019. Photo: Mike Kittrell.

and models to envision or reframe how transformative spaces can galvanize Black life, from the kitchen to the front porch, the street, and the spaceship.

Black people have grappled for years with what Black community means, what it looks like, and whether it is even necessary in a "post-racial" America. "It's been really hard for Brown and Black people to imagine a future in this country," said one designer in the MoMA exhibition. "It's been a real challenge, because Black people in America are not given the space to even just *be*," said another.[1]

In Mobile, the *Clotilda* discovery again brought to the surface the fact that slavery is an ugly stain on the myth of American democracy and egalitarianism. Like the protests and unrest that roiled America in the late 1960s and upset the international view of the country, a new generation of citizens – who have had no personal experiences with or even awareness of the humiliations and horrors of slavery, Jim Crow, and the violent whitelash against Black success – have again been forced to reexamine history and what America truly means if its Black citizens must protest yet again repeated generational injustices. Can America be "great again" when this new generation is learning how some of their countrymen burned prosperous Black communities to the ground or drowned them in man-made lakes? How some terrorized successful Black citizens and diminished their voting power to create public policies that could lift them out of poverty? How others designed highways that ran right through the middle of Black neighborhoods and business districts? How some turned a blind eye to the growing scourge of drugs, then created policies that would incarcerate millions of undereducated, unemployed, impoverished Black people in a multibillion-dollar prison industrial complex?

1. "Reconstructions: Architecture and Blackness in America," YouTube video, 1:05, posted by The Museum of Modern Art, March 8, 2021, https://youtu.be/NKFqFjtlj9g.

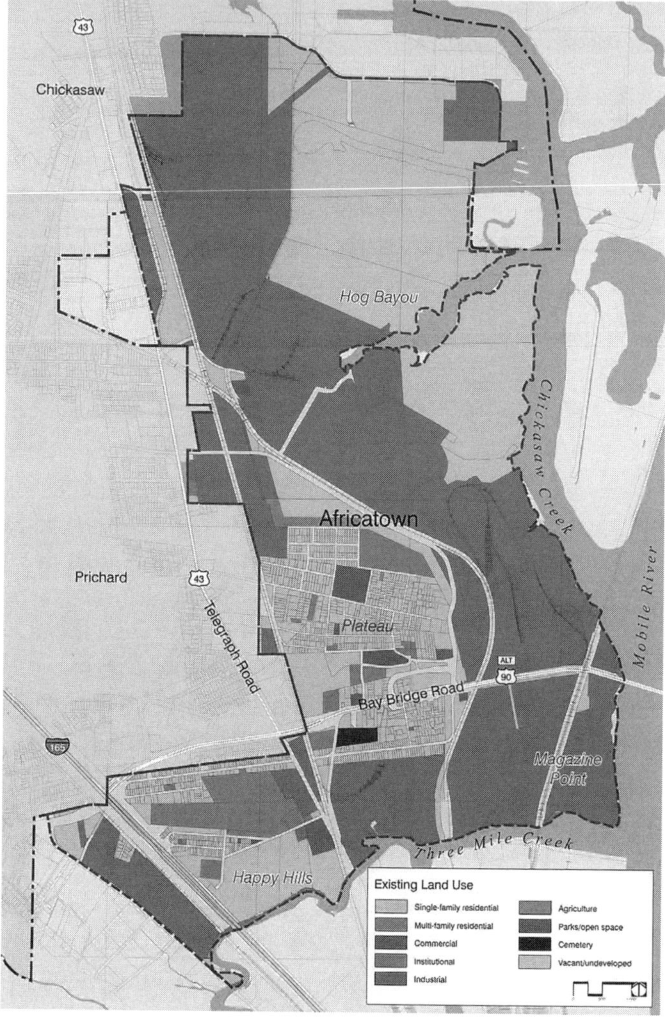

With the words of Young still reverberating in the ears of American architects, and despite the number of Black architects trained since 1968, how relevant is the profession in meeting the challenges of spatial justice in this round of American history? And what would Africatown add to the conversation?

Her children would tell today's designers, "Here is your chance to make your mark, an opportunity to help us reimagine our community, founded as a 19th-century settlement built after the Civil War by our ancestors, who were kidnapped by the king of Dahomey and sold to the *Clotilda* captain on a local plantation owner's bet, brought to toil mercilessly on plantations from Mobile to Selma." You would see the sadness in their eyes, but also a steely determination to thrive.

Unlike the children of enslaved Africans, who were born and literally bred like livestock in America, the *Clotilda* Africans

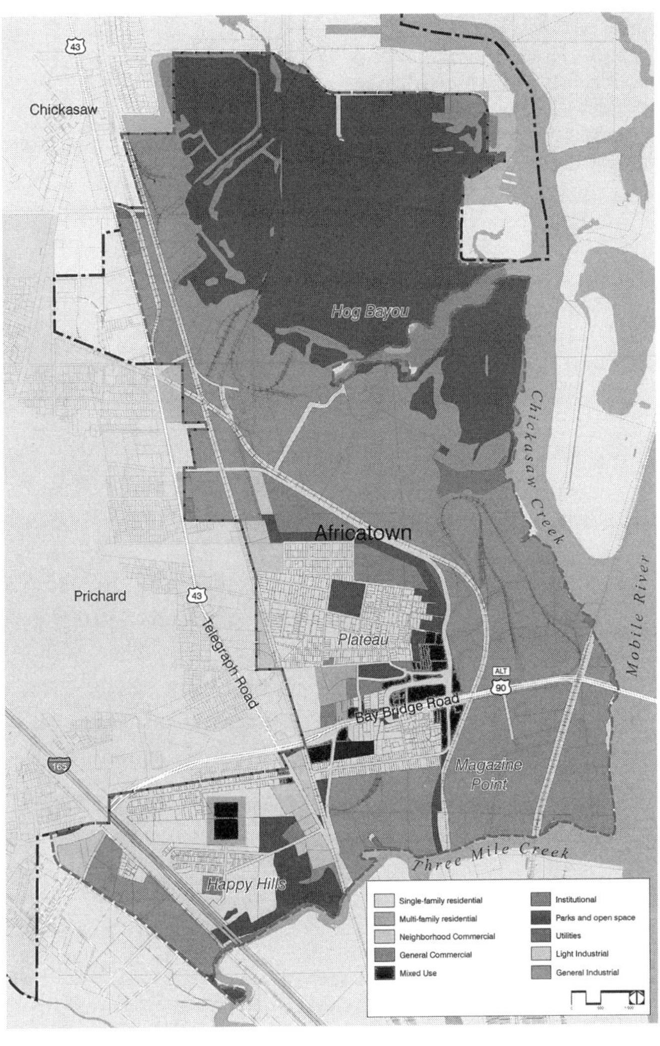

remembered their native lands and longed to return home. It was their dying wish, unfulfilled. But like other emancipated slaves, they too felt the weight of being a "problem" to the larger White society, even to other native-born African Americans. So they stayed to themselves; 32 *Clotilda* survivors settled down, worked to buy land from their former slave masters, and built the best lives they could during the Reconstruction era.[2]

The *Clotilda* Africans built their own churches, the first becoming Union Baptist. They built their own school – Mobile County Training School – with the help of Sears, Roebuck and Company philanthropist Julius Rosenwald and Tuskegee Institute's Booker T. Washington, the renowned Black leader of disciplined self-help who was determined to turn former slaves into hardworking, well-educated Black citizens who could ably run the affairs of their segregated communities.

2. See Sylviane A. Diouf, *Dreams of Africa in Alabama: The Slave Ship* Clotilda *and the Story of the Last Africans Brought to America* (Oxford: Oxford University Press, 2007), 154–55.

Cudjo Lewis with great-granddaughters Mary Lumbers and Martha Davis, twins born in 1923. Wilson C. Burton Collection. Photo courtesy The Doy Leale McCall Rare Book & Manuscript Library, University of South Alabama.

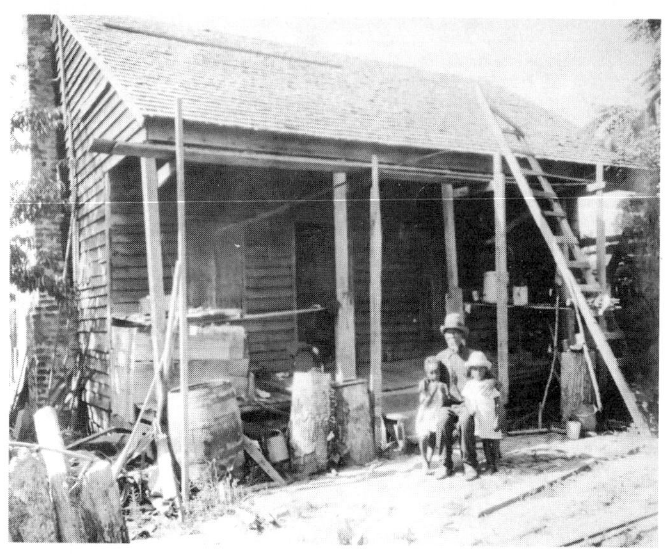

The *Clotilda* Africans managed to keep some folkways from their homelands, setting up their own governance structures, building each other's houses, and settling affairs without outside aid. Their collaborative efforts not only helped them to survive, they also built community pride that older residents and descendants fondly remember to this day.

Visions of the Past

Darron Patterson, a fifth-generation descendant of enslaved African Pollee Allen, spent the first 14 years of his life (1952 to 1966) in Africatown. A cofounder and president of the *Clotilda* Descendants Association, whose pride has been renewed since the slave ship's discovery, Patterson knows exactly what his beloved birthplace would say about itself:

As time went on those young, newly minted and now educated Africans grew me into a thriving community. All around were houses of people who all knew each other. By now thousands of neighbors who all had each other's backs!

Most of all, I remember the people… good people, happy people… sitting on their porches, with smoke billowing from old oil drums filled with damp rags set on fire to keep mosquitoes away. People were coughing and had red eyes from the smoke, but there weren't any mosquitoes. As cars drove by on Bay Bridge, the smoked-out porch-sitters would wave and horns would honk in response.

Those were good days.

Watching parents walk their kids to Whitley Elementary School, or the bigger kids walking in groups over to the iconic Mobile County Training School, all of them dressed in crisp uniforms… the girls in blue skirts and white blouses, the boys in dark

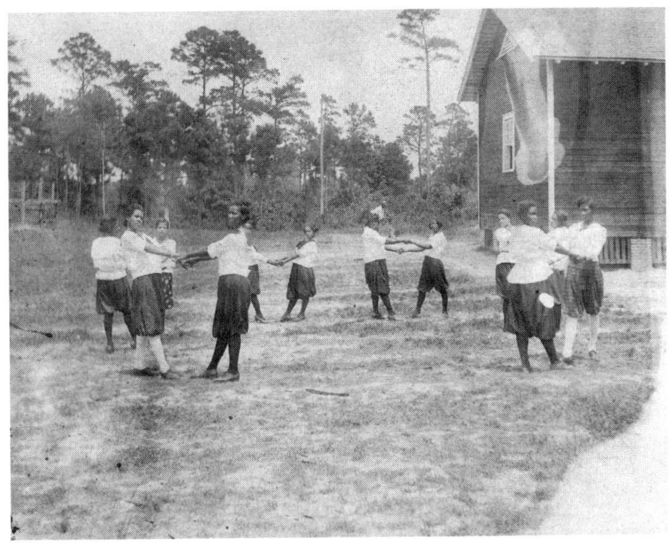

pants, with white shirts and dark ties.

The kids may not have known it at the time, but County was one of the historic Julius Rosenwald schools.

There was Randolph's Store and Clarence Allen's Store, one less than a quarter mile from the other on the main road, Bay Bridge, where the gas station, drive-in and…yes… even Mr. Day's United States Post Office all were.

Two more churches had been established, Yorktown and Hopewell, and would later be joined by a Catholic church, Our Mother of Mercy.

Deeper into the community there were even more stores, including Hubbard's, and down the street from there was where Mama Thelma Shamburger lived… the community midwife and closest thing to a doctor I had.

I can't possibly mention everybody who made me what I was, because there were just too many good folks who were the offspring of those Clotilda Africans, as well as some who had already settled here from days gone by.

A lot of those who made me what I am are still buried not far from the streets they used to walk and halls like the Elks Club where they used to dance.

I'm sad that so much roadway was taken by the city to widen Bay Bridge Road and I'm virtually sure some of those buried there in the Old Plateau Cemetery were bulldozed under, like discarded trash.

Giants like International and Scott paper companies were polluters, and Haas-Davis Meat Packing Company would spew the foul smell of slaughtered cattle so often that you eventually got used to it as just a part of another day.

How in the world could people here stay so happy, even when they had to rush to get their freshly washed clothes off the line so brown spots wouldn't get on them every time International or Scott decided to pump its filthy smoke into the air?

How could the people who lived in Happy Hill or Lewis Quarters, neighborhoods right at the back door of Haas-Davis, continue to smile when every breath they took on "kill days" was full of the smell of cooked animal flesh and boiling entrails?

You'd have to know my well-documented history very well to understand how all of these atrocities that the City of Mobile allowed to happen to me didn't matter.

But I have renewed hope that I will once again rise to the pinnacle of pride so many still have in me. Because I am Africatown, standing proud as a tribute to those who built me, for there will never be another community like me.

Africatown began facing environmental challenges from heavy industry after Augustine Meaher Jr. – grandson of Timothy Meaher, the man who had illegally shipped 110 Africans to Mobile in 1860 on a bet that he could get away with the crime – leased the land he owned along the Mobile River to large paper mills, International Paper and Scott Paper, starting in 1926. In doing so, the younger Meaher displaced hundreds of shotgun houses his family had leased for nearly 100 years to Africatown's poor Black residents, including some of the *Clotilda* descendants that his grandfather had owned after commissioning the pirate ship that brought them there in the first place. In a 1968 article about the displacements, Augustine Meaher dismissed claims that his tenants were complaining about moving to another Black community far from Africatown, saying, "You know, that's the way with n----rs. They'll be happy in a community – everybody together. They try and go back to African tribal life. He don't need garbage service – a darkie will feed it to his pigs. He don't need a bathtub – he'd probably store food in it. Wouldn't know how to use it."[3] His rental houses had no plumbing or foundations, and he relocated some of them north of Africatown to delay bringing them up to code after Mobile annexed Africatown into its municipal limits. He had doubts about the paved streets, garbage pickups, and other amenities the city brought, as well as code enforcements. "The water and sewage bill could easily run as high as rent," he said. "Besides, people have lived perfectly healthy and happy for years without running water and sewers."[4] Seen through the rose-colored lenses of his privileged childhood, Meaher said his family's Negro tenants were "very frugal people," making do with small gardens and a few hogs and

3. Jonathan Gordon, "Hard Times for Poor Folks," *Southern Courier*, March 16–17, 1968.
4. Roger Rapoport, "Grandson of Slave Ship's Captain Rents Houses to Negro Families," *Southern Courier*, June 17–18, 1967.
5. Ibid.

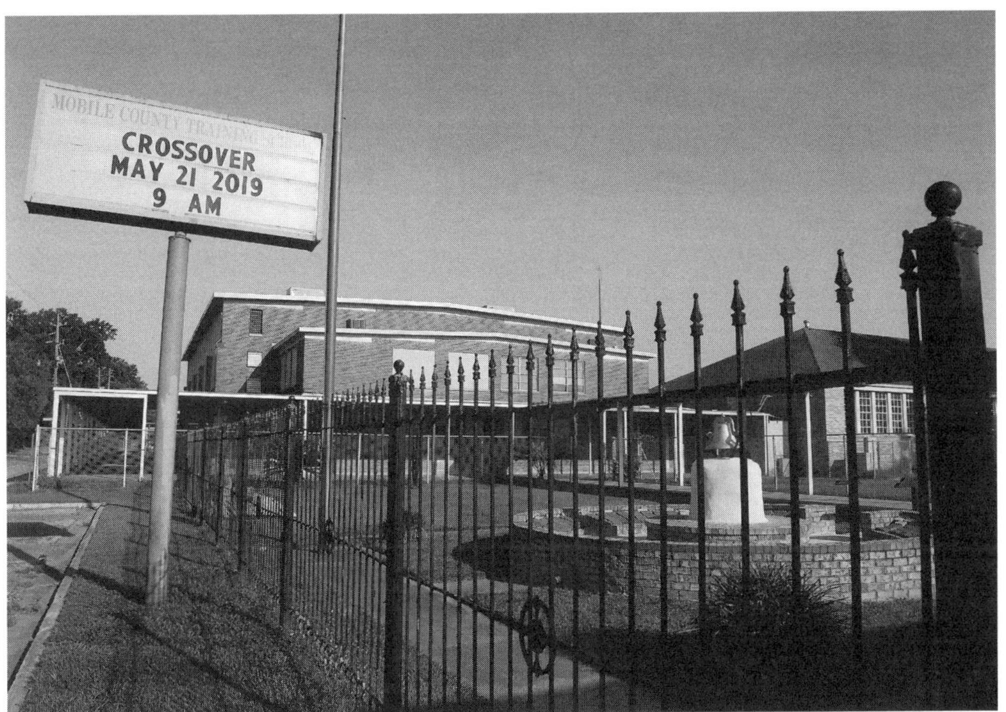

Africatown's Mobile County Training School, Mobile, Alabama, 2019. Photo: Mike Kittrell.

chickens in the yards around the shotgun houses that they rented for one dollar per week. "They always had a great time out there in Plateau, laughing and singing from Saturday night to Monday morning," he recalled. "I used to go there myself sometimes on the weekend and had some of the best times ever."[5]

Mobile's annexation of Africatown brought more highways and more industrial encroachment that led to soot falling from the sky like snow, as Patterson mentioned. Native son Joe Womack, a retired US Marine major and environmental justice advocate who heads the community nonprofit Africatown-CHESS (Clean, Healthy, Educated, Safe, Sustainable), recalls seeing the downward spiral of his beloved community. He follows in the footsteps of elders who fought to save their unique community from further industrial encroachment:

After I returned to Mobile from college and a stint in the military, I found Henry Williams and others fighting for and defending Africatown against industrial takeover and the loss of land within the community. I would go to City Council meetings and watch as Henry Williams, Mrs. Arealia Craig, Tommy Ballard, and others would yell at Mobile's City Council, letting them know how mad they were to have these issues come up over and over and over and over again.

Visions of the Future

For decades, Africatown had the unique advantage of know-ing the power of her history. Her leaders used whatever means they could muster to build the kind of environment around that history that would attract tourists and the money they would spend in Africatown to help revitalize the community.

In a 1981 *Mobile Press Register* article, Henry C. Williams, known as the father of Africatown and president of Africatown's Progressive League, envisioned a "total historic spot" that could include businesses, a library, a museum, a bank, and perhaps a "'little safari,' or a natural park." John Smith, mayor of the nearby city of Prichard, who had worked closely with Williams and other Africatown political leaders, envisioned "the largest Black historic preservation district in the United States," and the potential for it to have a sizable impact on the local economy.[6]

Back then, Africatown had the help of Black political leaders who worked on novel ideas such as creating a free trade zone and Africatown State Park in Prichard, on land International Paper sold to that city for one dollar, to estab-lish cultural and trade ties with West African countries, particularly Benin, which had been actively engaged in the

6. Cammie East, "Africatown works toward its future, honors its past," *Mobile Press Register*, July 5, 1981.

transatlantic slave trade with European colonizers of the New World. In 1999, Benin's president apologized profusely for its role in the slave trade. One of its kings of Dahomey, whose female soldiers often overtook nearby villages, had sold kidnapped Africans to the *Clotilda* captain. Africatown's civic and political leaders also worked to have a portion of Africatown placed on the National Register of Historic Places.

Today Africatown residents use the Africatown Neighborhood Plan, a visioning document commissioned through the City of Mobile in 2016, as a shield against developments they have agreed they do not want and as a guide to promote the kinds of developments they do want to see:

- an upgraded Mobile County Training School and more opportunities for youth
- a better-maintained historic cemetery
- less residential blight and more new homes
- Africatown as a tourism destination with attractions
- more landscaping and wayfinding signs in the district
- greater access to technology
- more businesses, including a grocery store
- more cultural activities

Joycelyn Davis – a sixth generation direct descendant of Oluale (whose enslaved name was Charlie Lewis) and Maggie Lewis, vice president of the *Clotilda* Descendants Association and organizer of the annual Spirit of our Ancestors Festival every February – has held scores of interviews since the *Clotilda* discovery. She keeps her heart firmly rooted in her family and community history, while looking forward to the future:

I have lived in the Africatown area for over 40 years now, and I love my neighborhood and telling the story of how my ancestors survived the middle passage, enslavement, Jim Crow and segregation.

Africatown is and will always be a part of my life, and I am now proud to pick up the baton of our history and carry it forward in my generation.

The newly found discovery of the last documented slave ship in the United States, the Clotilda *has put the Africatown community on the map. As a little girl visiting my great grandmother in Lewis Quarters and my grandmother on Railroad Street, you couldn't have told me that one day the ship would be found.*

But it's not about the ship, it's about the people, as I have told reporters who have flocked to Africatown only because the Clotilda *was found. This new attraction has the potential to give Africatown its chance to become more of the self-sustaining community I once knew as a child.*

I envision Africatown with affordable homes for first-time home owners, a veterans' home, a daycare center with senior services, tutoring facilities, increased enrollment numbers in our feeder schools, restaurants, salons, barbershops, laundromats, museums, performing arts studios, historical markers, murals – the list is endless. I envision Africatown will look like no other neighborhood in the Mobile area. Africatown should resemble Africa, the land my ancestors could not return to, the land I hope to see one day.

The Future Seen Through a Design Challenge

In 2018, our nonprofit M.O.V.E. (Making Opportunities Viable for Everyone) Gulf Coast Community Development Corporation commissioned studiorotan, a cultural heritage/civic design firm, to explore a range of planning tools that could unite divergent Africatown community interests under a single big idea as well as leverage the *Clotilda* discovery to launch a long-desired community revitalization. It would include what Africatown wants for herself – affordable housing to attract new residents, a workforce program including arts and technology at Mobile County Training School, a mixed-use development on an abandoned public housing site, eco-trails along 14-plus miles of waterways called the Africatown Connections Blueway, and the Benin House Project in nearby Prichard, a dream of reunification initiated with Benin.

These concepts are integral parts of the big idea, pulled together in the Africatown International Design Idea Competition, launched on Juneteenth (June 19) 2021. In addition to being a master-planning tool, the competition explores design as a spatial justice tool based on Africatown's unique cultural identity. Thus, it harnesses the power of design to create culturally significant architectural solutions within a well-defined matrix of various Black spaces – monuments, memorials, interpretive sites, and amenities. The competition is organized around four sites, each with four venues that vigorously pursue the design of sacred places, where Africatown can be honored and her history explored through immersive and interactive interpretive experiences across three cities and along 14 miles of waterways. The story also spans two continents by reestablishing cultural and commercial exchanges between the enslaved and those who sold them into slavery, Africans reconciling with African Americans and the worldwide diaspora and producing their own Afrofuturistic paths forward.

The Africatown International Design Idea Competition invites all designers to participate in creating ideas for a new community-regenerating tourism system that transforms Africatown into a 21st-century, technologically advanced and culturally connected African American community. Personally, I envision that African countries will one day send ships to the Port of Mobile with containers of minerals and agricultural products that can be processed and distributed in the US and worldwide. I imagine seeing these countries leading cultural arts exchanges with the descendants of those whom they sold into slavery, reconciled in peace and working in mutual cooperation on the global stage to make life better for Black people on both sides of the Atlantic. I call it Africatown 2.0 as Wakanda, with advances in clean energy, high-speed broadband, and sports and recreational facilities, where man and nature live in a balanced environment. It is an Afrofuturistic vision for Black lives that has yet to be designed and built.

However, as organizers and promoters of this grand vision with the Africatown community, who are all African American – and we hesitate to ask the question, but we must – is such a utopian, Afrofuturistic fantasy for the 21st-century iteration of Africatown, and for other Black neighborhoods and districts, even possible in America, as several exhibitors in MoMA's "Reconstructions: Architecture and Blackness in America" wondered out loud? Would these spaces be safe spaces for Black lives? Is the spectacle of communities full of Black joy, positive cultural expressions, political prowess, and economic success in America still vulnerable to violent whitelash? Or might they be made to suffer from a more benign form of disdain or cultural neglect in a White-dominated society that sees no value in Black places like Africatown, apart from their potential to attract tourists and their dollars for purely capitalistic reasons?

The keepers of Africatown's memories, its storytellers, its dreamers and visionaries, its advocates and protectors, see the intrinsic value of their ancestors' legacies. They feel the beckoning call of Mother Africa to share the story and tell the whole truth, so that she too might be set free from the karmic consequences of her past actions and repair relations with the children of those whom her leaders unknowingly sold into the worst forms of chattel slavery, and in doing so, were also poisoned by the insidious toxin of White superiority through colonization.

It is up to the current and next generations of architects – of all hues, in this circle of American history come round again – to decide that our future depends on their ability to competently dream, design, and build a world where Black people's aspirations are possible, not just in Africatown but in all historic Black communities that dot the country, in various states of repair or disrepair, especially those seeking heritage preservation and regeneration. In doing so, they will create opportunities for all of humanity to learn the full story of America and to grow from her past mistakes, just as the US is being led to do now in this cycle of its history.

The Design Brief

In portions from the competition program overview and brief, Kemp-Rotan writes that the visions designers are challenged to imagine for Africatown include:

sacred public spaces and interpretive landscapes, signature education facilities and preserved historic housing, welcome centers and museums with performing arts centers, boathouses and yacht clubs, walking paths in a mixed-income neighborhood, with water-edge taxis that take you along the Africatown Connections Blueway toward Prichard's enchanted forests in Africatown State Park, which opens up to a world-class concert hall, an Africa museum, luxury hotel, business centers and African tourism agencies, gateways and parks on an international trade complex built to further reconciliation and reconnection between former slave-trading nations along the coast of Africa and the African Diaspora, all while preserving Africatown's heritage and promoting its future with memorable narratives for the Africatown community, the city, and the world.

Taken together, all of these stories on all of the sites and venues are designed to tell an authentic and unique African American narrative in what we call The Africatown Cultural Mile. It is designed to serve as a physical, economic and cultural network built on tourism that reshapes the perception of Africatown – from that of a singular and discrete place to a geopolitical narrative about social justice, American slavery, discovery of the Clotilda, *celebration of Africatown Founders and* Clotilda *descendants, preservation and promotion of Africatown for cultural tourism, destination planning and the economic vitality of the Africatown community, City of Mobile, State of Alabama, this region and the world. Wakanda forever.*

So, designers, Africatown offers you the chance to make a meaningful contribution to its future, and by extension, to other Black communities struggling to revive, thrive, and just *be*.

Vickii Howell, a former award-winning journalist with the *Birmingham News*, is president and CEO of M.O.V.E. Joycelyn Davis is an education specialist working with special needs students. Darron Patterson, a prize-winning sportswriter for the *Detroit News*, was the first African American sportswriter at the *Mobile Press Register*. Joe Womack, a passionate environmental justice advocate for Africatown, writes a blog about community issues.

Deborah Gans

What Does It Mean to Be Safe?

1. See Étienne-Louis Boullée, *Architecture, Essay on Art*, ed. Helen Rosenau, trans. Sheila de Vallée, in Helen Rosenau, *Boullée & Visionary Architecture* (London: Academy Editions, 1976), 95.
2. Ibid., 97.

In his 1785 design for a theater on the Place du Carrousel in Paris, Étienne-Louis Boullée envisioned how an architecture of almost cosmic grandeur could ensure public safety in the event of fire. The primary structure was to be fireproof construction of metal and stone. Any wood scenery or interiors that caught fire would fall into a "large reservoir" beneath its floor and thus be extinguished.[1] Boullée describes how the circular plan sponsors a radial array of doors to provide the audience with escape routes equally positioned without regard to their tier of seats in the theater or situation in society.[2] This architecture is at once a rational response to potential physical danger and a symbolic trope of the social and spatial preconditions for democracy that would soon be implemented (if briefly) by the French Revolution of 1789. The fire from which the citizenry would flee signified the triple threat of the monarchy's absolute power, the unstoppable force of a social disruption that ultimately led from the Revolution to the Terror, and the existential annihilation of the individual subject in the fire's all-consuming flame. For Boullée, the theater's power to bring order to chaos depended on its fireproof materials and on a new, scaleless form of beauty uncoupled from humanist proportions as well as on a new engineering capable of simulating the enormity and force of nature, as conjured by the lakelike reservoir. He describes this architecture as one of "sublime beauty" in the sense of engendering awe rather than the terror that accompanies social disaster and individual death. Other philosopher aestheticians, such as Edmund Burke and Immanuel Kant, similarly understood the subjective power of the sublime as a challenge to the previously rational order of beauty. But, whereas Burke recoiled in fright from the release of the sublime force of the American Revolution, Boullée dared to propose it as the necessary antecedent to a new social order that would be characterized and facilitated by this "sublime beauty."

Boullée's work resonates in our particular moment with its similarly existential risks of fire and flood and the need for a new, revolutionary order by which to manage them; but our responses fall short of his sophisticated vision. Thus far, we have managed the concoction of man-made and natural forces that fuel our version of *"le déluge"* with technocratic regulations, which are beholden to the political economy of market risk. Our flood insurance policies are a prime example of how we attempt to control threats to society and nature through actuarial and financial calculation. In 1968, the United States government created the National Flood Insurance Program though the National Flood Insurance Act. This act requires that the government both pay for losses due to flooding from federal funds and reduce those losses by demanding that states and cities adopt local floodplain management measures; in this way, it explicitly links insurance to urban planning and architecture. To qualify for either government funding or flood insurance, residential construction within floodplains must be built above the height of the so-called 100-year flood, meaning a flood with a one percent risk per year or 30 percent risk over the life of a mortgage. Localities use federally issued flood maps and regulations, largely determined by the Federal Emergency Management Agency (FEMA), as the basis for their floodplain management. While cities often script even stricter design guidelines to account for sea level rise induced by climate change, they also challenge the federal maps and redraw them to exempt land they want to develop. New York City has made such challenges. In other words, the planning of our cities takes place in a battle between local development interests and FEMA actuaries, both of whom see our future in terms of economic risk. The potential collapse of a settlement in the wake of climate change is measured no differently than, for example, the impact on fish and the fish industry in an over-harvested watershed; both are simple market failures.

A visual scan of neighborhoods rebuilt in floodplains after disasters from Houston to New York reveals a new vernacular of a society preserved and defined through flood insurance. Rows of bungalows and ranch houses hover on stilts above the mandated flood elevation in blithe indifference to the fact that, in the event of the 100-year flood, the residents will still confront impassable streets and flooded backyards, this time from the risky isolation of their individual stairs. Even on a sunny day, the heightened social isolation of neighborhoods without street-level corner stores is palpable. These vulnerabilities at the scales of the block and the neighborhood flow directly from the structure of flood insurance itself, which reimburses the building owner only for building damages. There are exceptions, most notably the United States Department of Housing and Urban Development (HUD) National Disaster Resilience Competition, which funded innovative large-scale infrastructures developed with community support, as in the necklace of coastal wetlands for the southern tip of Manhattan, called The BIG U, or the acupuncture of parks, pumps, and green streets planned for Bridgeport, Connecticut. However, to date, our national investments in flood management have neither fully embraced Boullée-scaled engineering of enormous floodgates nor the more incremental infrastructures envisioned by HUD; rather, they rely on federal community block grants that, despite their nomenclature, fund only reconstruction on an individual lot and are unable to address even the infrastructures of water, sewage, and power that serve it. This policy reflects the American devotion to private property as the fundamental source of our wealth and well-being, self-protection and identity; it privileges a concept of safety derived from protective powers of homeownership, rather than from, as Boullée argued, our civic and common life.

New Orleans after Hurricane Katrina has played out both the obvious shortcomings and the more insidious social implications of our actuarial approach to risk. The first, short-lived initiative of the Urban Land Institute (ULI) designated entire low-lying neighborhoods that had been decimated by the storm as at risk and proposed the complete erasure of their human settlement in preparation for their reclamation by a natural habitat conceived of as authentic and spontaneous wetland. But, because ULI inscribed this post-Anthropocene vision as a series of perfect green circles over a map of larger New Orleans, the plan read not as a shift in the balance of natures but rather as the gesture of a sovereign political power, like a reboot of urban renewal or the implementation of a demilitarized zone. Equally damning was their choice of locations for those circles, many of which wiped out poorer neighborhoods of color while allowing wealthier, more White, equally submerged neighborhoods to persist. Public outcry put an end to it, although the slow-moving and inadequate funds to rebuild individual homes, and the absence of resources to rebuild social infrastructures like schools, ultimately led to a disorganized and dispersed flight from these neighborhoods in any case. Former First Lady Barbara Bush infamously implied that Katrina was a success in that the diasporic population landed in places with more job opportunities, like Houston, and coincidentally produced a less Black, less poor, and less Democratic New Orleans.

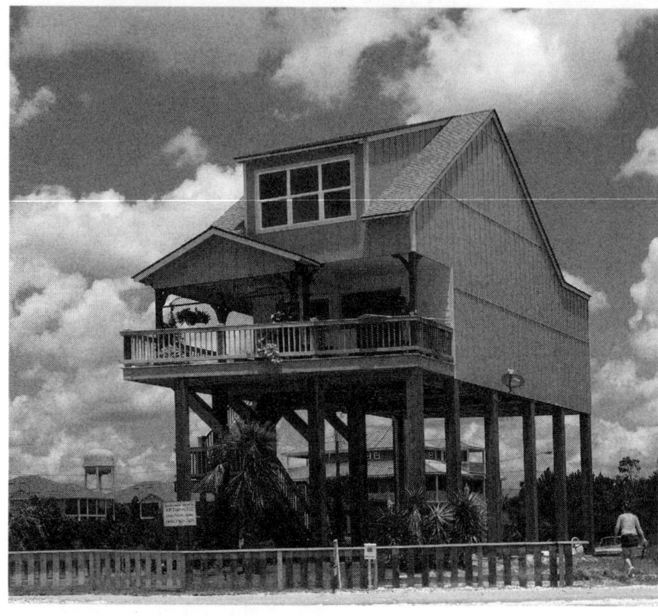

3. For histories of the Vietnamese in New
Orleans East, see Christopher A. Airriess
and David L. Clawson, "Versailles: A
Vietnamese Enclave in New Orleans,
Louisiana," *Journal of Cultural Geography*
12, no. 1 (1991): 1–13; Karen J. Leong et
al., "Resilient History and the Rebuilding
of a Community: The Vietnamese
American Community in New Orleans
East," *Journal of American History* 94, no. 3:
Through the Eye of Katrina: The Past as
Prologue? (December 2007): 770–79. For
a detailed case study of Village de L'Est,
see Annemarie Gray, *Community-Based
Rebuilding in New Orleans: The Story of
Village de L'Est*, Resilient Cities Housing
Initiative, MIT, June 15, 2014.

Despite the challenge of remaining, some of the vulnerable chose to stay because they considered ad hoc displacement and the dispersion of their community networks to be the greater threat to their safety than flooding. One such neighborhood, Village de L'Est, a vast suburban territory established by a single developer in the 1950s, had slowly shifted over time from a largely White and middle-class population to one of mixed race and economic strata. The Village has a large Vietnamese population who, sponsored by the Catholic Church, arrived as refugees in the 1970s and remain bound together through religion, language, their shared practices of gardening and fishing, and a fear of further displacement.[3] Through the Catholic Mary Queen of Vietnam Church and its priest Father Nguyen The Vien, the community asserted their identity and credentials as a culture that knew how to live with water and had already effectively adapted those practices to their new watery location along Lake Pontchartrain and could do so again.

The current language for discussing the human response to climate change is that of adaptation, mitigation, and retreat. Adaptation usually refers to reactive strategies, such as the elevation of a house in response to a floodplain, while mitigation implies active measures of environmental control, like carbon sequestration, and retreat signals abandonment. But when reconsidered in its stronger, biological sense, adaptation refers to the active adjustment of organisms to their environment to improve their chances of survival, inclusive of

4. See Charles Darwin, *The Descent of Man, and Selection in Relation to Sex*, 2nd ed. (London: John Murray, 1882), 75–86 and throughout.

5. See Peter Kropotkin, *Mutual Aid: A Factor of Evolution* (London: William Heinemann, 1902), 153–86.

their culture and social behavior. Contemporary discussions of sociobiological adaptation increasingly embrace Charles Darwin's concept of "sympathy" in a community of a species as intrinsic to its survival. While he is best known for the principle of natural selection, wherein survival and evolution derive from individual advantage (a principle that actually originated with Herbert Spencer, as Darwin acknowledged), his late book *The Descent of Man, and Selection in Relation to Sex* is a lengthy paean to the sociability of many animals, the services they render one another, and their "heroism," all of which contribute to the emergence of increasingly large, complex communities.[4] The framing of our capitalist culture of individualism as a social Darwinism evolving through the survival of the fittest is only the first half of Darwin's story. The complement is mutual aid, so called by Peter Kropotkin in his 1902 book of the same name, a vision of radical sociability derived from the biological role of cooperation in *The Descent of Man*.[5] Kropotkin describes the human models of successful sociability in terms reminiscent of other turn-of-the-century theorists like Ruskin and William Morris who gravitated toward a somewhat mythologized interpretation of the medieval village. Kropotkin's medieval inspirations are the commons, an agriculture-based organization of property held and worked collectively to everyone's mutual economic and environmental benefit; the guild, its urban manufacturing equivalent; and the marketplace, where the production of the village is sold to the stranger. But Kropotkin also provides examples of sociability from his native prerevolutionary Russia that stand in opposition to the emerging European industrialized capitalist culture. He describes a roving association of peasants who travel from village to village implementing a distributed infrastructure of large machinery like threshers, industrialized principles of crop rotation with artificial meadows, and strategically linked drainage and irrigation in order to incrementally establish the equivalent of factory farm production without disrupting the socioeconomic structure of the preindustrial commons.

The citizens of Village de L'Est secured their habitat and their right to remain through such principles of adaptation in this sense of sympathy and mutual aid, and of sociability of a complex sort. Under the leadership of their priest, they formalized their preexisting loose social associations and eventually created a community development corporation, MQVN CDC, for their mutual benefit. As a cohesive lobby, they successfully prevented the opening of a local garbage dump, which could have endangered their gardens, and subsequently won reparations after the BP oil spill polluted the water and soil in 2010. But this process also required them to find sympathetic allies beyond their immediate community, the largest and most powerful being the sustainability movement. The selling of garden vegetables in a local produce market is "organic permaculture" in the lingua franca of sustainability. In a subsequent project of MQVN CDC, Viet Village Urban Farm, the translation between the local and generic culture of sustainability is simultaneous, and the adaptation mutual.

MQVN CDC obtained a 28-acre site in order to consolidate and relocate the community's ad hoc individual gardens, some of which were illegally situated on the banks of a nearby canal. It was to include areas for livestock, small family and large commercial farm plots, and a series of restrained but monumental sheds to host a produce market for the 3,000 visitors who arrived on weekends to wander among the blankets and tailgates loaded with vegetables in the shopping center parking lot. The project descriptions present the farm's award-winning design by Mossop + Michaels Landscape Architects as a conflict-free melding of "the traditional Vietnamese way" with sustainable, low-tech farming practices of biofiltration, which requires little or no electricity to pump and filter water used in the fields, integrated pest control, crop rotation, and other sustainable techniques.[6] The urban farm is both an ecological and cultural adaptation of Village de L'Est to a new reality and an adaptation of the American coastal suburb to the more communal ways of Village de L'Est. As previously noted, Village de L'Est was established before the arrival of the refugees and named in reference to its village-like vision of suburbia in New Orleans East; but that name now came to denote the "imaginary," as anthropologist Allison Truitt describes it,[7] of a rural, specifically Vietnamese way of life that eschews market forces in its communal practices. This "imaginary" somewhat disguises the facts that many of the refugees came from Saigon's urban fish industry and that they sought to expand their economic and political power in the New Orleans establishment through this consolidated enterprise. As in Kropotkin's vision, the residents saw their commons not as antithetical to late capitalism but rather as a competitive alternative whereby they could use the evolving technological means and social norms of sustainability to retain their internal self-rule and negotiate with the stranger in the marketplace. The images of empty cultivated fields and of Saturday shoppers

6. "Analysis and Planning Award of Excellence: Viet Village Urban Farm," ASLA 2008 Professional Awards, American Society of Landscape Architects, https://www.asla.org/awards/2008/08winners/411.html.
7. See Allison Truitt, "The Viet Village Urban Farm and the Politics of Neighborhood Viability in Post-Katrina New Orleans," *City & Society* 24, no. 3 (2012): 321–38.

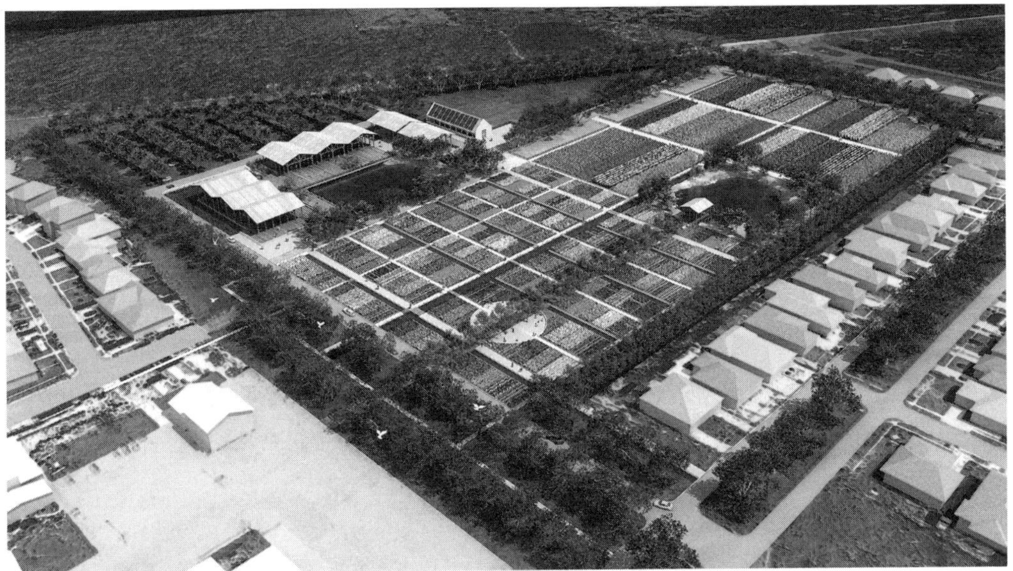

Mossop + Michaels Landscape
Architects, Viet Village Urban Farm,
New Orleans, 2007–11. Aerial perspec-
tive. Drawing courtesy the architects.

roaming among garden plots leave the forms of agricultural
labor indeterminate; the crops could be harvested by machines
and weeded by robots as easily as by grandparents wearing
straw hats. This indeterminacy precisely describes the community at that moment, which had previously kept to itself
as a way of protecting its identity but now realized that its
survival depended on a rapprochement with the politics of
greater New Orleans and America at large. While the project
was not realized – ironically because the property turned out
to be a brownfield – the images worked in terms of realpoli-
tik; a resident of Village de L'Est, Cyndi Nguyen, elected in
2017, became the first Asian American on the New Orleans
City Council.

The design for the sheds of Viet Village Urban Farm purposely renders the market stands, the fecundity of the farm
itself, and the once anonymous suburb, which ULI considered of little value, as heroic. This heroic narrative posits
the mutual adaptation of the suburb to the imaginary of the
farm and of the refugee to the American capitalist, if green,
economy. What is missing is mention of Hurricane Katrina
and the inevitable future of flooding due to climate change.
The landscape architects describe how the site's serious environmental challenges from nonpermeable soil, an absence of
positive drainage (it's flat), a high water table, and concomi-
tant frequent flooding led to their creative and expert design
of bioswales and systems of stormwater runoff; but they dare
not provide a long-term prognosis. Additionally, Village de
L'Est was resettled so quickly by residents intent on returning

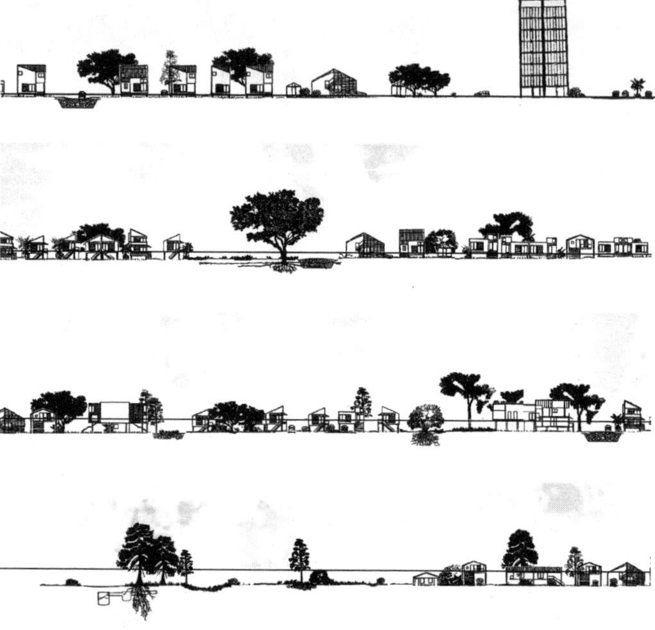

from Houston that most homes were simply repaired with homeowner savings rather than elevated with federal insurance money; thus the entire village remains a grounded ranch house suburb at risk. The renderings of sheds hovering over cultivated but empty fields suggest the presence of a vibrant community tending a substantial landscape. But the same view if rendered after "the deluge," with the sheds and fields abandoned to wetland, would not look so different. The scene contains the suggestion of its own eventual ruin along the trajectory of sea level rise.

Another plan for a similar community in New Orleans East, Plum Orchard, did directly confront the future of houses on an inevitably sinking terrain. The residents of Plum Orchard belong to that other imaginary of New Orleans, the multigenerational Black enclave, which Katrina thrust into view with its disaster imagery of the Lower Ninth Ward, but in fact also exists in the banality of the suburb. The Black neighbors of Plum Orchard arrived from the Lower Ninth Ward prior to the suburbanization of New Orleans East as owners of fishing shacks, then rebuilt them as ranch-style homes and bungalows in order to claim a piece of the American Dream denied to them in the adjoining tract-built White suburbs. Many of the current residents descend from the original families and own multiple properties. The superficial anomie of the suburban fabric disguises these long-standing social networks, which have served as a safety net in the absence of the state. Long before Katrina, the residents had established local community economies and infrastructures, renting apartments, selling homes, employing one another, lending money, and watching each other's children. Like the Vietnamese community, they too concluded that displacement presented the greater threat to their socioeconomic safety and chose to remain.

In Plum Orchard, as in Village de L'Est, the adaptive strategies took the form of a new commons but of a character particular to the residents' understanding of their landscape and property. As multigenerational citizens of New Orleans, they understood that, even in the city's low-lying territories, every inch of elevation counts in ways that FEMA flood maps do not register. A local community developer, the Association of Community Organizations for Reform Now, and their planners and architects (of whom I was one) took up this alternative reading of their landscape in order to challenge the authority of the FEMA flood documents, producing a much finer-grain mapping of elevation that revealed additional changes in grade across the eight blocks of the neighborhood.[8] High ground suitable for multistory residential and commercial development appeared along the literal highway of Chef Menteur; reasonable elevations for individual homes could be established between that highway and the low ground toward Lake Pontchartrain destined to eventually return to wetland. The family holdings of multiple lots allowed the residents to imagine the redistribution of their houses according to this map and to embrace the idea of rebuilding at the scale of the enclave, despite the federal policy that only funded the rebuilding of owner-occupied houses on their pre-storm individual lots. Even without financial support for large infrastructure, they could reshape their backyards without regard for property lines, as a shared water management landscape of plantings, swales, and dry wells. Engineering runoff calculations demonstrated that this collective landscape would allow the neighborhood to perform as a self-sustaining system to retain and drain a 10-year flood, although to accommodate the 100-year flood mandate required the additional rehabilitation of a city-owned pumping station at the lower end of the site. The project developers and designers then lobbied the district planners, who included this pump along with other civic-scaled infrastructures like a rapid transit bus route along Chef Menteur in their long-term plan.[9]

The architecture proposed for the resettlement of Plum Orchard is largely bungalows and sheds on stilts in

8. This project was executed by Pratt Center for Community Development, Ron Shiffman, Brad Lander, Deborah Gans, James Dart, Darius Sollohub, and Denise Hoffman Brandt along with students from Pratt Institute, New Jersey Institute of Technology, and the City College of New York under a HUD grant. For a more in-depth description of the work, see Carol McMichael Reese, Michael Sorkin, and Anthony Fontenot, eds., *New Orleans Under Reconstruction: The Crisis of Planning* (New York: Verso, 2014).

9. The engineering of the neighborhood was performed by Darius Sollohub and students of the Master of Infrastructure Planning program of New Jersey Institute of Technology and incorporated into the Planning District 9 Recovery Plan by St. Martin Brown & Associates.

acknowledgment of the financial limits on investment in this provisional landscape. Its material restraint presents *ars povera* as an alternative heroic gesture, akin to that of the Viet Village Urban Farm market shed. However, the real monumental work here is the reshaping of properties as a collective wetland and new commons that can preserve their individual value in the face of extreme risk. The most significant representation of the project is a cut taken just beneath the sill plate of the repositioned homes at design flood elevation. The neighborhood appears as an unencumbered field of pilotis inscribed on a continuous field of flora and fauna that it barely impacts. The residential property lines remain, but because the houses are raised, they are somehow disengaged from these lines.

This disengagement of a community as a whole from its ground, but not from its sense of self or place, speaks to an emerging reality beyond the extreme conditions of climate change. In these two tales of New Orleans, Village de L'Est and Plum Orchard, residents chose adaptation rather than retreat, in part because they couldn't afford to leave either their homes, which often represent their entire equity, or their communities, which provide their social safety nets. Their belief in the power of the commons to provide for their physical and social safety prevailed over actuarial assessment of individual risk. Indeed, current identity politics frames safety in similar terms, through a collective that protects the individuals within it and negotiates as a social commons with larger external systems. As Darwin wrote, "As man advances in civilization, and small tribes are united into larger communities, the simplest reason would tell each individual that he ought to extend his social instincts and sympathies to all the members of the same nation, though personally unknown to him . . . until they are extended to all sentient beings."[10] In the case of New Orleans and other geographies impacted by climate change, environmental crises will most likely force these inhabitants, already partially unmoored from their property, to depart and adapt again. They will abandon their territories to other sentient beings and become the strangers dependent on the hospitality of others. It is beyond the scope of this essay to imagine this future shift in status of our suburban denizens from villager to refugee or the shape of the commons that could welcome them; but through their steadfast occupation of a landscape of instability at the threshold of unmanageable risk, they have opened up new understandings of what it means to be safe.

10. Darwin, 122–23.

Deborah Gans FAIA is principal architect of Gans & Company and professor at Pratt Institute School of Architecture. Her writings on related subjects can be found in *Cities without Citizens*, *Urban Omnibus*, and *Places Journal*, among others.

Matthew Soules

UHNWIs and The Superprime

Editor's note: This essay is an excerpt from Matthew Soules's book Icebergs, Zombies, and the Ultra Thin: Architecture and Capitalism in the Twenty-First Century *(Princeton Architectural Press, 2021).*

Housing, and architecture along with it, is at the center of the 21st century's growing inequality. Architecture has always been a primary means to manifest and display wealth, but as the rich get richer and more money flows into the built environment in this era of heightened economic extremes, it is becoming synonymous with marketing and real estate. As a result, architecture appears significantly different than it did during the relative economic equality of the 1960s.

Increasing Inequality

A useful frame in which to consider the correlation between inequality and finance capitalism is the Organisation for Economic Cooperation and Development (OECD). The 37 OECD member nations include those commonly accepted as possessing the world's most advanced capitalist economies, which for the most part exhibit pronounced attributes of finance capitalism.[1] Inequality has risen over the past 25 years in all OECD countries but Turkey, Chile, and Mexico.[2]

Economist Thomas Piketty argues that whenever the rate of return on capital is larger than the rate of economic growth over a significant period of time, wealth inequality increases.[3] Piketty believes that the concentration of wealth is a fundamental quality of capitalism itself and that it was only under a unique set of conditions that the wealth gap decreased between 1930 and 1975. Yet it is a compelling correlation that the current ascent of finance capitalism started around the same time as the current growth in wealth inequality.

Piketty's core position is that capitalism is structurally predisposed to favor returns on investment over wages from labor. The development of finance capitalism since 1980 emphasizes investing as the preferred form of capitalist activity, accelerating the rate of return on capital and therefore generating heightened inequality between investors and wage earners. As inequality has increased, so has the sheer number of wealthy individuals. The finance industry refers to exceptionally wealthy people as *high net worth individuals* (HNWIs). An HNWI is an individual with financial assets in excess of $1 million, excluding the value of a primary

1. OECD's member nations include countries in Europe and North America, along with Japan, South Korea, Colombia, Chile, Turkey, Israel, Australia, and New Zealand.
2. See "Inequality," Organisation for Economic Cooperation and Development, accessed May 31, 2020, http://www.oecd.org/social/inequality.htm.
3. See Thomas Piketty, *Capital in the Twenty-First Century* (Cambridge: Harvard University Press, 2014).

4. See Merrill Lynch and Cap Gemini Ernst & Young, *World Wealth Report 2001* (2001), 3. http://www.in.capgemini.com/m/in/tl/pdf_2001_World_Wealth_Report.pdf.

5. See Capgemini, *World Wealth Report 2018* (2018), 8. https://www.capgemini.com/wp-content/uploads/2018/06/Capgemini-World-Wealth-Report.pdf.

6. See Vincent White et al., *World Ultra Wealth Report 2018* (New York: Wealth X, 2018), 10.

7. Ibid. See also, Capgemini and RBC Wealth Management, *World Wealth Report 2013* (2013), 7. https://www.cap-gemini.com/se-en/wp-content/uploads/sites/29/2017/07/wwr_2013_1.pdf.

8. White et al., 11.

9. Ibid., 13.

residence – essentially, a person who has more than a million dollars available for investment. Since 1996, the French multinational corporation Capgemini, in collaboration with various financial institutions, has produced the annual *World Wealth Report*, which describes the investment needs of HNWIs. According to the 2001 report, there were six million HNWIs worldwide in 1998, owning a total of $22 trillion in financial assets.[4] By 2007, that number had grown to 9.5 million HNWIs with $40 trillion in assets, and by 2017, it had mushroomed to 18.1 million individuals collectively holding more than $70 trillion.[5] In 17 years, both the number of HNWIs and their collective wealth tripled.

The unprecedented scale of superwealth led to the creation of new subcategories in banking parlance. *Very high net worth individual* (VHNWI) describes those with between $5 and $30 million in assets; *ultra-high net worth individual* (UHNWI) defines those with more than $30 million in assets. In 2017, standard HNWIs accounted for 88.3 percent of all wealthy individuals, while 10.6 percent were VHNWIs and 1.1 percent were UHNWIs.[6] The latter held 34 percent of all HNWI assets – more than $31 trillion in 2017.[7] In fact, the number of UHNWIs grew by 12.9 percent and their wealth grew by 16.3 percent in just one year, between 2016 and 2017.[8] These 255,000 UHNWIs represent the wealthiest of the top one percent and possess a radically disproportionate accumulation of capital. Wealth-X, a company specializing in data and analysis of the very wealthy, projects that the UHNWI population and its assets will grow by 41 percent between 2017 and 2022.[9]

The history of architecture is intimately related to concentrations of wealth; that the very wealthy have a major impact on the built environment is nothing new. However, a number of factors have conspired to realign the spatiofinancial ecosystem. Most of these are straightforward, yet in combination they engender Doppler-like amplifications. First is the unprecedented population growth of both HNWIs and UHNWIs – wealth managers refer to the HNWI as "the millionaire next door." Second is the relatively widespread geographic distribution of these individuals. Third is the interconnectivity of global financial practices and the communication and transportation systems that enable them. It is easy to forget how radical and recent a development it is for relatively large numbers of wealthy individuals to purchase real estate in globally far-flung locations en masse. These three basic conditions precipitate what might be called urban impact multiplication, in which the serial purchase of real estate in select cities multiplies, or greatly expands, the urban and architectural footprint of the superwealthy.

This also occurs because the very wealthy locate proportionally more of their wealth in real estate than do average investors. The average investor has historically tended to locate the majority of investments in stocks and bonds, whereas UHNWI investment portfolios are reported to allocate an average of 24 percent to real estate, the majority of which is in the form of direct ownership of residential real estate.[10] This investment is in addition to homeownership for personal use; the global average UHNWI owns 2.4 homes for personal use. Asian and Russian UHNWIs have an average of three personal-use homes.[11] These investment behaviors allow the London-based global real estate brokerage Savills to state: *Global real estate is mostly residential and held by occupiers. But in the world of traded investable property, private owners are becoming more important than institutional and corporate ones. . . . Accounting for just 0.003% of the world's population, the real estate holdings of . . . UHNWIs . . . total over US$5 trillion, or around 3% of all the world's real estate value. . . . Privately wealthy individuals are becoming an increasingly important force in the world of real estate.*[12]

The Emergence of Superprime

Around the time that UHNWI entered the lexicon of finance and banking, *superprime* property gained popularity in real estate parlance. The demographic segment of the extremely wealthy needed its correlative in real estate. The superprime designation depends entirely on price, and this determination is largely about promotion and marketing. A superprime building always has units that are expensive – sometimes a $1 million unit qualifies, at others a $10 million unit. A whole subindustry within real estate now specializes in superprime, and buildings are explicitly marketed as such – the term itself signifies a structure's status. Frequently celebrity architects design these buildings. Richard Rogers's One Hyde Park in London, Rafael Viñoly's 432 Park Avenue in Manhattan, Herzog & de Meuron's Beirut Terraces in Lebanon – all superprime.

A prerequisite for the high cost that defines superprime is the perception of scarcity. At its most fundamental, this is a scarcity of location. First, the city is considered in relation to other cities: Is it highly livable, an alpha global city? Second is neighborhood, then site, and finally the specific location

10. See Knight Frank Research, *The Wealth Report: The Global Perspective on Prime Property and Wealth* (London: Think, 2014), 61.

11. Ibid., 11, 61.

12. Savills World Research, *Around the World in Dollars and Cents: How Private Money Moves around the Real Estate World* (2014), 2–3. https://pdf.euro.savills.co.uk/residential---other/privatewealth.pdf.

within a building. A penthouse with a view of London's Hyde Park is superprime by location alone. Given a prime location, the architecture could be anything. But it is not anything – it is specific, at least in certain ways.

When it comes to what occupies a residential site, whether it is an entire lot or a three-dimensional volume in the sky, the prevailing conceptual and formal logic is that of differentiation: the design is meant to heighten the perception of scarcity. There is only one London and only one Hyde Park, so how can this site be even more prime? The essential role of design in the context of superprime is to add hyperbole – to make it more super, finer, to add excellence and amplify luxury. Symptomatic of housing's complete submission to the demands of real estate, the spatial qualities of superprime residences are almost entirely a metrical matter. As Reinier de Graaf writes, "Through the general deployment of the term 'real estate,' the definition of the architect is replaced by that of the economist."[13] Cost itself is the primary metric, which both arises from a unit's inherent superprime qualities and produces the very perception of those superprime qualities. Closely related to cost is size: How many square feet? How many bedrooms? How many bathrooms? Add to this the age of the structure (either really new or a specific vintage upon which scarcity has been ascribed) and one has the entire metrical array of significance – the determining factors of superprime. Then there is the view, perhaps the next most significant design attribute beyond overt metrics. While the view plays a strategic role at the nexus of metrics and location, it is fundamentally premised upon an in situ human experience; ironically, superprime structures may not be regularly inhabited, meaning their viability as investments is premised on the potential for pleasurable inhabitation.

Beyond metrics and views, architectural design qualities both matter and don't. Physical design attributes are mainly about achieving exceptionalism in two ways: material finishes and details and formal/aesthetic differentiation. Architecture as a signifier of luxury tends to focus on the building's exterior, whose sole purpose is to appear distinct and original. The best results of this emphasis on novelty are beauty and surprise, but distinction and originality also produce no shortage of vapid banality, of freaks and oddities all shouting, "Invest in me!" And it is not just top-heavy forms and proliferating cantilevers that achieve exoticism – sometimes minimal simplicity alone does it. A totally silent aesthetic can often provide the singularly unique structure on the block. Architecture as

13. Reinier de Graaf, "Architecture Is Now a Tool of Capital, Complicit in a Purpose Antithetical to Its Social Mission," *Architectural Review*, April 24, 2015, https://www.architectural-review.com/essays/viewpoints/architecture-is-now-a-tool-ofcapital-complicit-in-a-purpose-antithetical-to-itssocial-mission/8681564.article.

asset differentiator is entirely agnostic and supremely promiscuous when it comes to architectural qualities like color, shape, and style.

One Hyde Park, an Example of Superprime

Rogers Stirk Harbour + Partners' One Hyde Park, in the London district of Knightsbridge, is about as superprime as it gets. Superprime is a marketing and cultural construct, and popular media offer a good barometer of a building's superprime status. Newspapers frequently label One Hyde Park as London's, Europe's, or even the world's most "elite" and "exclusive" building. A penthouse here was refinanced for £160 million ($213 million) in 2018 – reportedly making it the most expensive home ever sold in Britain.[14]

Situated directly on Hyde Park and in one of London's most expensive neighborhoods, the tower occupies the scarcest of locations and offers all the requisite metrical qualities of superprime. The larger unit of the 86 apartments occupies roughly 9,500 square feet and includes five bed-rooms, eight bathrooms, two kitchens, breakfast room, din-ing room, media room, study, large principal reception room, and second reception room. Residents and staff have separate entrances, and the building is serviced by the adjacent Mandarin Oriental hotel.

The formal design logic of One Hyde Park amplifies the perception of scarcity to achieve the qualities of the superprime. The building comprises four separate blocks, or pavilions: one is 13 floors, two are 11 floors, and the shortest is nine floors. They are connected with glass circulation cores. The overall effect is four almost identical minitowers. At 700,000 square feet, One Hyde Park is large for any residen-tial structure, but exceptionally so for a superprime building. (By comparison, SHoP's 111 West 57th Street project in New York City is 315,000 square feet.) So, what is often touted as the world's most exclusive residential address is also one of its larg-est. This is one of the conundrums of the UHNWI condition of finance capitalism: how to satisfy the demands of the increasing legions of the very wealthy while maintaining the perception of scarcity in the context of dense luxury. By breaking the build-ing into discrete pavilions, the architects divided one potentially massive block into a series of smaller structures.

The arrayed pavilions also increase the envelope-to-area ratio, thereby increasing exposure to views. The plan of each pavilion is akin to a lozenge made of two mirrored trapezoids. Rather than running perpendicular to the street, the long

14. See Rupert Neate, "UK's Most Expensive Home Valued at £160m," *Guardian*, October 9, 2018, https://www.theguardian.com/uk-news/2018/oct/09/record-160m-paid-for-uksmost-expensive-home-ever-sold.

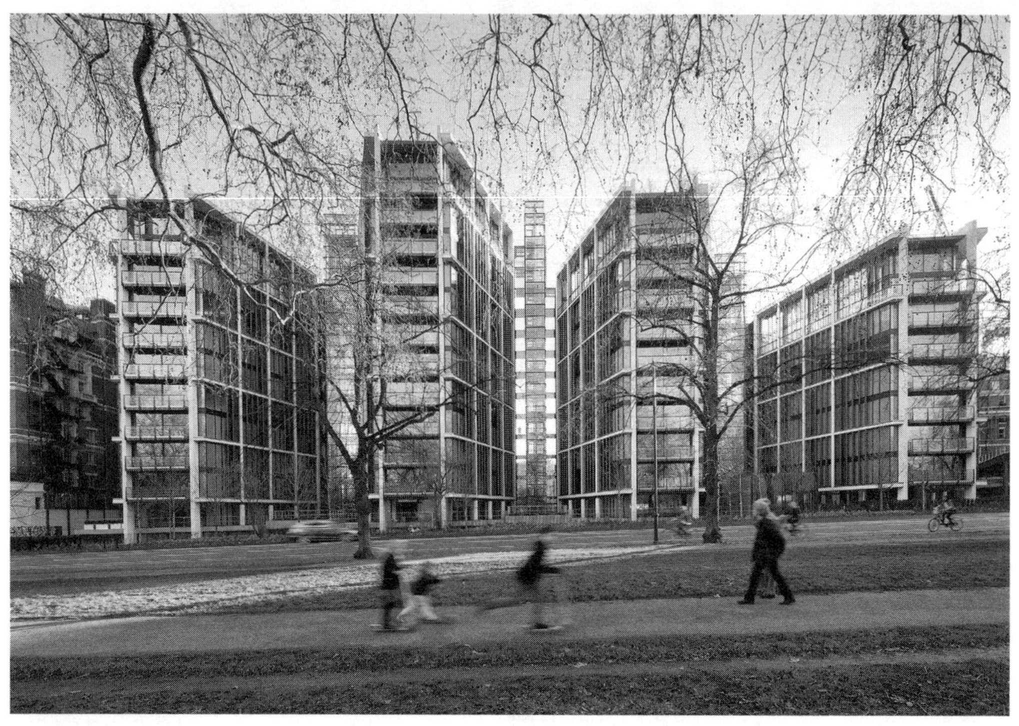

Rogers Stirk Harbour + Partners, One Hyde Park, London, 2011. Photo: Paul Raftery. Opposite page: Level-five (typical) floor plan. Drawing courtesy the architects.

15. See "One Hyde Park," Rogers Stirk Harbour + Partners, https://www.rsh-p. com/projects/one-hyde-park/.
16. See Douglas Spencer, *The Architecture of Neoliberalism* (London: Bloomsbury, 2016), 64.
17. Patrik Schumacher, "The Concept of Style and Parametricism as Epochal Style," Patrik Schumacher website, 2016, http://www.patrikschumacher. com/Texts/The%20Concept%20of%20 Style%20and%20Parametricism%20as%20 Epochal%20Style.html.

faces are angled, allowing for full perimeter views of Hyde Park to the north and Kensington to the south. To reap the benefits of this view-optimizing geometry, the building skin is floor-to-ceiling glass. Each apartment's main living space occupies the narrow outer edge of the trapezoid, in what the architects call the promontory,[15] which provides panoramic views and the illusion that no other unit surrounds it. In other words, the number of units was concealed through the careful management of the view.

Two Positions on Architecture and Capitalism

It is useful to contextualize One Hyde Park in relation to the work of Patrik Schumacher and Pier Vittorio Aureli, both of whom combine active design work with writing about capitalism. Schumacher is the principal of London-based Zaha Hadid Architects (ZHA), and Aureli is a partner at the Brussels-based architecture practice Dogma. Schumacher leads design work at ZHA and occasionally teaches, while Aureli engages architecture primarily through design propositions, teaching, research, exhibitions, and publications.

Parametric design, and the complexity associated with Schumacher's brand of it, is rhetorically associated with post-Fordist organizational principles and their progressive potentials.[16] Schumacher argues, "Parametricism is the only

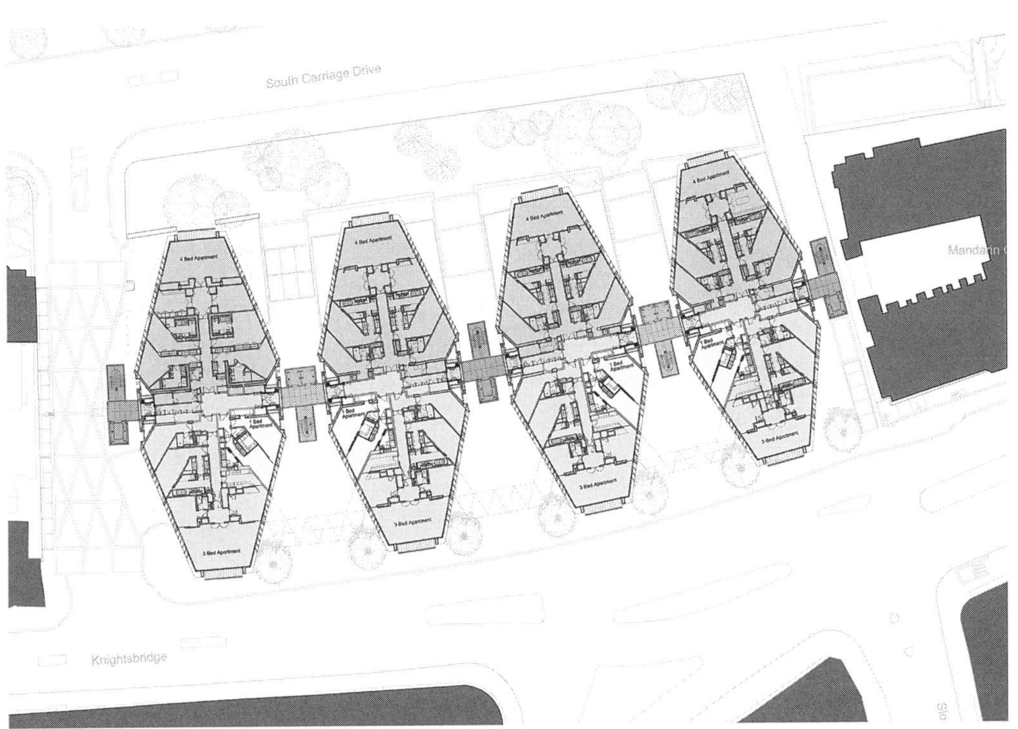

plausible contemporary candidate to become the global epochal style for the twenty-first century."[17] He does not use the term *finance capitalism*, preferring *post-Fordism* to describe contemporary capitalism. But finance capitalism is a more accurate description of current conditions and captures post-Fordist managerial practices under its umbrella. From Schumacher's position, the formalism of parametric complexity is the spatial correlative of contemporary capitalism's logics.

While Schumacher and ZHA are best known for cultural and civic structures, the practice is increasingly involved in luxury housing projects, including One Thousand Museum in Miami, completed in 2019, and 520 West 28th Street in New York City, completed in 2017. The latter sits alongside the High Line and incorporates 39 condominium units in a basic 11-story extruded L shape. Units range from 1,500 square feet, with two bedrooms and three bathrooms, to an 11,000-square-foot penthouse with six bedrooms and six bathrooms. With condos selling for more than $3,000 per square foot during presales in 2017 and 2018, this is a superprime building in terms of location, unit size, and price. However, the L-shaped massing of the building and plan of each unit are entirely standard. The only interior organizational element that differentiates it from other condominiums of its size is the absence of hallways. Instead, two strategically placed cores

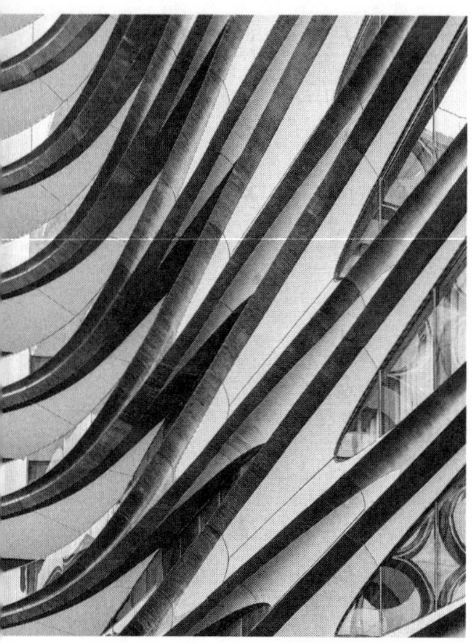

Zaha Hadid Architects, 520 West 28th
Street, New York City, 2017. Chevron
shapes on the building's exterior skin.
Photo: Hufton+Crow. Opposite page:
Level four and five floor plan. Images
the architects.

18. "520 West 28th," Zaha Hadid Architects,
video, https://www.zaha-hadid.com/
design/520-west-28th-street/.
19. Pier Vittorio Aureli, "A Room
against Ownership," in *Real Estates: Life
without Debt*, ed. Jack Self and Shumi Bose
(London: Bedford Press, 2014), 42.
20. Ibid., 44.
21. Pier Vittorio Aureli and Martino
Tattara, "Barbarism Begins at Home:
Notes on Housing," in *Dogma: 11 Projects*
(London: AA Publications, 2013), 90.

give the impression of private elevator lobbies for each unit.
Parametric geometries can be seen in the entrance lobby and
swimming pool, but are otherwise confined to the building's
skin. In the units themselves, only the kitchen island represents the sculptural differentiation of parametricism.

Derived from the architects' impression of the site, the
building's layering provides the opportunity for parametric
"emergence." The floors in one bar of the L are offset by half
a level from the floors in the other bar. This split creates the
opportunity for the building's main architectural operation:
the resolution of the split levels through the chevron form. As
Zaha Hadid said, "The chevron comes from this idea of split
levels. But because we don't stagger them, they become one
single line."[18] The result is a skin that has a swooping metamor-
phosis in which one offset side fuses into the other around a
zipper-like nexus. Since it is largely relegated to the skin, parametricism here seeks solely to differentiate the building from
its context and provide scarcity in terms of exterior appearance. In contrast to One Hyde Park, which operates mainly as a
place from which to experience a view, 520 West 28th is a sculptural object of desire to be perceived from the outside.

Far from celebrating the parametric style as an embodiment of the current political economy, Aureli foregrounds
the use of architectural space in general and housing in
particular. His particular notion of use is influenced by the
Mendicant order of the Franciscans; he writes, "A fundamental tenet of their rule was the refusal to own things as a way
of refusing their potential economic value and thus the possibility of exploitation of others."[19] As an example of architecture "against property," Aureli cites Swiss architect and
Bauhaus director Hannes Meyer's 1924 Co-op Zimmer in
which the domestic space is reduced to a single room containing "only the essentials": "Co-op Zimmer reveals what could
be seen as an architecture of use against the architecture of
property. While the latter must always be a reflection of the
owner, Meyer's room is radically generic and anonymous.
Precisely for this reason, it promises its inhabitant the possibility of a life liberated from the burden of household property."[20] This focus on use pits a potential architecture against
the basis of capital: ownership.

For Aureli, architecture should "become destructive in
a symbolic sense, by ridding itself of illusions: for example, a
wall has to be a wall and not an analogy for anything else. In
performing this act of destruction, the architecture of housing can clearly state both its function as containment and its

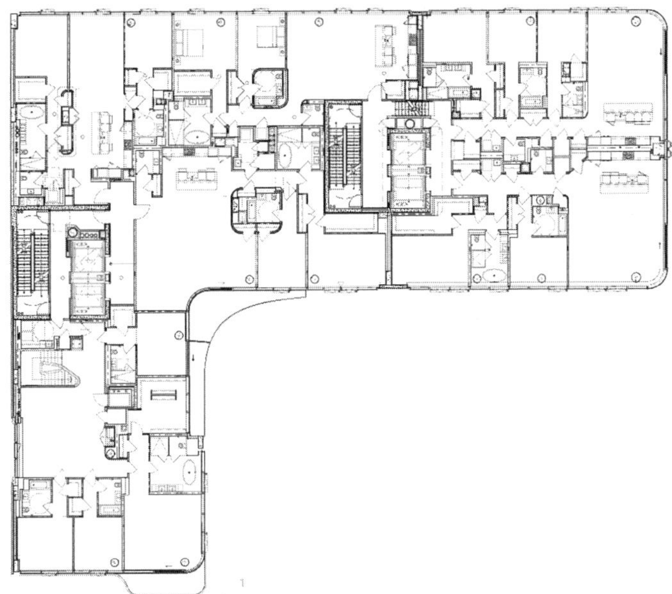

potential to formulate new and unforeseen forms of life."[21] Aureli's architecture is exceedingly reduced. Its basic increment at the urban scale is various formations of the rectangular bar: sometimes low, other times high, sometimes bent to form an L. These bars are generally composed with an unyielding, visible grid that is both organizational and aesthetic. Enacting a mandate of repetition and achieving a sublime austerity are the discrete elements of this simple architecture: flat floor slabs, vertical columns, and walls. A wall is simply a wall – an overwhelmingly elemental schema.

For an invited competition for 44 units of social housing in Westerlo, Belgium, Dogma proposed Frame(s), a pair of two-story bar buildings pushed to the edge of an existing meadow, thereby making space for a shared garden. Each unit has the same volume, what Dogma calls a single tunnel space, which is framed by a thickened service wall that incorporates a cooking area, stairs, bathrooms, and closet. It allows the rest of the unit to be clear and open – a background against which life can unfold in an undetermined manner. The narrow and deep rectangular dimensions of each unit, in combination with fully glazed end walls, reduce the envelope-to-area ratio (to lower construction costs) while extending the living space out to the exterior. The exterior elevations communicate the interior plan condition – a simple rhythm of service wall and tunnel space for living. Each unit is essentially an open space where the primary role of architecture is to provide a container for life.

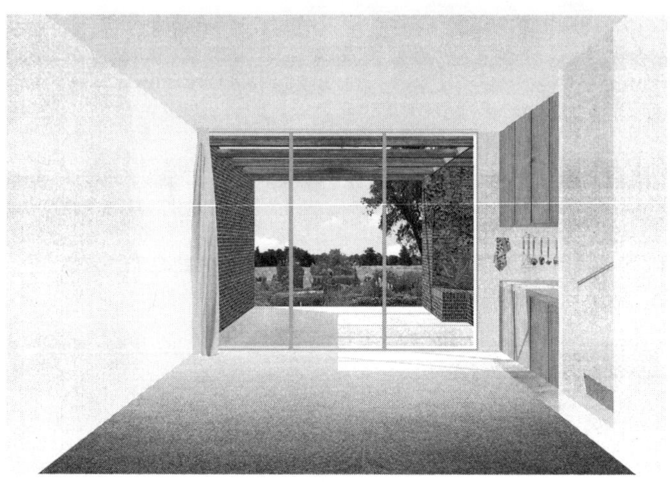

One Hyde Park and the Empty Interior

Aureli and Schumacher occupy opposing poles, with elemental form aligned with use at one end and complex parametric form aligned with ownership and speculation at the other. Dogma's Frame(s) project foregrounds the simplicity of architecture in service of the occupied interior, while ZHA's 520 West 28th Street finds its primary architectural purpose as a sculptural object to be perceived from the exterior – a reduced frame for social housing versus a zippy superprime skin.

One Hyde Park and 520 West 28th are against use in the Aurelian sense. They possess a modus operandi that is outside of themselves and therefore outside of actual domestic utility. One Hyde Park's architecture is primarily geared toward viewing, while 520 West 28th is primarily concerned with being viewed. They are both organized around vision and are relatively incorporeal. As Aureli has written:

If we see how the political economy has worked over the past decades, we discover the significance of housing as a question of representation. . . . This phenomenon has been a major contributor to the financialisation of households: in other words, our economy of debt is also driven by the image of housing. The radical stylistic wealth of architecture in recent decades is also a by-product of this condition. Ironically, the more standardised the building industry becomes, the more architecture takes on the role of offering a "personalised" image.[22]

Superprime can thus be characterized by two versions of relinquishing the interior: one is the stylistically omnivorous elevation of differentiation; the other is the building operating as a view machine. Any emphasis on bodily use is antithetical to the investor-oriented, largely unoccupied architecture of the superprime.

22. Aureli and Tattara, 89.

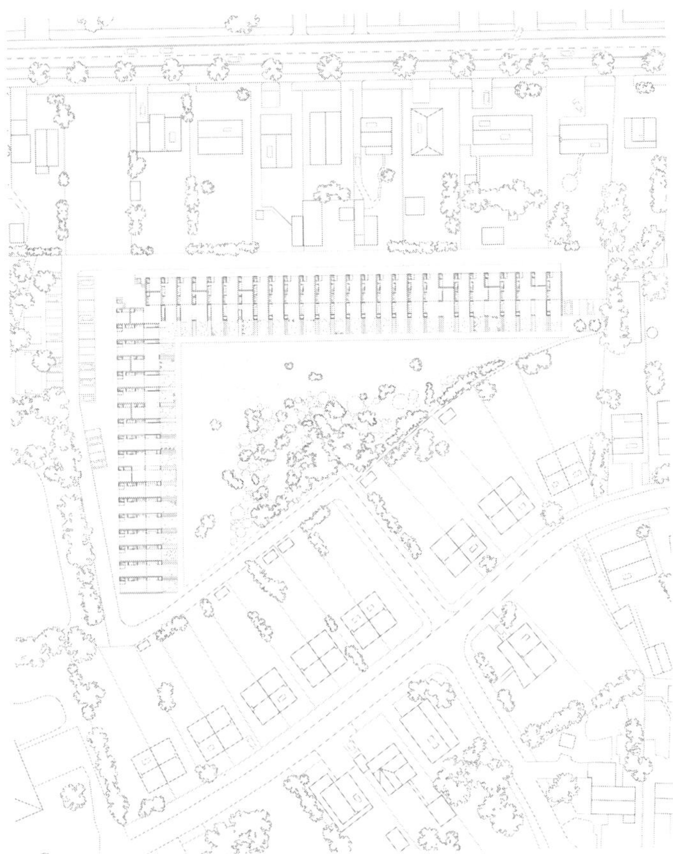

Style Omnivores and Sheltered Taxes

The inequality described by Piketty is itself accelerated by
the schism between more affordable, use-based housing and
superprime investment housing. Aureli's identification of
the use and ownership dyad plays out across the spectrum of
UHNWI investing. Architecture serves as a spatiofinancial
object alongside such things as paintings, wine, and antiques;
all are being financialized. It is no coincidence that companies that specialize in selling valuable objects also play an
important role in the luxury housing market – Sotheby's and
Christie's, for example. Just as housing prices have dramatically escalated in much of the world, so has the value of many
luxury investment commodities.

A compelling parallel to UHNWI investment in real estate
is the storage free port, where as long as an artwork stays
within a warehouse, the owner can indefinitely postpone
value-added tax and customs duty payments on it. There
are major art-focused free ports in Switzerland, Singapore,
Monaco, Luxembourg, and Delaware. A tax shelter is often
also at play in superprime architecture. In Manhattan, for

23. See Kriston Capps, "Why Billionaires Don't Pay Property Taxes in New York," *Bloomberg CityLab*, May 11, 2015, https://www.citylab.com/equity/2015/05/why-billionaires-dont-payproperty-taxes-in-new-york/389886/.

instance, New York's property taxes result in luxury condo owners paying far fewer taxes than the occupants of more moderately priced condominiums and cooperative units. For example, the buyer of the penthouse of One57, which at the time of its sale was the most expensive home sale in New York's history, paid one-hundredth of the average property tax rate in the United States.[23] Superprime architecture is like a free port, units are sheltered from taxes, and, frequently, taken out of use.

In the current postideological condition, in which the logics of real estate have free rein, perhaps the true ideology is that of hyperbole – or hype. While superprime is a distinct category, because of its tight relationship with elite architecture and the urban-multiplier effect of UHNWIs, its shadow is long. The architectural ideology of the now might represent nothing more than the maintenance of systems of wealth and power and the propagation of the inherent scarcities that they necessitate.

Matthew Soules is associate professor of architecture at the University of British Columbia School of Architecture and Landscape Architecture and the director of Matthew Soules Architecture.

Patrick Templeton

The Cost of "Public" Space

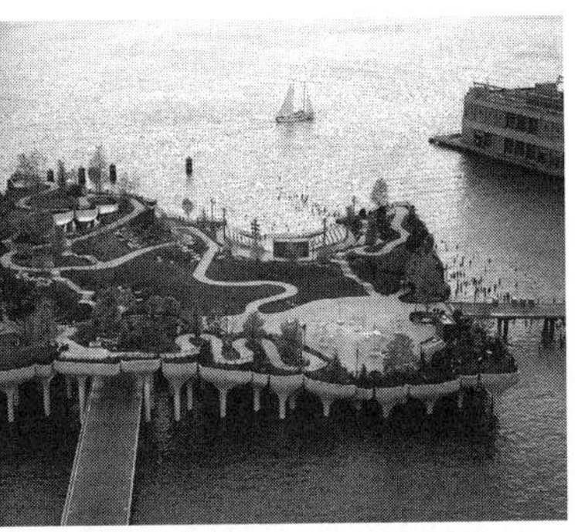

Heatherwick Studio, Little Island, New York City, opened May 21, 2021. Photo: Michael Grimm.

The spectacle is capital *to such a degree of accumulation that it becomes an image.* – Guy Debord, *Society of the Spectacle*

As designer Thomas Heatherwick's second privately commissioned folly opened in New York City this summer, his first closed. The city's newest green spectacle, Little Island is an artificial landscape built on the site of the historic Pier 54 in the Hudson River, standing on 132 tulip-shaped concrete piles. The pier, where survivors of the *Titanic* disembarked and from which the *Lusitania* departed on its final voyage, was a haven for the LGBTQ community in Chelsea beginning in the 1970s, but it fell into disuse after being severely damaged by Hurricane Sandy in 2012. Originally tasked by media mogul Barry Diller to design a pavilion to rejuvenate the derelict pier, Heatherwick – dubbed the "billionaire whisperer" by *New York Times* architecture critic Michael Kimmelman – convinced Diller to instead replace it with an entirely new type of public space that would be an "immersive experience with nature and art." The cost subsequently doubled from $130 to $260 million, with Diller committing another $120 million for maintenance over the next 20 years.

The greenery of Little Island, designed by landscape architect Signe Nielsen, combines all of the features of a picturesque landscape set in a 2.4-acre square: serpentine paths climb hills planted with 290 varieties of grasses, perennials, vines, and bulbs; overlooks afford views of both the city skyline and the ruins of Pier 54's submerged piles; at what could be called a ha-ha, the artificial ground plane suddenly drops to form a 687-seat amphitheater; there is even a grotto of sorts – providing the only real shade until the 35 species of trees grow in – where the "tulips" cover one of the two wood bridges that connect the island to the Hudson River Park bike path. It's all charming.

Eminently photogenic, Little Island has been largely met with praise, drawing crowds just as the city reemerged from the COVID-19 pandemic. But in the few months since it opened, there is mounting evidence that this green spectacle is neither as public as it claims nor particularly resilient: daily attendance is limited; visitors must reserve free timed tickets for entry in

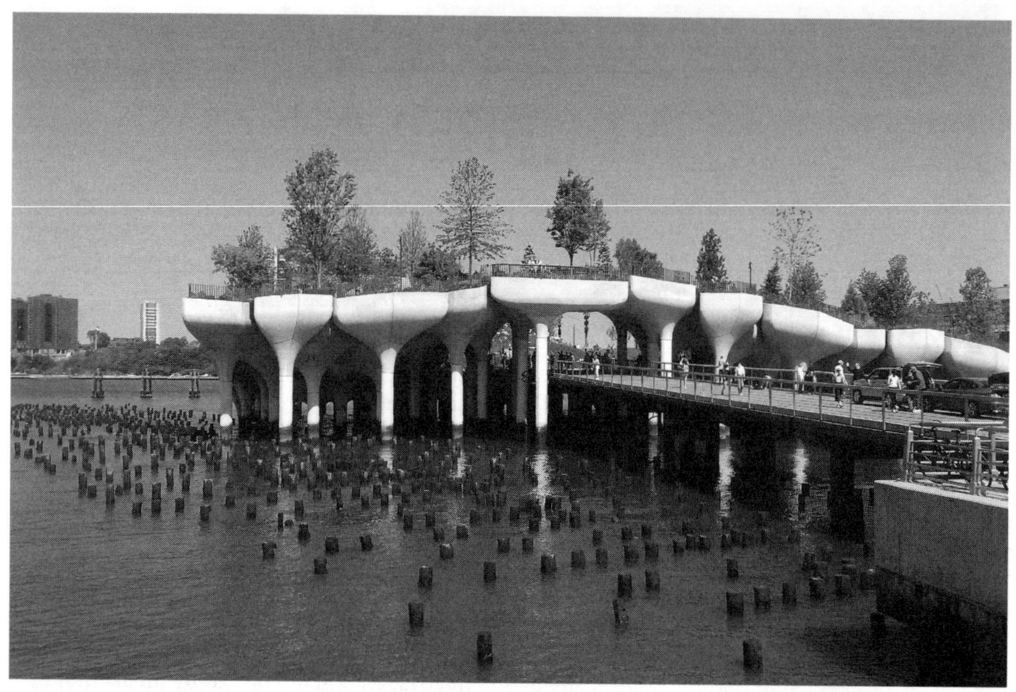

The south entrance to Little Island. Opposite page: Heatherwick Studios, The Vessel, 2019. Westward view over the site of the second phase of the Hudson Yards development. Photos: Patrick Templeton.

the afternoon; bicycles, scooters, cigarettes, and dogs are all prohibited; the park has been evacuated several times due to lightning in the area; and the lawns are mostly cordoned off due to heavy foot traffic.

Just a mile stroll up the High Line from Little Island sits Heatherwick's Vessel, which faces an uncertain future. On July 29, a 14-year-old boy visiting the Vessel with his family jumped to his death, becoming the fourth suicide since it opened in March 2019. Stephen Ross, the billionaire chairman of Related Companies, the real estate developer behind Hudson Yards and its centerpiece, said that the Vessel – a structure he once billed as "New York's Eiffel Tower" – would be closed for a second time and might never reopen.

When the design of the Vessel was unveiled in 2016, Heatherwick described his $150-million folly as a jungle gym for locals to climb for a unique view, as "something that everybody could use, touch, relate to," and as a mile of public space coiled up 154 flights of stairs. The design, which Ross personally commissioned, approved, and concealed until its much-hyped unveiling, was immediately criticized for its lack of accessibility for anyone in a wheelchair, pushing a stroller, or with bad knees. Less than a year after the Vessel opened, the US Attorney's Office for the Southern District of New York reached a deal in which Related "agreed to commit *substantial resources* to install a platform lift that will allow individuals

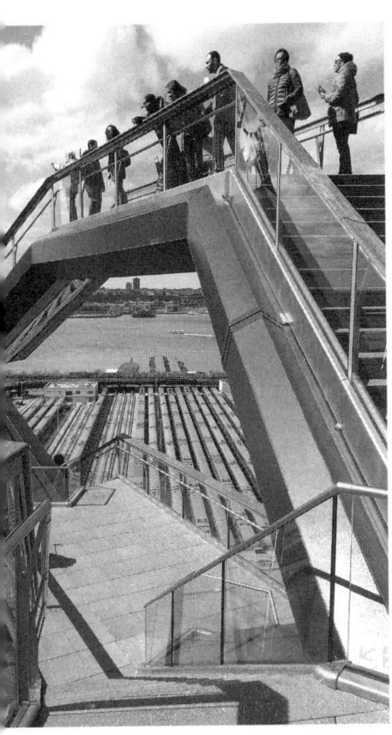

with disabilities to enjoy 360-degree views from the Vessel's top level." This pricey view, however, is one mostly blocked by the surrounding Hudson Yards skyscrapers, and the current panorama looking west, toward a Whole Foods Market in Weehawken, New Jersey, will be blocked when the second phase of the Hudson Yards development is completed.

The Vessel was closed for the first time in January of this year, when a 21-year-old man from Texas jumped to his death – the third suicide in just 11 months. To reopen it, Related implemented a $10 entrance fee and a buddy-system policy as deterrents but rejected design modifications (perhaps to avoid further significant expense). In less than three months, however, these deterrents proved ineffective.

No longer free, not easily accessible, offering no real view, and, for now at least, closed to the public, the Vessel is hardly the post-jog-on-the-High-Line Stairmaster or local hangout it was promised to be. At worst, the Vessel is a billionaire's ill-conceived vanity project; at best, it is an exorbitant backdrop for tourists' selfies. Will the same prove true of Little Island?

The Vessel is nothing more than an image. As *New Yorker* critic Justin Davidson wrote in his call to dismantle it, "When an icon fails, iconoclasm is the only reasonable response." Perhaps Heatherwick's second New York folly will fare better, but considered apart from the spectacle of greenery rising out of the water, it is already clear that Little Island offers very little: a concert venue that seats a few hundred (for comparison, the Prospect Park Bandshell accommodates 9,000); some concession stands no better than the food trucks parked across the West Side Highway; and a bit of extra green space in a wealthy neighborhood that already has ample access to parks, including Battery Park and the High Line (which were also privately developed).

Despite their promises as public amenities, these expensive follies constitute a spectacle urbanism incapable of addressing the city's real needs. Pocket parks and other urban regeneration efforts deliver on the accessibility, flexibility, and community that Heatherwick evokes to sell his follies but at a fraction of the cost. Given that the annual budget of the New York City Department of Parks and Recreation was recently slashed 14 percent, to $503 million, due to the pandemic, which also highlighted the vital importance of public space, Ross's and Diller's hundreds of millions could certainly have been put to better use.

Patrick Templeton, managing editor of *Log*, regularly goes for walks around his local public park.

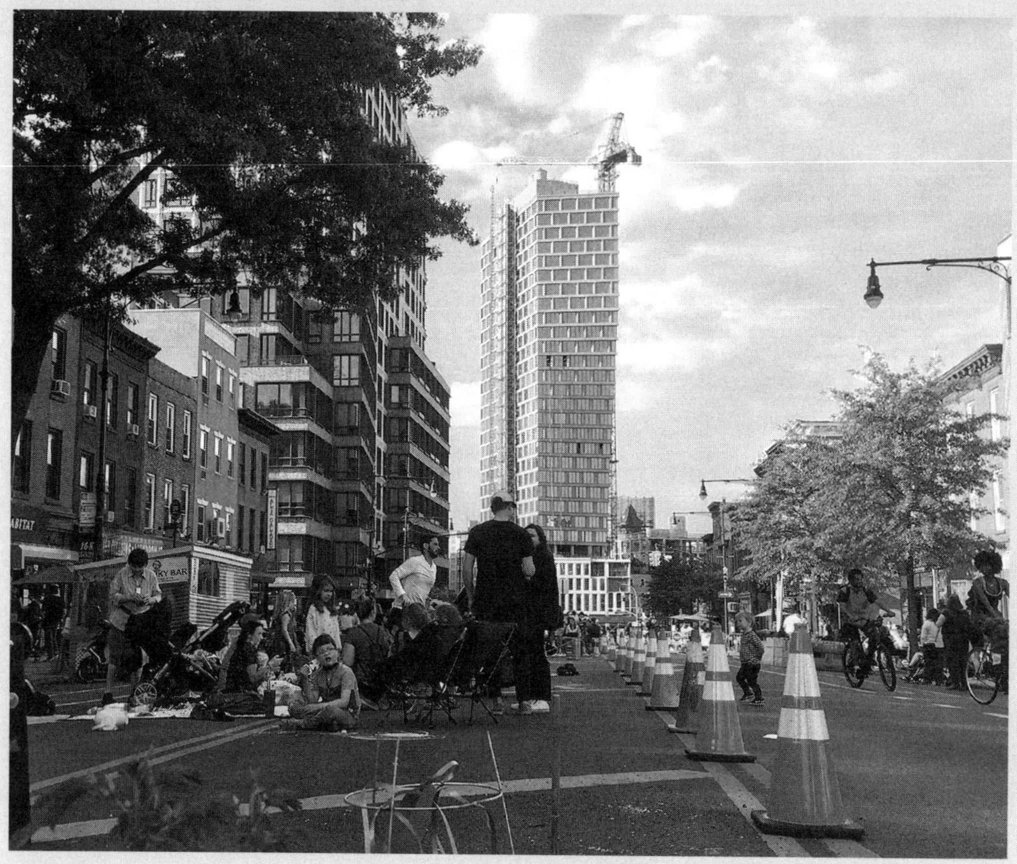

Prospect Heights, Brooklyn, May 2021.
Photo: Kate Heath.

It's a Friday evening in May, and Vanderbilt Avenue in Prospect Heights, Brooklyn, is closed to cars. The closure started last summer once it became clear that the pandemic would stay awhile. Replacing the cars are restaurant tables, crowds of pedestrians, and a steady stream of bikes, strollers, and scooters. Some accelerate past as though they have places to be, but for most, the street seems to be the destination.

The warm air feels particularly charged this evening — for the first time in recent memory not with anxiety or dread but a tenuous yet electric optimism.

The new CDC guidance issued yesterday recommends that the fully vaccinated can forgo masks and social distancing.

Almost every passing group seems to illustrate the uncertainty of this recently updated reality. For every person with a mask, there is now one without, a ratio unheard of yesterday.

A group of families spreads out blankets and unfolds camping chairs. The parents set up a machine that spews bubbles to entertain their kids and then talk excitedly, catching up with each other, perhaps finally sensing "normal" on the horizon. They are so lost in unmasked conversation that several kids chase the drifting bubbles past a line of cones into the stream of bike traffic. Distracted hands quickly extend to shepherd them back into the herd.

The kids are as oblivious to the cone boundary as they are to the significance of yesterday's milestone. Their world is that of the present and immediate. To them, today is just another day to ride their bikes, to play in the street, to chase bubbles floating on the warm breeze.

– Kate Heath

Thomas de Monchaux

All Things Seen And Unseen

Representation is a double-edged word. One side of it speaks, in a narrow architectural discourse, to the mysteries of drawing: the matrix of projections and rules that enable architects to see what is or is not yet there, and to visually communicate, with seemingly objective and measured means, the subjective and immeasurable experiential effects of places. Half a millennium or so after Brunelleschi, perspectival projection remains, for its credible immersion of one person's visual field into another's, an everyday miracle. The other side of the word *representation* speaks to inclusivity and interdependence among individuals and communities, across the intersecting lines constructed by class, race, creed, sexuality, gender, neurotypicality, and more, along every kind of spectrum and shade of gray. In the architectural profession – still so residually beholden in its mythologies to old White men, and to the celebration of the lone genius at the cost of more accurately centering the radically collaborative and intersubjective creativity at the heart of most best practices – this broad meaning of *representation* is ever more urgent.

Traditionally, the architects devoted to either edge of representation aren't supposed to meet: the former group an unworldly congregation, deep in a hall of mirrors or a cave of shadows with only dog-eared pages of Robin Evans to guide them, and for whom capital-*A* architecture may be merely an end in itself; the latter group a more worldly delegation, who in their admirable righteousness cherish design of the built environment less as an arcane and fragile folklore than as an instrumental means to the betterment of society. But these two groups of devotees recently found each other down on Forsyth Street in Lower Manhattan, at a narrow basement gallery daylit only through a heavy glass door. The occasion was "Linee Occulte: Drawing Architecture," a small but acute spring/summer 2021 exhibition and installation at Citygroup, curated and designed by Studio Ames principal Daisy Ames.

The show featured drawings commissioned from nine emerging designers around the theme of the hidden line – or as Sebastiano Serlio called it in Book II of his 1545 treatise *On Perspective*, "linee occulte." This obscured line is what

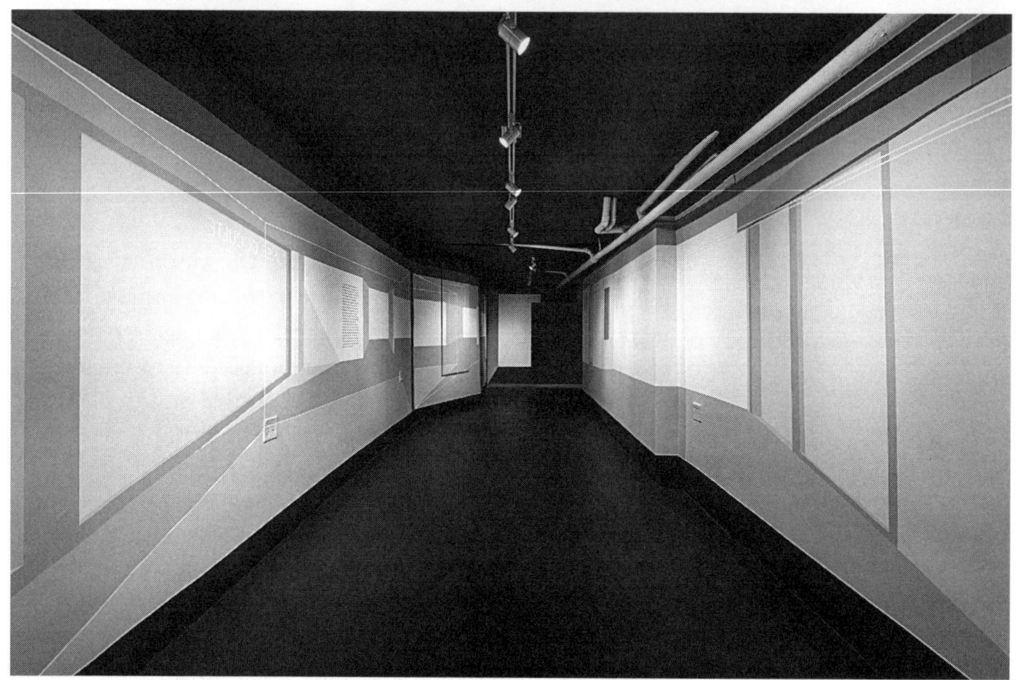

Studio Ames, "Linee Occulte: Drawing Architecture," mural, Citygroup, New York City, 2021. Assembled with Betsy Clifton, Hanneke van Deursen, Leonard Fuchs, and Matthew Wagstaffe. Opposite page: mural on the north wall of the gallery with Melissa Shin, The Hidden Perspective, 2021. All photos: Alan Tansey. Courtesy Studio Ames.

draftspeople today call the construction line: the palimpsestic trace, deliberately erased or else artfully retained in the construction of a drawing, that represents not the drawing's nominal subject but the systematic conventions and constraints of its own making. Ames associates this line with psychoanalyst Christopher Bollas's idea of the "unthought known": our catalogue of formative developmental experiences that, because they precede language acquisition, are internalized but unthinkable in ways we are accustomed to thinking through words. Figures from Slavoj Žižek to Donald Rumsfeld have ruminated on similar unknowns and their consequences. Gratifyingly for architects who care about the geometry of adumbration, the work of Freud, from which much of this discourse of inarticulable knowledge derives, is full of allegories about casting into shadow.

The drawings in "Linee Occulte" were case studies in the visual expression of conditions that, to the extent that they are verbally unspeakable or indescribable, might otherwise be incommunicable. In her drawing Lignes Blanches, Iman Fayyad translated Platonic solids of cones and cylinders through orthographic operations that start familiarly but end in a gestalt uncanny. For Hybrid Object: Unmasking Domesticity, Mersiha Veledar defamiliarized and dematerialized potentially gendered artifacts from the domestic landscape into clouds of contours and convolutions. And Stephanie

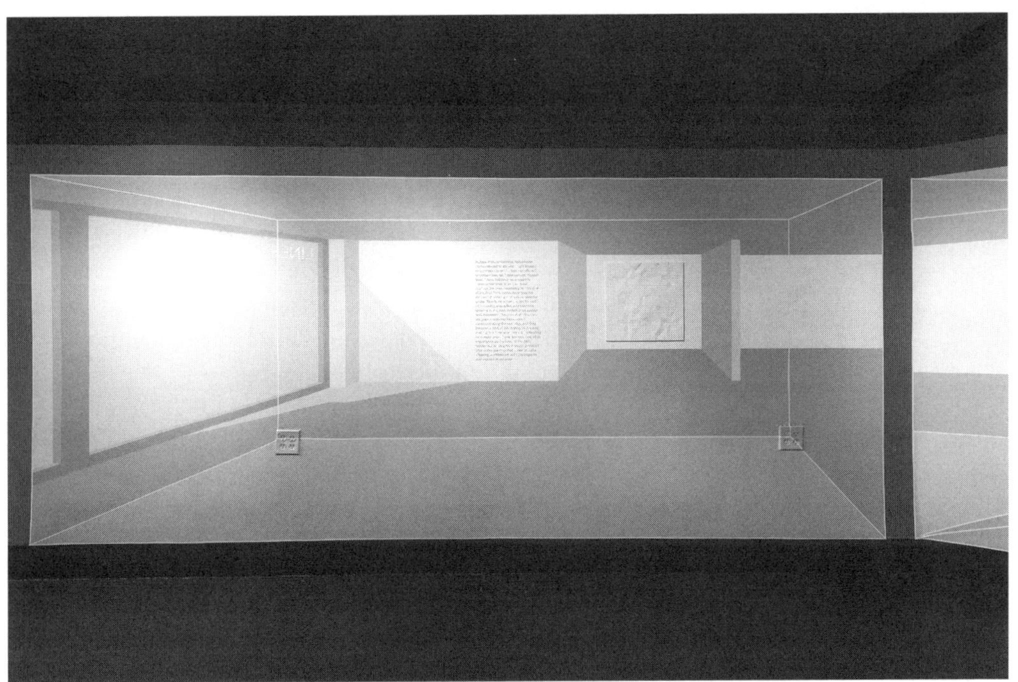

Lin's Digital Fresco No. 2 was a drawing of a drawing that studies the ambiguous excavation of a surface image by the decay of its underlying media. The self-referential singularity of each of the exhibit's singular visions was both their great strength and their eventual weakness. Each could be decoded by long looking, yet for all their shared but differently signified visual vocabulary of dashes and hatches, each was also a closed world and a bell jar. One could hope that future curatorship on this theme might look at how such works could become more mutually intelligible and their systems of notation ever more an open-source code.

The drawings were mounted within an immersive mural: an X-ray wireframe perspective of all the underground spaces in the surrounding building and block, rendered at one-to-one scale and projected semi-anamorphotically from several station points in the cramped gallery. Shadow lines in this projection corresponded to the singular late-afternoon moment when, like solstice sunbeams into a prehistoric tomb, low light transected that semi-subterranean glass door. In a painterly Agnes Martin palette of moody grays, the mural phenomenally dissolved the space in a way that recalled Vito Acconci and Steven Holl's more mechanical operations at Storefront for Art and Architecture a few blocks away – raising hopes that the relatively new Citygroup may build its own outsized legacy (and that it may keep the mural).

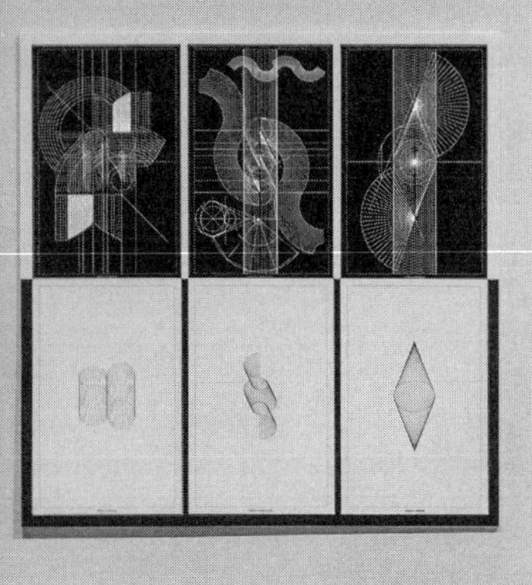

Iman Fayyad, Lignes Blanches, 2021. "Linee Occulte" participants also included Daisy Ames, Lindsay Harkema, Kevin Hirth, Alfie Koetter, Stephanie Lin, Melissa Shin, Mersiha Veledar, and Lindsey Wikstrom.

Thomas de Monchaux teaches design at the Columbia University Graduate School of Architecture, Planning and Preservation and is the 2021 inaugural *Places Journal* critic-in-residence in architecture.

"Linee Occulte" briefly coincided with the Museum of Modern Art's significant exhibit, "Reconstructions: Architecture and Blackness in America," in the light of which much contemporary architectural research and curatorship can usefully be seen. Certain projects in "Reconstructions" developed critical techniques that called to mind the moment, circa 1990, when some architects drew from post-structuralism and deconstruction in literary criticism in search of analogous visual, spatial, and material practices to defamiliarize, dematerialize, and destabilize systemic and structural conditions in the built environment. The reappearance in both "Reconstructions" and "Linee Occultee" of these techniques of excavation, superimposition, and excision – developing deliberately ambiguous field conditions subject to multiple readings between appearance and essence – may suggest in our times a new currency for architectural analogues to literary deconstruction, even distinct from the formalist style with which such techniques were once popularized. Thus the work of representation in its narrowest sense of visual transcription can serve representation in its broadest definition. In its particular attention to transformative operations of perception and depiction, such work speaks today to the useful belief by architects that – especially when they find themselves beyond words – the first step to changing the world is representing it.

Whitney Moon

Making Room For Architecture

In "No More Room," a spring 2021 installation at the SCI-Arc Gallery in Los Angeles, BairBalliet destabilized our understanding of an otherwise overwrought type: the architecture exhibition. Although much has been written about the history of exhibiting architecture and the challenges of displaying architecture in the context of museums and galleries (absent the building itself), BairBalliet leveraged the medium not only to represent and communicate architectural intent but to serve as a generative model for architectural production. Rather than relegate their role to that of exhibiting subject, exhibition designer, or curator, BairBalliet exploded our understanding of these categories, offering instead something entirely different: split screen scenarios for an architecture predicated on incompleteness and the in-between.

The exhibition occupied both the physical and virtual realms in real time, challenging our assumptions about architecture by interrogating the images we consume and how we consume them. Following our cultural obsession with split screen aesthetics, such as HGTV's before-and-after comparisons or the glitch space between Instagram stories as we swipe right to left, BairBalliet transposed two static images into a three-dimensional filmic space. In subverting the autonomy of an image by pairing it with another, a generative model was created, spatializing nonlinear images as a territory for architectural invention and inhabitation.

Both in situ and online, "No More Room" was, and continues to be, a multiscalar, multimedia spatial paradox that celebrates, even exploits, the ephemeral nature of exhibitions. Engaging the contemporary condition of consumption in a state of perpetual distraction, BairBalliet employed both the material, physical installation and the immaterial, digital compositing realms to broadcast an array of architectural effects. At its core – both literally and figuratively – the gallery installation included a massive white cylindrical element (an additive extraction) and three figured blue screens (that served as the physical backdrop for the exhibition's three discrete animated episodes, whose visual content was digitally modeled and superimposed virtually using chroma-keying).

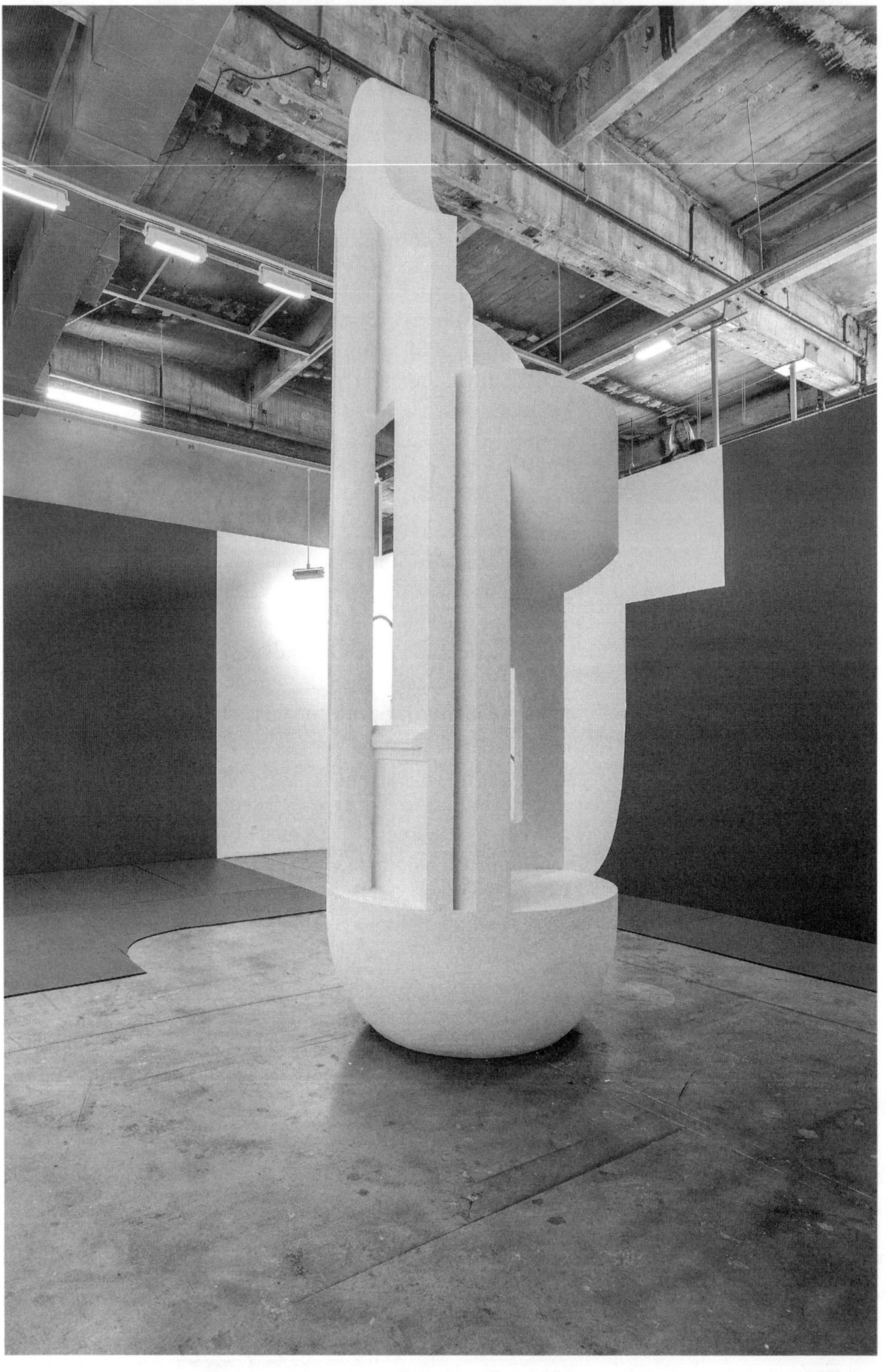

These architectural elements, both objects and subjects, established a multitude of frames and surfaces for meditation on the ways we encounter and experience rooms. Here, the physical gallery served as a stage set for the cinematic unfolding of virtual rooms within rooms, made visible exclusively through online viewing.

For BairBalliet, core is both an architectural concept and an object. They define *core* as a key moment highlighting "a territory with the most spatial consequence," as opposed to architectural conventions such as vertical circulation and service areas. This concept of core lies between architectural fact and fiction. Rather than extractions, as in a conventional geological core sample, these are additive operations akin to those of a kaleidoscope. The designed core generates endless visual and spatial effects yet works within the controlled parameters of an apparatus of vision.

Each of the three episodes of "No More Room" – More Cores, Enfilades, and Paperthin – locates the physical core at the center of its frame, yet its virtual content varies drastically in its conceptual aims and exhibitionist effects. Viewed online, the left side of the split screen is a mock security feed of the physical gallery; the right image merges the physical space of the exhibition with content designed using visual effects. "No More Room" posited a nested, scalar, and multiperspectival experience as it mediates between the physical and virtual lives (and perspectives) of the gallery space. The result expands the exhibition into an ambiguous architectural space that resides somewhere between the real and surreal, generating silent possibilities for architectural occupation. In its negotiation between center (core) and periphery (enclosure), "No More Room" consumed the entirety of the gallery yet left infinite space for both its physical and virtual occupants/viewers to contemplate an architecture of incompleteness.

In the opening virtual episode, More Cores, the built core sample, a physical element to be viewed in the round, is the central character. Privileging proximity, the designed core leverages familiar architectural attributes – stair, column, handrail, window – to invite the viewer in as a gallery visitor (left screen) and as an online observer (right screen). The core's rough-hewn stucco reaffirms its presence as a physical (and labored) work in the gallery, and it is a counterpoint to the smooth Yves Klein–blue hue of three perimeter graphics objects, likewise articulated to be anything but barely there. Appropriating these surfaces as spatial portals, other related core samples make cameo appearances as slow films while the

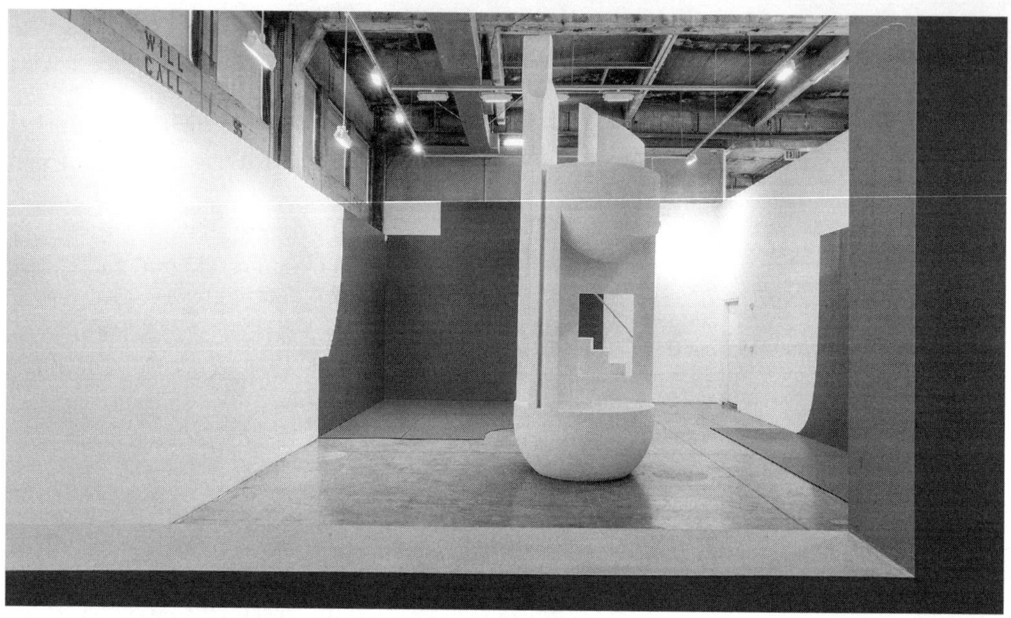

BairBalliet, "No More Room," SCI-Arc Gallery. Photo: Joshua White. Opposite page: SCI-Arc, "No More Room," film still, https://www.sciarc.edu/no-more-room.

1. "BairBalliet: No More Room," SCI-Arc, streamed live on April 9, 2021, 50:39, https://livestream.com/sciarc/events/9579578/videos/219761369. The exhibition's opening, defined by BairBalliet as a "variety show," featured a variety of guest acts: a welcome from Hernán Díaz Alonso (SCI-Arc director); a gallery talk with Kelly Bair and Kristy Balliet; "how it started how it's going" with John McMorrough and Julia McMorrough; "behind the scenes" with Irvin Shaifa, Malvin Bunata, and Melody Chu (SCI-Arc students); "fresh talks" with Jackilin Hah Bloom, Marcelyn Gow, and Marrikka Trotter (SCI-Arc faculty); and "real talk" with kids.
2. Similar to the work of contemporary photographer and sculptor Thomas Demand, whose elaborate paper sets restage and spatialize familiar images that circulate through various media, BairBalliet reconstitutes the pictorial frame as a means to both reengage the viewer as an active spatial participant and to meditate on its embedded content. That is, by revealing the thinness of the image, both Demand and BairBalliet produce a desire (if not longing) for the absence of the physical thing itself.

architectural "variety show" (as the opening online event was named) unfolds.[1]

The second episode, Enfilades, speculates on potential rooms from which the core emerged and how they can be experienced as a virtual promenade. Speculating on a form of genetic coding for future architectures, "Enfilades" is simultaneously voyeuristic and immersive. One catches glimpses of architectural elements – now envisioned in expanded and spatial instantiations – as the viewer is led through the filmic enfilade of rooms with misaligned doors. Unlike in a video game, the viewer has no agency to control their point of view or position.[2] Thus, one feels simultaneously inside and outside of the exhibition.

In the third episode, Paperthin, the viewer occupies the physical core of the gallery space, and as a result, can no longer see the core as a discrete object. Here, the core is the framing device, reifying the viewer's position in space through which projected content is witnessed as animated fragments. As the camera slowly rotates the field of vision clockwise, the exhibition unfolds in unanticipated ways, expanding and contracting as it reveals the flatness of digital renderings and the atmospheric effects of an animated environment. Viewers are transported through three different, partially constructed worlds, each with its own scale, speed, and implied portals into other rooms. Oscillating between surface and mass, and revealing their artifice, these paper-thin simulations are ruminations on an architecture of incompleteness. This final episode posits a

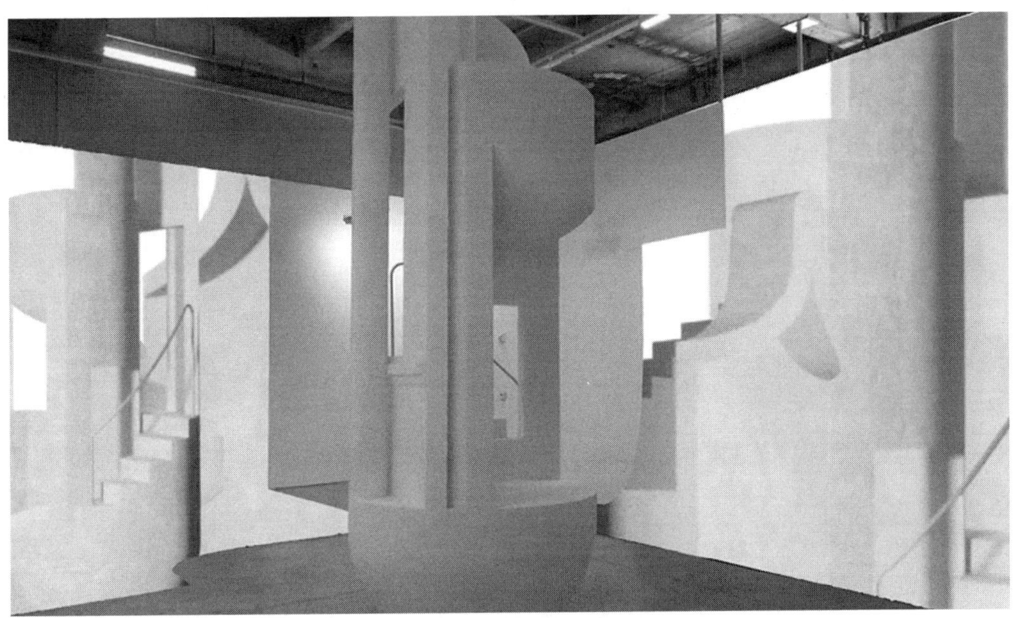

netherworld for architectural speculation, akin to an e-mail draft – a message in the process of being composed but in need of further action.

Timely in its capacity to address how we mediate our physical and virtual existence, BairBalliet's exhibition explored the generative potential of new media and how it expands our understanding of the ways architecture is constructed, communicated, and experienced. The slow yet evolving nature of this show, which unfolded in three acts over 60 days, demanded from its audience a form of architectural attention. Not unlike the communications blackouts that occur during the reentry of spacecraft into the Earth's atmosphere, "No More Room" leveraged and leverages silence as a space-time continuum, breeding anticipation as it isolates us from the white noise of all that is our contemporary condition. The effect is a hypnotizing sequence of spatial musings in the round, where the observer – whether in situ or tuning in – is implicated as both an occupant and voyeur. BairBalliet adeptly suggests that in the interstitial spaces between gallery and screen, plaster and pixel, mass and void, volume and line, presence and absence, there is anything but "No More Room" for architecture.

Whitney Moon is an architect and assistant professor of architecture at the University of Wisconsin-Milwaukee, where she teaches history, theory, and design.

A stand of Atlantic white cedar trees is slowly decaying in Madison Square Park in Manhattan. One could say the city is to blame for the trees' dire condition and not be entirely wrong, but the scene in question is a temporary installation by artist and architect Maya Lin, commissioned by the Madison Square Park Conservancy, called Ghost Forest. *Past annual installations in the park have ranged from sculpture to architectural follies, but Lin's piece eludes those classifications. Instead, she chose to demonstrate the effects of climate change with natural elements that are otherwise invisible to most city dwellers.*

The grove of pines originated in the coastal Pine Barens in New Jersey, where, due to sea level rise, salt water is seeping into the soil. The increased salinity slowly kills the trees, producing the phenomenon known as a ghost forest: eerily lifeless trees still standing as they decay. Lin selected 49 of the Pine Barens trees for their scars and ruggedness before they were cut and transported to Manhattan, where they were positioned as if they were a small forest, their trunks then "replanted" eight feet deep into the park's Oval Lawn. The scale of the installation — the trees are all around 40 feet tall — and its relationship to the deciduous trees around it echo the extent of the human impact on the planet's ecosystem. The simplicity of Lin's installation underscores the fact that our climate changed reality is no longer an ecological forecast and that the time has come not to project devastation but to witness the damage already done (a premise Lin also explores in her multimedia project What is Missing?*).*

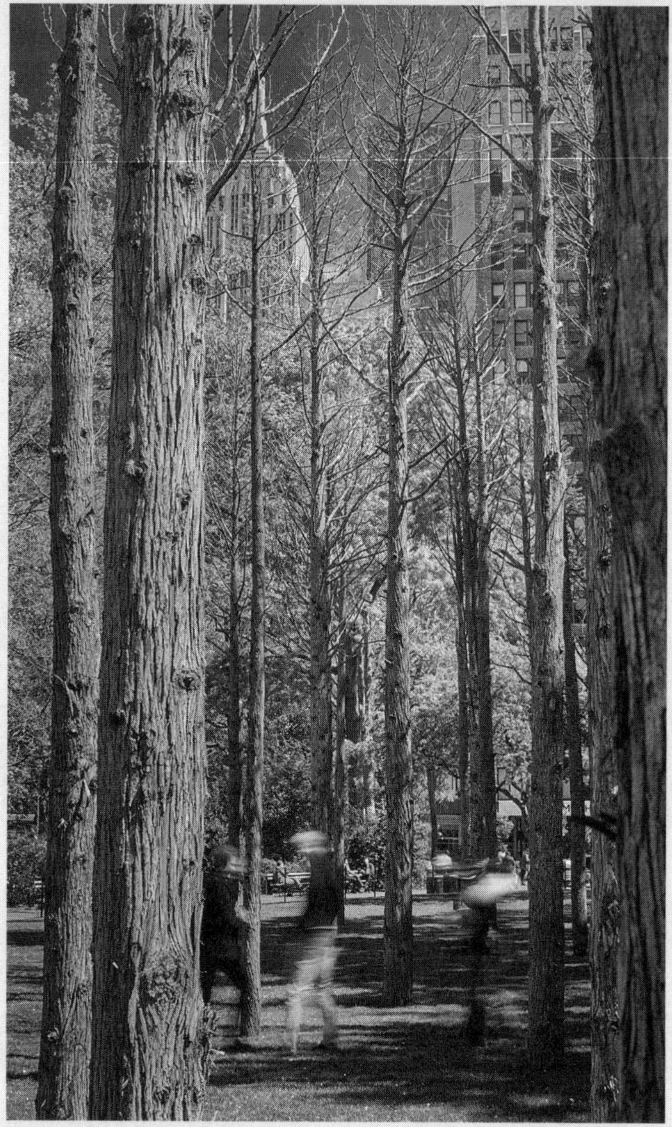

Maya Lin, *Ghost Forest*, New York City, 2021. Photo © Andy Romer.

Ghost Forest *was originally scheduled to open in the summer of 2020, but it was postponed due to the COVID-19 pandemic, which ultimately endowed the piece with a new meaning. As Lin said, "The pandemic and climate change are kindred disasters."*

— Osvaldo Delbrey Ortiz

Cynthia Davidson

The Environments Of Emilio Ambasz

NEW YORK, NOVEMBER 17, 2020 – The Museum of Modern Art announced today the establishment of The Emilio Ambasz Institute for the Joint Study of the Built and the Natural Environment. The goals of the Institute, through a range of curatorial programs and research initiatives, are to foster dialogue, promote conversation, and facilitate research around the relationship between the built and the natural environment – making the interaction between architecture and ecology visible and accessible to Museum visitors and the wider public while highlighting the urgent need for an ecological recalibration. – MoMA Press Release

With the announcement of the Ambasz Institute last fall, architect Emilio Ambasz is, in a sense, coming home, back to the place where, in 1969, he became a curator of design; a place where his graphic design work entered the collection even earlier, and where both his industrial and architectural projects are in the museum's collections. A peripatetic individual who says he feels most at home "in my shoes," Ambasz agreed to two transatlantic Zoom conversations in June, 2021, to discuss the new program at MoMA, which he endowed with a $10 million gift; his work as a curator in the early 1970s; and his exceptional career in architecture and industrial design. What follows is an edited transcript of those conversations, giving some insight into the life and mind of a man whom many call the father of green architecture – an achievement that the University of Bologna recognized this year with an Honorary Doctorate in Architecture and Engineering. – CD

CYNTHIA DAVIDSON: How did a boy born in the provinces of Argentina get himself to Princeton University in 1963?

EMILIO AMBASZ: When I was 11, I knew without knowing that I wanted to be an architect. I was only interested in toys having to do with architecture. When I was about 15 or so, I started listening to the courses at the university in Buenos Aires. It had about 6,000 students of architecture, so nobody noticed me. I also bought Frank Lloyd Wright's *In the Nature of Materials* and Bruno Zevi's *Saber ver la arquitectura*. I told my parents that I would go to America, because America, for me, was the stage of the world. Is it still in the 21st century? I sadly nurture doubts. Anyway, I did everything possible to connect myself with architecture. Mainly, the great thing was Amancio Williams, an Argentine architect who was a great poet [of architecture]. I thought one would learn poetry from a poet, so when I was 15, I presented myself to him and he accepted me in his office. So I could be in his office in the morning and afternoon, I went to high school in the evening. I really gained his trust, he even trusted me to go to Uruguay to find an architect of record for a building he had designed for the richest industrialist family in Argentina. I got Eladio Dieste to be the architect of record, who told me, *Young man, I don't do that, but I will do it for Amancio.* And also a brilliant self-taught structural engineer, Mr. [Leonel] Viera.

Now, having done all of that, and getting to a certain age, I started applying to American schools, and knowing quite well that competition was severe, I applied to about six or seven. I can't remember exactly. The most interesting one was Rensselaer Polytechnic Institute, which replied, *We know you're going to be accepted somewhere else, and that's the reason we're not accepting you.*

CD: Really?

EA: But I was accepted by Princeton. They gave me an absolutely immense scholarship. When I came to Princeton, I thought I was coming to the Institute for Advanced Study. I looked around for Einstein, but he was probably in another part of the campus.

CD: Yes. The institute is a separate entity.

EA: I couldn't stand the fact that I had to sit with the freshmen in Commons, which was the name of the dining room, and listen to kids saying, *Pass the butter, please,* or other such profound statements. I started as a freshman in the School of Architecture, but thanks to a few professors, mainly Peter Eisenman, I was moved from freshman to senior in the first semester. Because I went to class with a coat and a tie, people asked Peter if I were very rich. And Peter said, *Oh, yes, Emilio's father is in the oil business.*

CD: I've heard that story. It's a good one.

EA: Because it was true. How did the son of a gas station attendant get to Princeton? The rational answer would be luck, luck, and luck again. The second answer is a much more historical one. There was a gentleman at Princeton by the name of Alden Dunham, who was in charge of admissions. That was his first year, and he managed to convince the university that it was populated by WASP boys, all of them sons of rich alumni, and that he had to create a class that was more varied and mixed. So that is why I was accepted with an absurdly large scholarship, absolutely large, okay? And the third answer is that it was simple, single-minded perseverance on my part.

You should have seen me, a young, little student sitting at a seminar table, trying to look intelligent so they wouldn't ask me questions because I barely could speak English. When I came to America, my first girlfriend said that I spoke like Gary Cooper. I didn't study English in Argentina, because under Perón, you couldn't. English was a capitalist language and it wasn't taught in school. So I would listen to television, cowboy films, and repeat every word. I had expressions like "How you like them apples?" that were absolutely laughable. Anyway, that is the story of the boy from Argentina. Born not in the Pampas, I assure you. Where I was born is a subtropical climate. At 4:00 pm it rains. At 4:30, the clouds come out from the sidewalk and go up.

CD: So that's how you got to Princeton. You're infamous for graduating in one year.

EA: The second semester, I was in graduate school. And at the end of the first year, I went directly to graduate school in a more formal way. I had a four-year scholarship that was so big it covered everything. The man in charge of matters in the School of Architecture, a professor by the name of Henry Jandl, said, *Pay nothing, and just keep on enjoying the scholarship.* But at the end of the first year, I said I was going to Yale, at which point they said, *What do you want?* And I said, *I don't want anything. But since you ask in such nice terms, I want Colin Rowe.* And they got Colin Rowe. Of course, I was introduced to the idea of Colin Rowe by Peter. Before Colin arrived, I collected all of his essays – all of those I could collect – and out of my not very meager scholarship, I paid to print them in offset form and gave it to all my classmates so they would know who he was. When he arrived and saw that, he said he was going to sue me for copyright infringement. I should have received him with a bottle of cheap scotch, although kerosene might also have been acceptable.

At the end of my master's – I'm coming to the end of this – Robert Geddes, dean of the school, asked me to join the faculty. Kenneth Frampton told me that the appointment was quite disputed, mainly by Graves. Graves and I were like cats and dogs. I disliked his way of teaching, and I didn't mince words. The students he would favor were the ones that made Michael Graves architecture. I thought that that was not a way to teach.

CD: So did you join the faculty?

EA: Yes, indeed. Then, at a certain moment, Peter [having left Princeton] began having conversations with the director of the A&D department at MoMA, Arthur Drexler, because he had done a show for him. Peter had the idea to create the Institute [for Architecture and Urban Studies]. I would wait for Peter when he returned from New York on the bus, and we would talk about what he and Arthur discussed. As a matter of fact, Peter suggested to Arthur that I would be a potential candidate to be a curator, because Mildred Constantine, who had been the associate curator of design, was moving to another position. So I went for an interview. Arthur had a few questions, including what did I think about Mies van der Rohe. I said, *Well, isn't it remarkable that a man that invented in reality the most refined and elegant architecture provided a formula for speculators who do very cheap buildings.* Anyway, that is what I remember from my conversation with Arthur. So I was invited to join the museum. But my invitation was 50/50, 50 percent of my time as associate curator and the other 50 percent as the associate director of the Institute for Architecture and Urban Studies.

CD: You joined MoMA on July 1, 1969, at the age of 26. The press release said you were responsible for industrial and graphic design, publications, and exhibitions. Did that mean curating, plus writing, plus designing exhibitions?

EA: Yes, I designed exhibitions. I did several exhibitions, but I was not forced to stay within the domain of graphic or industrial design. I did a few architecture shows. For example, I took a book by Peter Wolf on Eugène Hénard, who was an urbanist in turn-of-the-century France, a remarkable urbanist, in my opinion, and I did an exhibition of his work. So I was all over the place.

CD: You did a Luis Barragán exhibition, too, right?

EA: That was much later, at the end of my time at MoMA. The first show I did was

Eugène Hénard. I also did one on [Charles] Rennie Mackintosh and his chair designs.

CD: How did the concept of environmental design as opposed to architectural design enter your consciousness? As I understand it, you named the CASE group, Conference of Architects for the Study of the Environment, in the mid-'60s while still a student.

EA: This is absolutely true. I was a student then. But to go back to your question. You said environmental design as opposed to architectural design. It's not opposed. At that time, I was thinking of *environmental design* as one way of saying that architecture exists not only beneath its own premises and as a discipline, which is quite restricted to its priests, but in a larger sociocultural context. That's really what I meant by environmental design. I thought that we had to expand architecture's relation with the social and the cultural context where it operates and not as if it were a self-enclosed discipline.

CD: So you weren't necessarily thinking about the natural environment yet?

EA: I was thinking about the total environment. Not the green environment at that time, no. It included it, but it was not exclusively that, no.

CD: The environmental was the focus of your 1969 essay "The Formulation of a Design Discourse." The ecological as distinct from human endeavors is the focus of the Ambasz Institute. What is the difference between environmental and ecological, and why are you emphasizing the ecological today?

EA: The focus of "The Formulation of a Design Discourse" was on an analytical system, or system analysis, which understands problems in terms of systems and components of systems and how they influence one another, which brings us back to my earlier answer. That's really what the essay works out. The word *discourse* is used in the philosophical sense. You have a discourse if you have a set of values and meanings that are established and constantly reevaluated. But back to your question about the environmental and the ecological. Frankly, the *ecological* is something the museum's people wrote when they did the PR about the Ambasz Institute. In the contract I have with MoMA, the word *ecological* was put in by [architecture curator] Martino Stierli, probably, I suspect, because *environmental*, or something like that, bothered some people on the board of trustees. The board of trustees is made up of some people who are in the business of construction, and the notion of doing green architecture and taking into account factors like maintenance, which go beyond immediate building, is just a disturbing function for them. Probably he used the word *ecological* to avoid a certain amount of irritation. *Ecological* comes from the Greek word *oikos*, which means a dwelling, not only in the sense of a house but also in a temporal sense: to dwell or to wait.

CD: If MoMA is now emphasizing the ecological, that's very interesting. In a 1993 interview with Sharon Zane, you said that MoMA "could provide institutional support, to actually become an impresario and trigger certain types of projects." Why would such a transformation of the institution be important?

EA: In my practice as a curator, I distinguished two types of curators, the farmer and the hunter. The farmer curator plants, harvests, and collects the seeds. He sells part of the harvest; the seeds that he collects he will plant again for next year's harvest. The hunter curator is one that proposes the subject, then goes out and makes it happen. I believe that in a museum, the curators in painting and sculpture and photography should be farmer curators – that is to say, they should harvest and they should collect seeds, which they should classify and evaluate. The hunter curator, for me, is only possible in architecture. I was interested in the fact that the institution, MoMA, provides an immense platform that allows you to put into practice certain ideas that do not exist. Imagine the curator of painting who goes to see a painter and says, *Hey, take a look at this new type of plastic paint. Do me a painting with that.* Makes no sense, does it? But as a curator of design and architecture, I could go to Italy and say to the designers, *You are making beautiful furniture, but I know that you're deeply unhappy, because the furniture is only the beginning of your concern. You would like to be able to design at least the surrounding environment where that furniture operates, let's say the domestic environment, or domestic landscape.* I did that with Italian design, and I did it again with the taxi show, where I proposed the creation of a new taxi. I believe that the architecture curator can become an impresario. That is what I was trying to tell Sharon Zane.

CD: Essentially your first big project at MoMA, which you began formulating in 1969, was the Universitas conference in January of '72. What were you hoping to achieve with this?

EA: I was aiming to create an institution, a feasible institution. It was to be located in Jamestown, New York. It was a project that greatly interested [Governor] Nelson Rockefeller because he was interested in creating a State University of New York equal to the state university system in California, to Berkeley. He was planning to have a fast train from New York, and was arranging for trains to stop in Jamestown. The key for the whole operation was the Land Grant Act, whereby

most of the American agricultural universities were created in the 19th century. I saw that that law was still valid, and we could use it to create urban land-grant colleges and be granted approximately 70,000 acres of land that would be the experimental field for the university. I worked with some economists to try to figure out how that would work. We were quite advanced in the notion that it was possible to obtain enough funds to finance that type of university without selling the land but by leasing it, and that the university would be engaged in several things. Very important for me was preventive health care. I thought it was absolutely pivotal, so it wasn't only architecture I was interested in. The great misfortune was that Richard Nixon resigned, Gerald Ford became president, and he made Rockefeller his vice president. About 120 seconds afterward, Rockefeller, in the great princely tradition, lost all interest in the university. And poor Mr. [Anthony] Adinolfi, the building chief of the university, almost died of a broken heart.

CD: What relationship does the new Ambasz Institute have to these goals? Notably, your call for MoMA in 1972 was to develop a research arm, and your Program on Environmental Design was to be an independent program. Is that what you're hoping the institute will be?

EA: I can say the following: I'm a boy of few ideas, infinitely reformulated. That is an answer that Borges used to give, and I always liked it very much. He says it's always the same story, it's just reformulated differently every time. With *environmental*, I expected the department to be concerned not with architecture simply as a building but with the social-economical context in which architecture was operating. That's why I prefer to use the word *environmental* and not *architecture*, because architecture, for me, limits itself to thinking about the building and all of the canons of architecture, which are plenty, thank you very much. I wanted to expand to the sociocultural domain and even to the natural domain. Now, today, what I want to do with the institute is the following. For me, MoMA's architecture department has been the champion of modernism for 75 years, and that intellectual capital is almost exhausted – not completely, but almost. I thought that the department should renew its capital. I wasn't going to come back to be the curator, so I thought I could provide the funds to have an institution within the department that would be concerned with establishing a correlation between nature and architecture, understanding that everything we do is a contribution to man-made nature, which is replacing, overbearingly, the nature we were given.

CD: In a similar vein, you argued that transformation of society and culture, to have real effects, should take place within existing institutions. The Ambasz Institute seems a bit like planting a seed, since you're talking about seeds, for the structural transformation of MoMA, or at least the Department of Architecture and Design. How do you perceive it? Is it just another program at MoMA, or does it have transformative potential?

EA: The institute is a distinct institution within MoMA. It will become whatever they can make of it, okay? But the point was that the Museum of Modern Art has, for 70 or 75 years, been the champion of modernism. That intellectual capital is considerably exhausted, to be polite. I think there has to be a renewal of that intellectual capital. I put it in those terms. I wrote it in those terms and it irritated MoMA, but what can I do? I'm the rich kid, okay?

CD: Have you met Carson Chan, the first director of the institute?

EA: No. I don't even know who he is. He seems to be very enterprising and intellectually very ambitious, and that is very good. Because any institution will run as fast as the individual in charge of it. So we will hang from his coattails, and we will go with him.

CD: Given that you hit the ground running when you joined MoMA, it seems you've been playing the long game. When you launched the Program on Environmental Design, did this expand your purview beyond industrial and graphic design? Or was it a precursor to the concerns you would raise in "Italy: The New Domestic Landscape"?

EA: I proposed to Arthur that we do the show on the state of Italian design because they had been making very beautiful products worthy of being in MoMA's collections. But when I got to Italy and started observing the intellectual domains, I realized that the products were not what made the phenomenon of Italian design so interesting. The Italians had a far deeper understanding of design as one way of analyzing and criticizing society. Mind you, most of them were architects. They didn't have much work, which is also a circumstance that cannot be forgotten, so they had dedicated themselves to doing products. At the same time, there were groups of architects that refused to do anything, what I called the moratorium architects, who said, *You cannot do anything in society until society changes.* And there were others that said, *Well, maybe you can use objects in some way to try to change society, as a provocation.* This is why the show ended up covering a much larger domain than just the handsome products that you can see at MoMA and then run to a store to buy. How many Braun toasters were sent to me by people who, in furious letters, said, *Your pretty toaster burns toast!*

Now, to come back to one word that you used, *seeds*. From seeds sprout trees, trees

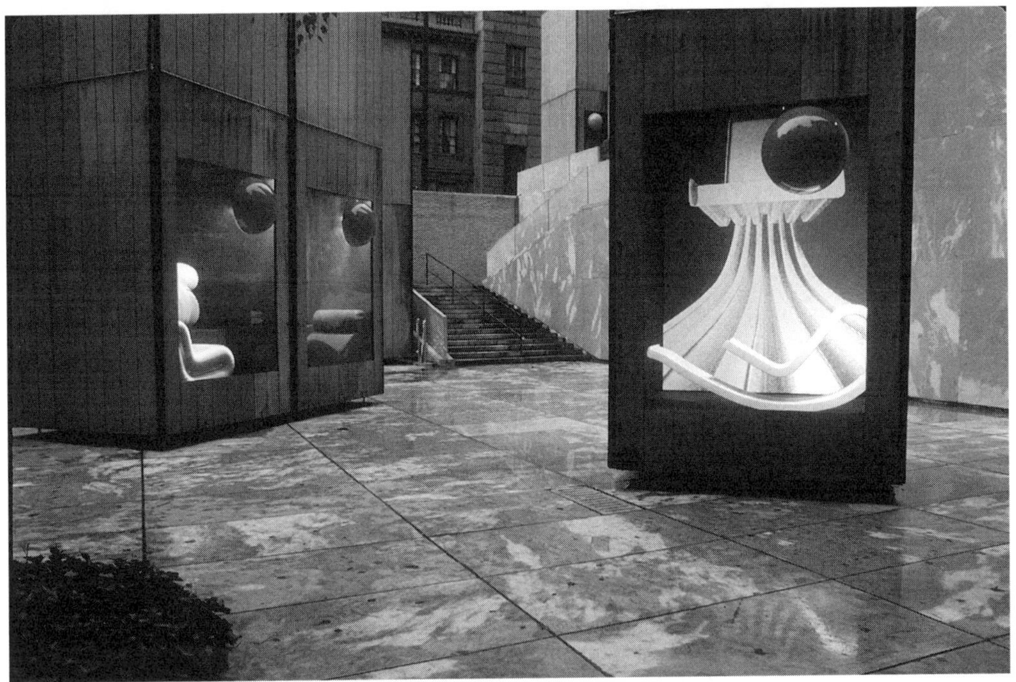

"Italy: The New Domestic Landscape," installed in the garden of the Museum of Modern Art, New York, May 26–September 11, 1972. Photo: Cristiano Toraldo di Francia. The Museum of Modern Art Archives. All images courtesy Emilio Ambasz.

sprout flowers, from flowers sprout fruits, fruits attract birds. The birds eat the fruits, they fly away and do their thing in other gardens. My notion is that you plant the seed and hope for the little bird to spread it to other gardens.

CD: It is said that the "New Domestic Landscape" exhibition introduced an expanded field of operation for architecture that was then eclipsed by the theory debates that arose after Drexler's Beaux-Arts exhibition. Why was Italian design at that moment a way to explore or demonstrate this expanded field?

EA: American designers were furious. To them, these were a bunch of Italian designers who were making very pretty objects while bending every possible rule, rules that they, in proper Bauhaus tradition, had been educated to uphold. And it's not that I did it purposely. I'm not an intellectual. I perceive and I act, okay? I make images. I am an intuitive person. And I am relatively observant. My idea was that Italy was producing the objects that MoMA had always celebrated in the Bauhaus tradition, but in reality, what they were making in Italy was something far more powerful. It implied, and this became evident to everybody, that design was a cultural production that covers many different aspects of society, not only the little pretty flower.

As for Arthur's show, I have no idea why he did it. Maybe because he was looking for something pretty to show. I used to think sometimes that it was just because all those drawings from the École des Beaux-Arts were available. I don't think it was an attempt to go back to that school of architecture. He was too lucid and too intelligent to pretend that an exhibition would do that.

CD: What lessons did you personally take away from "New Domestic Landscape" that influenced your own design work?

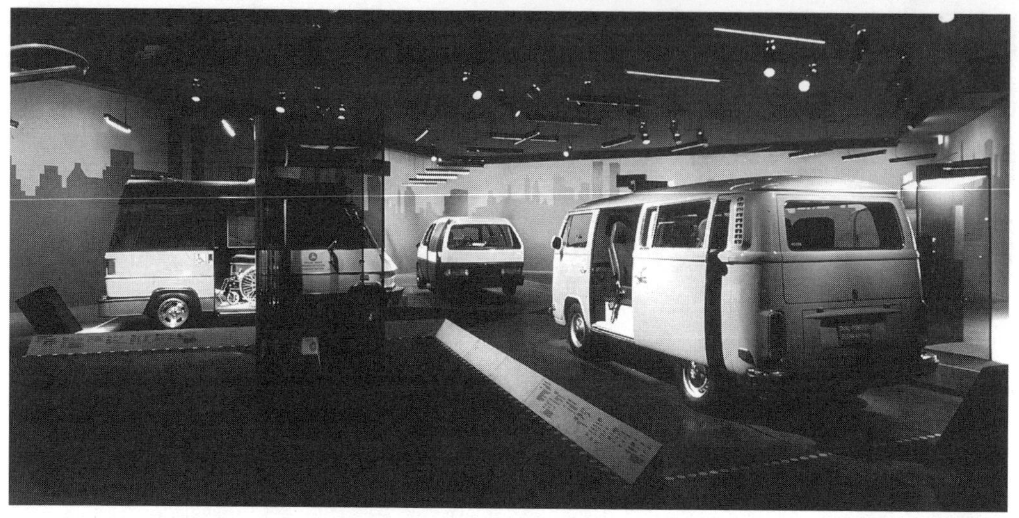

"The Taxi Project: Realistic Solutions for Today," The Museum of Modern Art, New York, June 16–September 7, 1976. The Museum of Modern Art Archives.

EA: That the designer can, in some way, introduce ideas with objects, and that objects are the containers of ideas. I also learned that I put much more trust in images than I put in words. I grant that ideas come wrapped in words but I distrust words, because when you deal with words, you're in the semantic domain. And in the semantic domain, you're in a conventional domain that is already agreed upon. That means it cannot be innovative. It can only be operating within an established culture. With images, you can start in some way to suggest a different mode of thought, a different mode of perception, and in some cases, maybe, a certain way of acting upon the present.

CD: That's very interesting, since I edit a journal that resists the seductive power of the image and puts its trust in the power of words.

In 1976, you curated "The Taxi Project." What happened to the prototypes you commissioned? How did they resonate in the world after the show closed?

EA: When I proposed to MoMA to do the taxi [prototype] show, they said, *You will have, of course, Detroit*, and I said, *Of course we will have Detroit*. In the meantime, I negotiated with Fiat and with Volvo to produce taxis according to a design program set by the Taxi & Limousine Commission for the type of vehicle the New York taxi should be. When I approached Detroit, Detroit told me to go jump in the lake. So I went to David Rockefeller, then the chairman of the museum, and said, *Mr. Rockefeller, we have a problem*. So he wrote to the chairman of General Motors, who wrote back saying, *David, I don't understand why you're bothering yourself with that. Pay attention to your bank. We sell 50,000 Chevrolets every year as taxis, and nobody has any problem with them*. At the end of the show, the press release quoted this statement by the magnificent chairman of General Motors, and the lawyers of General Motors came running, hoping that they could sue us for libel. I showed them GM's letter and they walked out.

In the meantime, I had designed a museum for Grand Rapids, and I became acquainted with Gerald Ford, then the vice president, who lived in Grand Rapids. He asked me, *How is that [taxi] project coming?* I said, *Sir, we are going to have a big problem, because the American car industry is not inter- ested in participating.* And he said, *What do you think would be necessary?* I said, *Well, you know very well how capitalism operates. They want to be underwritten, like in a socialist country.* So he got the Department of Transportation to make available two million dollars for two American companies. I flew back to Detroit and met with Chrysler, where they grace- fully told me they would do it, but would send a prototype made up of scagliola – that is gypsum, okay? And I said, *It will be marvel- ous. I can just imagine the opening day, when the television crews are there, and somebody opens the door of your scagliola taxi and it breaks and they end up with a handle in their hands. No way. We are giving you a million, that should be good enough for you to build a full-scale model.* They had no interest whatsoever. So the two million was adjudicated to two small American companies. One of them produced a hybrid car, and the other produced a steam- driven car, which took us back to the end of the 1800s. So where did it all end up? I had two units made for each of the vehicles pre- sented. The Department of Transportation took the cars and tested them. I don't know the results of the tests. But I can tell you that Volvo tested their prototype before sending it here. They designed it so that the taxi could also be an ambulance, because they couldn't afford to produce such a vehicle only for the taxi market. Fiat produced the Alfa Romeo prototype, which was designed by [Giorgetto] Giugiaro. Volkswagen refused to design a special vehicle, saying their Kombi was perfect as a taxi.

CD: When you compare the taxis in New York today to the photographs from the show, it seems that it took 40 years to get a better taxi. The shows you curated prove that MoMA is a powerful base of operations for architecture and design. So why did you leave the museum in 1976?

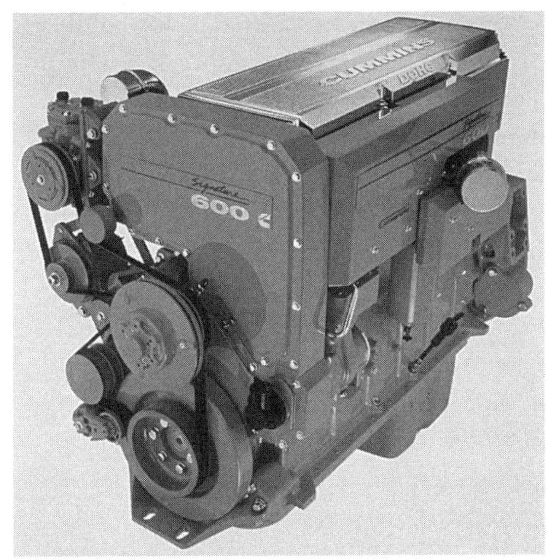

Emilio Ambasz, Cummins Engine Company Signature 600 Diesel Engine, 1996.

EA: MoMA was going to embark on a three- or four-year construction project. By that time, I was already 32 or 33, and I thought that I was too old to waste three or four more years at MoMA. And frankly, I don't think I was a good curator. I wanted to do architecture – after all, I had started playing with architec- ture toys. And I never ever looked back and never regretted it. And I had no idea of who I had been, or what my position was, until Gaetano Pesce called and said, *You're crazy, Emilio. You're resigning? You have power, you're my only friend with power.* I said, *Gaetano, I pre- fer poetical power to political power.*

CD: I heard that after the taxi show, after you left MoMA, that Cummins Engine got to you, and you started designing diesel engines.

EA: The situation was exactly like this. Mr. [Irwin] Miller, Cummins's chairman, who was really an enlightened industrialist, truly a remarkable man, had the idea that his diesel engines should be judged as archaeological entities by a culture that would come 100 years later. Those were his words. And that culture is produced from nine to five, not after five. Eliot Noyes had been the industrial design consultant for Cummins. When Eliot died, Mr. Miller asked a number of people about a new designer, including Cesar Pelli and Paul Goldberger. They, not knowing anything, said, Emilio. So he invited me to come to Columbus, Indiana, to meet with him. At the meeting was a very charming and kind man by the name of Mr. Schwab, who was the chief engineer. Trying to look intelligent, I asked Mr. [William] Schwab, in the presence of Mr. Miller, *When do engines die?* He looked at me and said, *Well, you know, we don't say they die, we say that we cannot overhaul them anymore. And we cannot overhaul them after usually 500,000 miles because they rust, and then they're beyond repair.* So I said, *To cool the engine, instead of using water, which rusts the engine, why don't we use oil? We can take the oil out of the block and cool it in a separate bronze or copper aftercooler.* At which point he stood up and said, *Marvelous idea,* which I assumed was meant tacitly to say, *Finally, someone said what I have been trying to do for the last 30 years. Since he seems to be a friend of Mr. Miller, I will say that this is the best thing ever.* And that's how we went into developing an engine that was cooled with oil.

CD: Emilio, how would you know to cool an engine with oil if you didn't have that early background in oil?

EA: Exactly. Imagine, how would I? Yes. Well, how would I?

CD: You have described yourself as an inventor, and your projects as prototypes. In fact, you hold 220 industrial and mechanical patents. How is your work in architecture and urban design related to and different from your work in industrial design?

EA: Architecture, for me, operates in the domain of poiesis. Or *poiēsis*, if I can be very Greek. The domain of industrial design is pragmatic. Industrial design products are always related to the body of the user. Whether it is a toothbrush, a chair, even a car, they all have to do with the body and the relation of that product to the body. Architecture's relation to the body is much more than use. Architecture deals with the body, yes, but also with the brain and with feelings. Therefore it is in the domain of poiesis and not solely in the domain of the pragmatic.

CD: Earlier you said objects contain ideas. Do you think of the object also as presenting an image?

EA: No, it's presenting its shape.

CD: So where does the image of the object come in?

EA: The image of the object is something you keep in your memory, but not before the shape has presented itself. In architecture, the idea does not exist until an image arrives. And the image, if it is worth anything, is prototypical and has to be decodified. I separate architects into three types. There is an architect artist, who invents architecture, and there is an architect professional, who takes what the architect artist has invented as a prototype and introduces it into the culture and operates with it as a type. So the prototype goes from the architect artist to the architect professional, and becomes a type. In time, the culture changes and the type becomes a stereotype. That is the way images are born, that's the way they die.

CD: Is the third type the stereotype?

EA: The third is the stereotype, a type that became a stereotype. The hack architect uses stereotypes. The professional architects – Skidmore, Owings & Merrill would be like that – they operate in the domain of types. And the artist architects – Frank Lloyd Wright or Mies van der Rohe or Le Corbusier – are in the domain of prototypes.

Novo, novo-, is a marvelous root word. *Novo* means new in Latin. That's what I seek. For example, you talk about the text. When I think, I think in terms of images. When I think of Le Corbusier or of Wright, do I care to dwell on their millions of words? Or do I take refuge in their prototypical images? Maison Dom-Ino, Villa Savoye, Ronchamp, Fallingwater – that's what matters to me. Not the words, some more skillful than others, certainly. Le Corbusier wrote much more aggressively and much more seeking to convert. Wright was another sort, he was preaching, which is completely different. He was not interested in converting. Maybe he knew that his character would not attract followers.

CD: Many of your peers consider you the father of green architecture. Assuming you are happy with that moniker, what is green architecture? How can we differentiate today between green architecture and the green-washing of architecture? What do you think of LEED certification?

EA: Okay, look, at present, for me, the green movement – let's call it that, okay? – is not a movement, it's just a label. It is a state of awareness, okay? It's not yet a conceptual reality because it lacks a precise system of discourse and it lacks a theoretical structure that would allow it to transmit a body of knowledge. And more important, it would allow it to be constantly reevaluated. It's an attitude, so far. It's not yet a principle. But I have no doubt it will become one. It will. I, of course, am immensely upset about all the people who have jumped on the bandwagon of green architecture. Some of them have been immediately successful and created really extraordinary practices by selling pots of plants on balconies

and calling that green architecture. That's not what I mean by green architecture. The main problem is that society is like a sponge and absorbs everything.

CD: What do you think of LEED certification? Is that helpful?

EA: Yes, LEED certification is useful. If anybody asked me to do it, I would not know how to do it. I would call someone to do it. I'm not a specialist in that. When I do a building, I work with many engineers and technicians. They're the ones that make sure that you respect the requirements of LEED. But I don't think it's sufficient. There has to be something more. If a building is sustainable and LEED-approved and blah, blah, blah, but does not move the heart, it's just one more building. An edifice, not architecture. To do a building, you need technology. To do architecture, you need art.

I'm all for sustainability. I find that little attempts, for example, a building that saves electricity by putting up a solar panel or things like that, are fine. But the real attitude should be a communal system of solar panel collectors, not a single building doing the solar energy collection. It would be more economical and more efficient. The strategies, I believe, need to be more social, more community-minded than individual. At present, that's the way it is done, but it's not enough.

CD: My friends in San Antonio love the garden you did there. How did you arrive at its glass forms? Are they in contradistinction to the softness of the landscape?

EA: Cynthia, it doesn't escape you that a greenhouse needs glass or the plants would die on you very fast. The client came to me and said, *I want you to do a greenhouse.* And I said, *Where?* He said, *San Antonio*, and I said, *But why do you need a greenhouse in San*

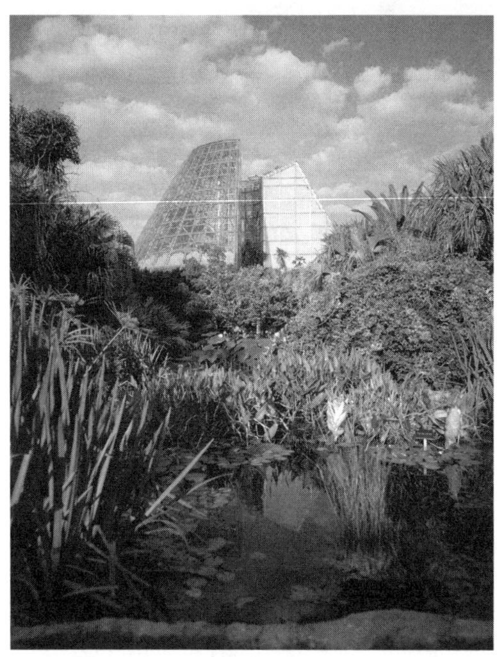

Emilio Ambasz & Associates, Lucile Halsell Conservatory, San Antonio, Texas, 1988.

Antonio? The climate is so good. So he said, *No, the problem is that we can get in three or four hours, a drop in temperature of about 15 degrees, and the plants cannot accommodate it and they die, or else we get very strong cold winds, which come down all the way from Canada, down the prairies, and they kill the plants. So we need to protect them.* So that's why the buildings are there. Now, at the same time, like all those clients of mine, they come with beautiful ideas, with splendid minds, and with very tight pockets. Therefore, there was not enough money to put in all the types of mechanical equipment that a building like that needs. So most of the buildings are surrounded by earth on the ground level to reduce the heat load. Now, the glazing is there for two reasons, not only for the lighting. Because there is too much sun, I hung curtains to filter the sunlight. This is probably one of the few greenhouses with curtains. Now, money was very tight, so I had to invent the glazing system. What we did was use the structure itself as the support for the glass. The glass was not in a frame, it

was just glued onto the frame with a lot of glue. If the building moved, the thick layer of glue would be enough to absorb the twisting of the building, and thereby the twisting of the glass, because, believe it or not, glass, to a certain extent, and in some dimensions, is elastic. It will bend – of course it will bend with very minor curvatures, but it will bend. Carlo Scarpa knew a lot about that. His main amusement, whenever anybody visited his buildings, was to hit the glass with his hand. It would create a tremendous amount of noise. And people would say, *What are you doing, you're going to break the glass*, and he would say, *No, glass is elastic.*

CD: The hospital you designed in Mestre, outside of Venice, is also largely glazed.

EA: Very much so. It's really a greenhouse. I have been in enough hospitals, and they are always depressing because you have a feeling that you're coming into a place that ignores you or into a warehouse or a military garrison. I wanted the hospital to receive patients with a bouquet of flowers. And when they are recovering, they should be able to walk between plants. So half of the rooms look directly into the greenhouse and half of the rooms have their own gardens. It has been quite successful, actually, really visited by everybody, because it was supposed to be the first green hospital. Now, I was aware that such a type of hospital wouldn't cure people, but my hope was that it wouldn't make them sicker.

CD: You have used the phrase "green over gray" to describe your work. Given the number of buildings today that sport trees, one could interpret "green over gray" as cladding, even window dressing. What do you mean by "green over gray"? And can you point to a particular project of yours to illustrate this?

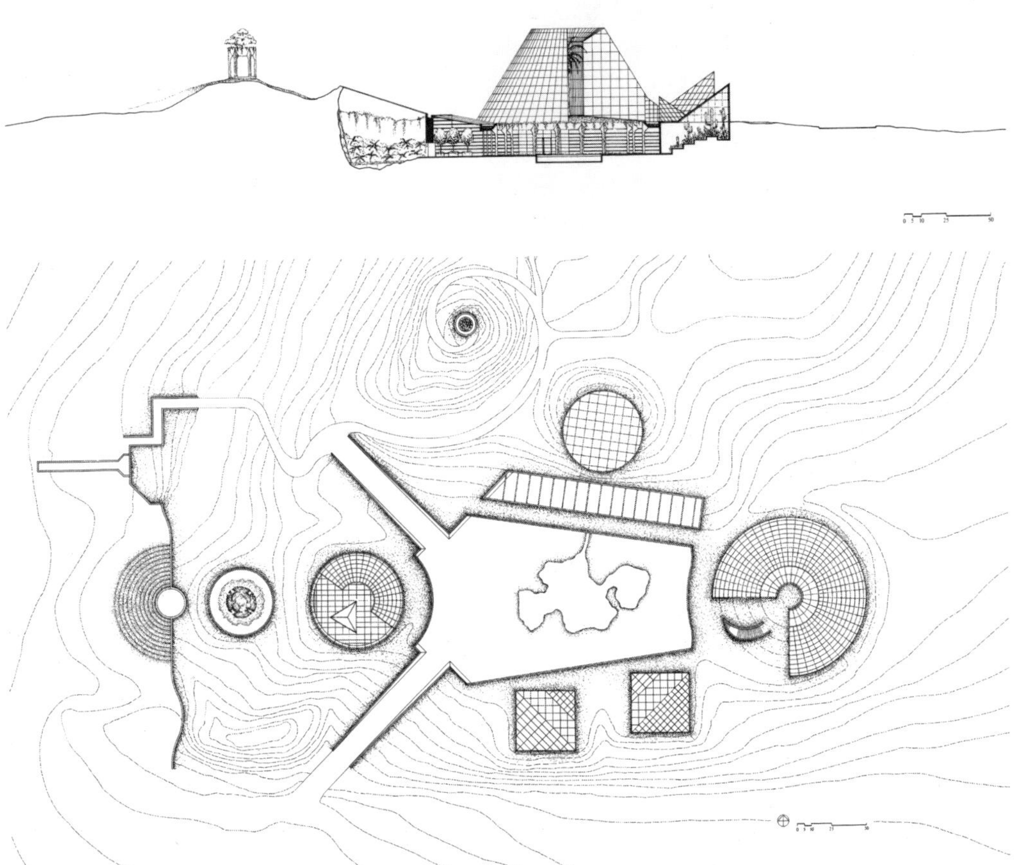

Emilio Ambasz & Associates, Lucile Halsell Conservatory, San Antonio, Texas, 1982. Section and plan.

EA: Well, there are a number of instances of the superficial uses of plants. There's nothing terribly wrong with covering the facades with greenery, it's just that they don't move the heart. If it doesn't move the heart, what type of architecture is that? By "green over gray," I meant the replacement of the notion of architecture as gray and the integration of architecture, which is man-made, with natural nature, which in some cases I've achieved. The project in Fukuoka is one where it worked out quite well.

CD: How was Fukuoka worked out?

EA: As I told you, I don't work by thinking or reasoning. I work by making images. And once I make the image, I try to understand what it means. Many times, I don't get it immediately. It takes time. In the specific case of Fukuoka, I was not aware when I made the image for Fukuoka that the city government was taking away half of the only park the city had, and that, unbeknownst to me, that fact was creating a great amount of unhappiness in the people of Fukuoka, who were protesting. When I did that image, I recovered almost 100 percent of the greenery that the building footprint was to cover. That is what made the building possible and that's why it won the competition. Everybody told me, *Don't bother, it will be won by [Kisho] Kurokawa.* The jury was 46 men, and their decision was supposed to be unanimous. Two of them did not vote for Kurokawa, they voted for me. Since it was not unanimous, instead of being

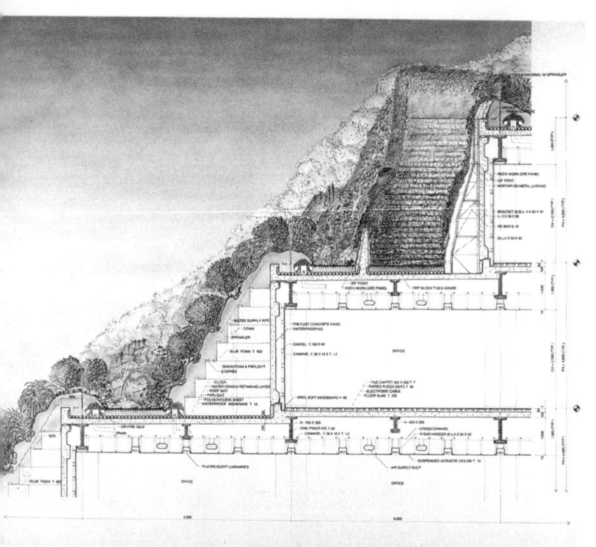

Emilio Ambasz & Associates, Fukuoka Prefectural International Hall, 1990. Stepped garden section detail.

sent to the mayor of Fukuoka, it had to go to the governor of the region.

At that moment, the newspapers in Japan, mainly *Asahi Shimbun*, got hold of that. And if you know Japan, you know how, inconceivably, terribly indifferent its people are because they don't think that they can change anything. It's very rare that they will protest unless they want to enter some negotiation. So the governor selected my project. My client took me by the neck, more or less, to put it in an image, and took me in front of the group that commissioned Kurokawa to convince them that my client never asked me to win, that I was a barbarian *gaijin*, which means a foreigner, and didn't understand anything. Now, because of that building, 25 years later the climate on the top garden, according to the owners of the building and the university that works with them, is about 15 degrees Fahrenheit lower in temperature. Fukuoka is in the south of Japan and therefore is quite hot. And did I plan for that? Certainly not. It just resulted in that, okay? It suits my privately held belief that perfect acts will generate perfect coincidences. I do not doubt that a statement like this is enough to irritate any logical person.

CD: That's interesting about the temperature. I thought you were going to say that it had a ripple effect in terms of more greening of the urban space.

EA: No. What it did was demonstrate that you could have greenery in the center of the city. You don't have to go to the periphery or to the suburbs. But again, it wasn't that I was set on a campaign to demonstrate that greenery in the center of the city is possible. My image was simply a building covered in greenery, and I was really lucky that I won the competition.

CD: How does the building at Fukuoka extend the park physically? It extends it visually, right? Can people in the park access the facade of the building?

EA: You can go up all the way to the very top by stairways, which start in the park and are within the greenery. And the beautiful thing, and that I really intended, is that when you get to the very top, you can see the bay of Fukuoka. It's very handsome, almost like the bay of Hong Kong. The City of Fukuoka has never given me back my original sketch, which was a section of the building. I am told they use it as the logo of the city.

CD: Let's continue with this idea of image. What do you want the image of your Casa de Retiro in Spain to convey?

EA: Yes. I made an image. I was not conscious of what I was generating, but once it appeared, I realized that what I had done was something I could derive a number of principles from. I didn't intend to make a building that was efficient from an energy viewpoint. I just wanted to insulate the building from the intolerable heat of Andalusia. I wasn't aware that I was designing a house that, once it was built, with the roof and

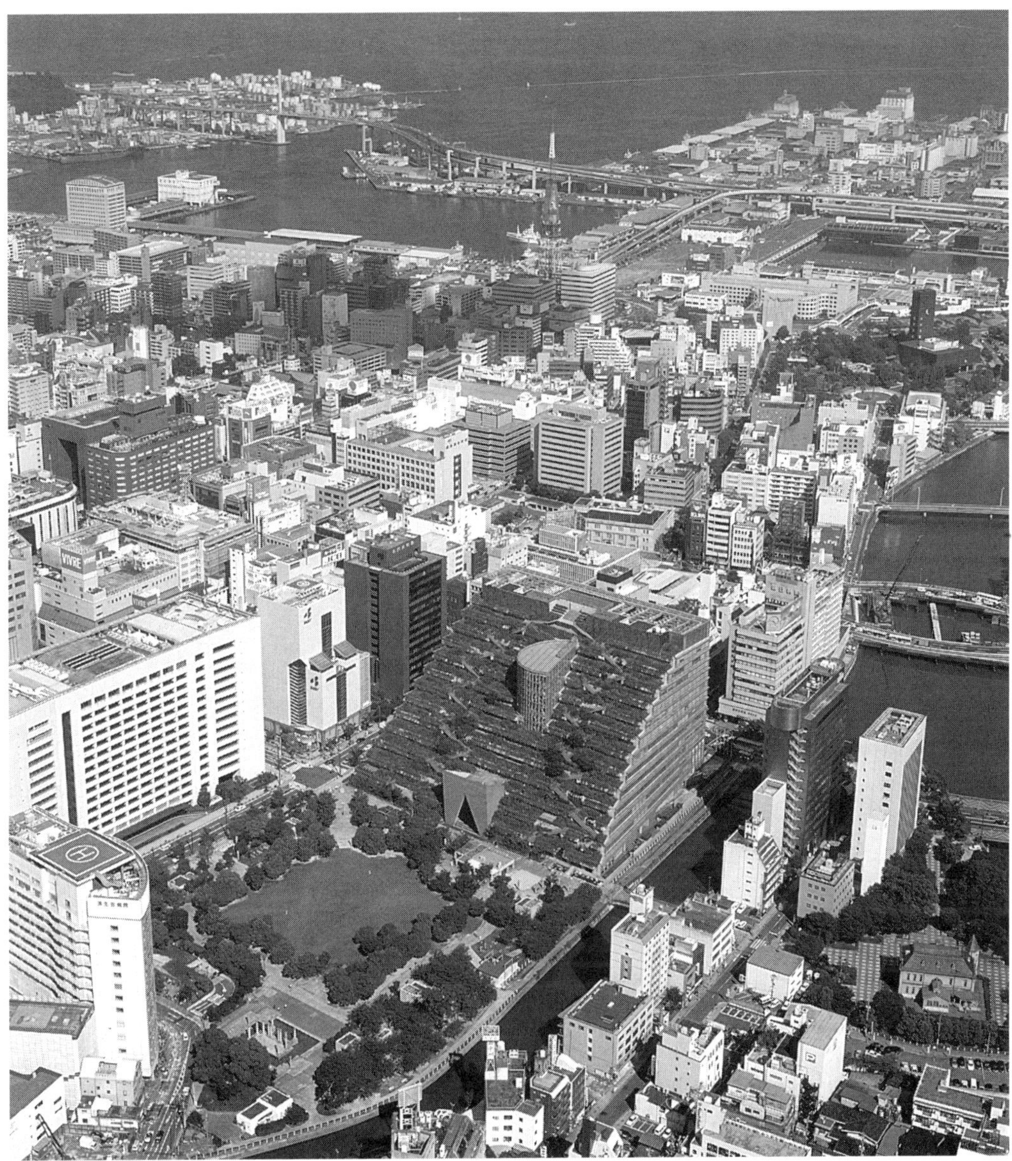

Emilio Ambasz & Associates, Fukuoka Prefectural International Hall, 1995. Photo: Hiromi Watanabe – Watanabe Studios.

walls covered in greenery, there wouldn't be any need for heating, there would be no need for air-conditioning. It was only afterward, after I designed that building, or I generated an image, that I started thinking, what does it really mean? And when I started to decodify or decipher it, I realized it harbored a number of ideas. One of the first ideas was to give back as much as possible the ground that the building covers and make it into gardens that are accessible to the users of the building and, better still, to the community. The second thing I realized is that I had designed a building that was so intricately related to the surrounding landscape that it wasn't possible to separate one from another. And third, I had created ornament that changes with the seasons. And I did it deliberately to decorate the building – *decoration*, that great taboo word, which should not be used, we were told. I believe greatly in decoration. In fourth place, putting earth and plants on the roof to create a garden allowed me to make a building that sings with a loud voice but with a closed mouth. What I'm trying to say is that I don't sit down to try to do buildings that really save electricity, that are sustainable, I just design the building, and then I try to think, what does the image imply, mean, represent? Because the key task is to develop a technique, an ineffable technique, and then leave yourself at the mercy of inspiration. Now, you cannot build a school on that and it's much more detested by professors, but that's the way I operate.

CD: But let me ask you, isn't the primary image of that house the two freestanding walls, the corner?

EA: Yes, very much so. It is a very essential image. I wanted to be able to evoke the totality of architecture, or the poetry of architecture, using very essential means, to reduce everything to the most essential things.

CD: But one could argue you don't even need those walls, so what do they mean for you?

EA: Do I need those walls? Yes and no. I have to tell you why yes. They stand for the pleasures of architecture. You need them also because you need light inside a house. If it were direct sun, you would cook inside that house. But the walls reflect a more subdued light, so the house's inside is full of filtered light that has been reduced considerably by the reflection from the walls.

CD: The Casa de Retiro and the computer research center in Mexico City were both designed in 1975, while you were still a curator at MoMA.

EA: Yeah, yeah.

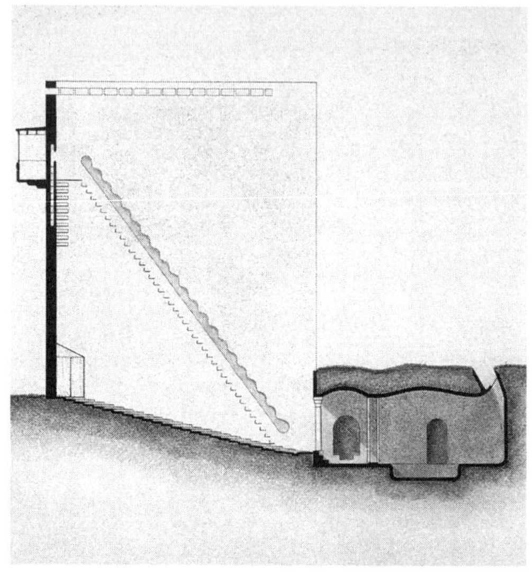

Emilio Ambasz, Casa de Retiro Espiritual, Córdoba, Spain, 1975. Section.

CD: Given how we've adjusted work space during the COVID-19 pandemic, I'm interested in something you wrote about the Mexico City project. You said, "Behind the design of this environment is the premise that nobody should have to work. At worst, one would work at home and not need a large building but rather a small one to simply house a computer and receive messages. The building has been conceived, therefore, as a set of elements that can be progressively reconfigured and recombined as the needs of the office vary over time." Did you make this idea clear in 1975? And why was the project not built? What other factors were at play?

EA: I made the idea very clear. And notwithstanding the fact that the group of people who had commissioned the building knew that I spoke Spanish, they said, *Está un poco loco*, which means, *He's a bit crazy*, when I told them exactly what you just read. I said, *There is no need to have the people coming here to work. They can work from home with their computers, so you will slowly be able to remove the barges and then leave only one barge in this image of the islands of Xochimilco*, which are really islands of flowers.

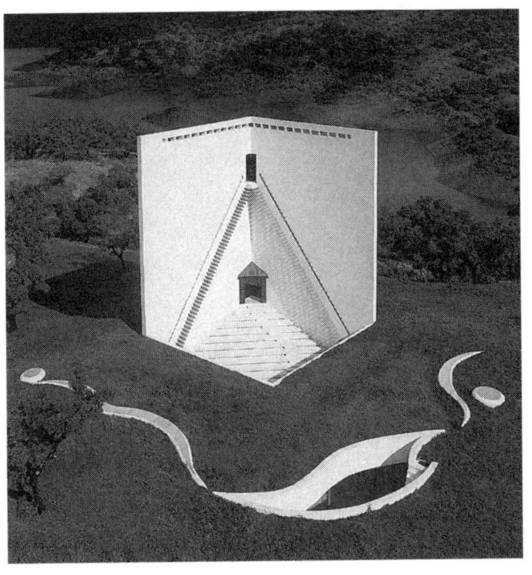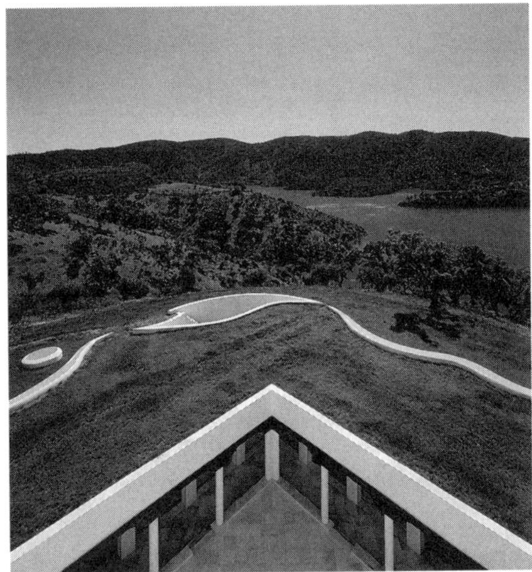

Emilio Ambasz, Casa de Retiro Espiritual, Córdoba, Spain, 2004. Photos: Michele Alassio.

CD: Islands of flowers?

EA: Xochimilco is not very far from Mexico City center. It is a place where people sell flowers from boats, so they are like floating islands of flowers.

CD: It seems like a prescient idea given where we are now, not only because of the coronavirus but ever since computation has become nearly universal. In 1975, no one had really a computer at home.

EA: Let me tell you the story of this project. I was doing the Barragán show, and I was with Barragán in his car, which was being driven by a chauffeur. He was telling me that he had gotten this commission and told me what it was. I took a piece of paper and said, *Well, Señor Barragán, you know how I would do it? I would do it like this.* So I put my two hands together, you can't see them, but they more or less simulated the two walls of the Mexican project, and added water because, I said, all of Mexico City before Cortés arrived was once a veritable network of water canals. That would solve the problem of drainage

and at the same time would allow the barges to change positions as the tasks they housed changed. He turned to me and said, *Your project is much more beautiful than mine, do it yourself.* But they commissioned not little me, they commissioned big Barragán.

CD: Did he build it?

EA: He didn't do anything. No.

CD: In 1971, you published three short essays in *Perspecta*, one titled "Manhattan: Capital of the Twentieth Century," playing off Walter Benjamin's "Paris: Capital of the Nineteenth Century." When did you discover Benjamin's *Arcades Project*? And how did it affect your view of cities at that time?

EA: There was a translation of Walter Benjamin's writings that I think Yale University Press published. I was smitten by Benjamin, because I believe in a distinction between the critic who is a belletrist writer and the critic who is a writer in the *Kunstgeschichte* [art historical] style. For me, Benjamin was a belletrist, like Baudelaire,

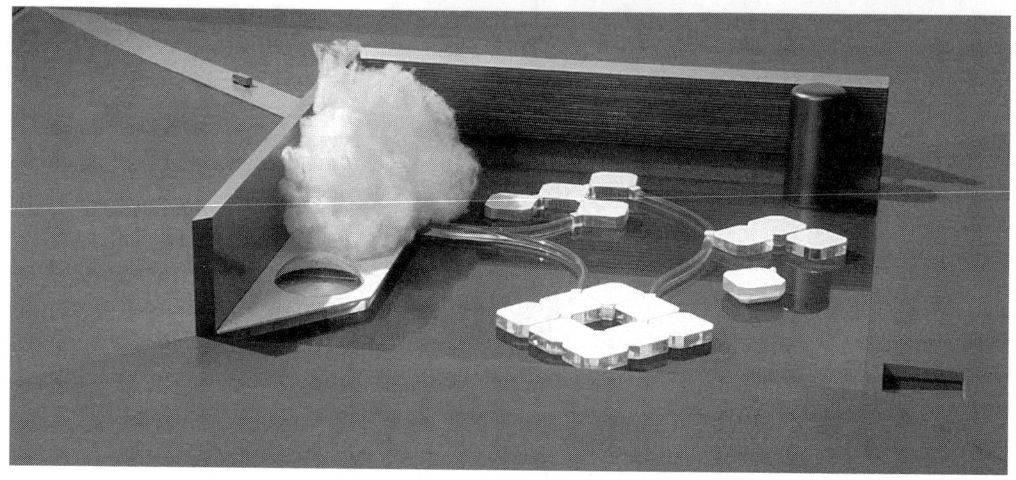

Emilio Ambasz, Center for Applied Computer Research, Mexico City, 1975. Model. Opposite page: Photomontage.

and I was fascinated by that mode of perception. A poetic mode of perception is far more insightful than a rigorously historical one. And, of course, it influenced me because I write fables. The first one was "Manhattan: Capital of the Twentieth Century," which, yes, picks up on "Paris: Capital of the Nineteenth Century."

CD: In the essay you write that the power of design is to question the present and give it new meanings or to restructure it. If architecture can only work in the present, what is its responsibility to the future?

EA: You can only make proposals for the future in the present. Therefore, any project that does not propose a better type of living, a better type of existence, is unethical, and it has to propose it in the present. That means it has to produce a type of building that probably is prototypical or experimental or whatever it is. But I believe very strongly that the architect's ethical obligation is that of proposing a better mode of existence, through architecture, and that can only be in the present. To have an effect on the future, it has to play in the present. We have to be courageous to change the present.

CD: What is your concept of the emerging city today?

EA: What is a city? I am immensely distrustful of undertaking, as an architect, the design of a city. For me, a city is an aggregate of many opposing wills, contradictory wills. The homogeneous idea of a city like Brasília hasn't succeeded. It has to be the result of a number of communities, their wills opposing and slowly modifying one another, to have a real city. Designing a building is a paramount undertaking, but designing a city is nerve to the point of effrontery, it is unadulterated chutzpah, unless you first design the infrastructure, the whole system of movement and of services, so that elements and buildings can be added later and removed. And these architectural elements have to be designed in such a way that when they are removed, they create the minimum amount of upheaval. But the design should only be that of the city's infrastructure. Over time, elements are added and elements are removed. And when you design the elements to be added, you have to be conscious that they will be removed. And that it costs to remove them, that you have waste, that you need energy to remove the components. That's why I was talking about "Manhattan: Capital of the Twentieth Century" as an extraordinary infrastructure,

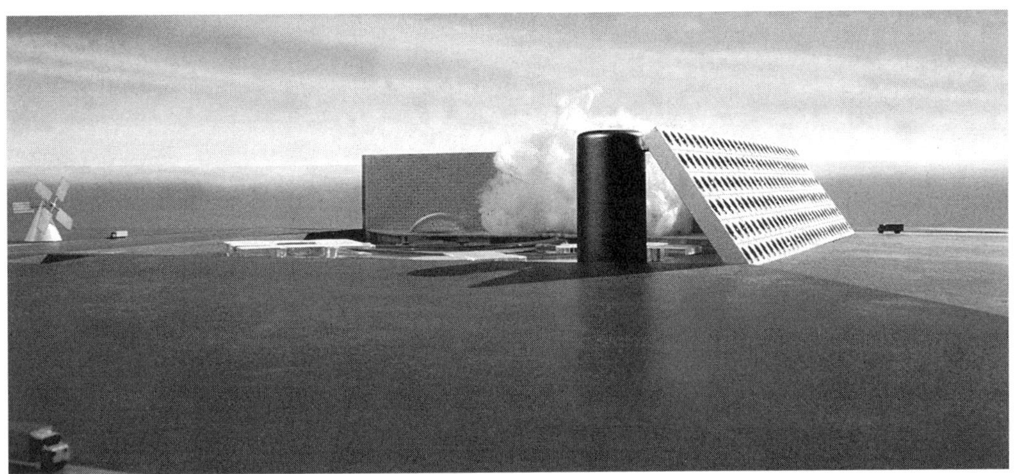

the grid or net on which you can put buildings and other such things and remove them, but the infrastructure remains standing there. Of course, an infrastructure is not just physical, the city is also a city of information. One of the advantages of information nowadays is that you probably don't need such rigid physical elements because it can now be transmitted by digital devices. Manhattan is a city of information and a city of culture.

CD: The Universitas Project raised questions about the relationship between design and science, with a working paper that said, "Design cannot prosper within the confines of the scientific worldview." What do you think about the role of science and technology in architecture today?

EA: Well, science operates in the domain of that which exists, trying to understand it, or trying to modify it. Design or architecture operates in the domain of visions, of proposing things that don't yet exist. It operates in the domain of *invention*. And that is a difference. The method for invention cannot be the method of science. It requires the methodology of science to evaluate what it has produced, it requires a methodology of science to evaluate what it is inventing. But there is no method of science to generate visions. I

believe only in visions, I believe in architecture as invention. I believe in architecture as the domain of artists.

CD: In that sense, if science solves problems, like how to deal with the coronavirus, does the professional architect also solve problems?

EA: The professional architect, of course, has to solve problems, because he's operating within a set of requirements, between sets of laws and regulations, and capital and society, let's say the public. Yes, he's solving problems that people have. And he's using visions or images that have been created by others, and tested, and probably, in some cases, even tested by science. It is one way of collecting experience and applying and reutilizing it, so it's not wasted. But the images that are being used, if they are of any quality, as I said, must be prototypical. If not, they are types, they are typologies. And the professional architect works within the domain of type. How many architects, and you know them very well, create prototypes? It's a terribly difficult question.

Take a look at, for example, nature as a concern of architecture in different periods. It has appeared in many a vision. Giulio Romano, in Palazzo Te, was desperate to run away from Renaissance strictures, so he upset the rules of the columns and the grid. Decades later, in a much better case, [Bernardo] Buontalenti made the geomorphic buildings in Pratolino for Francesco I de' Medici. This kind of concern for nature keeps reappearing with a different word to define its style. First it is called mannerism, later it's called art nouveau. For example, rococo furniture resembles nature, etc. The fact that now we're having a certain concern for nature really means that it's a pervading concern, which comes back in every culture. Nature is a substantial longing that keeps reappearing throughout the ages. I don't see anybody doing rococo or art nouveau architecture today. They're only trying – in a few cases – to reconcile nature as it was given to us with the nature we have been creating, okay? We have transformed nature to the point that if you find a tree today, it's there because somebody placed it there or someone left it there. There's almost nothing that man has not intervened in. So what you need now is a notion of architecture in which architecture is considered to be one element of the nature that we are creating. And it has to be in reconciliation with the nature that was given to us. The Greek notion that we have to conquer nature because nature is our enemy has subsided. The enemy is the nature that we have made, if we have made it badly.

CD: I have a last question, one that involves words rather than images. You have said that Lucretius's *On the Nature of Things* is one of your favorite books. Why? What is its bearing in architecture?

EA: I read poetry. I read Wallace Stevens, I read everything like that. Lucretius is an extraordinary Roman poet, before Christ, who thought about the universe in terms of atoms, who thought that gods did not exist and everybody was free to make their own destiny. That was quite remarkable when people were so superstitious and bound to adoring gods made of bronze. Lucretius had been a student of Epicurus, but his notion that man is alone in the universe is what I found so remarkable. And I find it remarkable that without ever mentioning him, Baruch Spinoza, the Dutch philosopher of the 1600s, had very similar words. I think that the great misfortune in our culture was the moment we put our bet on Descartes and not on Spinoza. As a matter of fact, I am now reading a novel on Spinoza, which has nothing to do with philosophy. It is an invention of his life.

CD: Why do you call your own writing fables? What does the word *fable* mean to you?

EA: A fable usually is an educational device. You write them to teach a moral lesson. In that regard, allow me to confess I am only interested in discovery, not in recovery; I am keen on invention, not on classification. In the uncharted realm of invention, taxonomy is a process yet to be born. In the same way, as I search for essentials and lasting principles in architecture, in opting to write fables rather than write theoretical essays I may have grasped something basic: fables remain immutable long after theories have crumbled. The invention of fables is central to my working methods, it is not just a literary accessory. The subtext of a fable, after all, is a ritual, and it is in the support of rituals that most of my work addresses itself.

It is said that *verba volant, scripta manent* (words fly away, while writings remain). But for me, it is images that transport the heart to higher domains.

Cynthia Davidson, editor of *Log*, enjoys a good fable. Anna Renken, editorial intern, was instrumental in doing research for and editing this conversation.

Kurt W. Forster

Leaps and Bounds, Grace and Gravity

Grace, one of the paired terms in the title of Lars Spuybroek's new book, is a special quality of human performance that belongs to the realm of life experience; the other, *gravity*, is a property that makes itself felt in matter and in things, something we have to deal with without being able to change it. Grave matters often address breaks, ends, and death; graceful ones help to move through dangers and dance across treacherous grounds. Beauty and grace are deeply connected, but take on conflicting manifestations, for we seek beauty in things and expect life to endow them with grace even though we remain fatefully enthralled to death. Every building is rigid but needs to house life, which is flexible; every work of engineering is calculated but aspires to demonstrate its power to harness threatening forces that could just as well bring it down. In a world where everything gains presence through media – in liquid stability and fleeting reflection – experience ultimately erases the distinction between life and death.

In Spuybroek's view, "Architecture approximates language, where thousands of years of interpretation and thought have structured its formal elements in such a way that even in its most quotidian use a deep structure of thought is anonymously at work."[1] Therefore, architecture doesn't make an apt subject of philosophical definition but rather becomes the very object of its own thought, or so one might agree as one delves into *Grace and Gravity: Architectures of the Figure*. Spuybroek's latest tome dwarfs his *The Sympathy of Things: Ruskin and the Ecology of Design* from a decade earlier, both in scope and in ambition. One-fifth of the new book's considerable heft is reserved for crisp notes, bibliography, and index, revealing the geology of Spuybroek's mind and the enormous range of his knowledge. *Grace and Gravity* bodes well, inviting readers into an enchanted philosophical *florilège* instead of abandoning them on the crabgrass of modern polemics. A lost cause? Not if you are willing to take a journey through millennia of thinking.

The first sentence of the first chapter poses a question like the 17th Venice Architecture Biennale's "How will we live together?" but with significant modification: "How do

1. Lars Spuybroek, *Grace and Gravity: Architectures of the Figure* (London: Bloomsbury, 2020), ix. Unless otherwise noted, subsequent quotations are taken from the book.

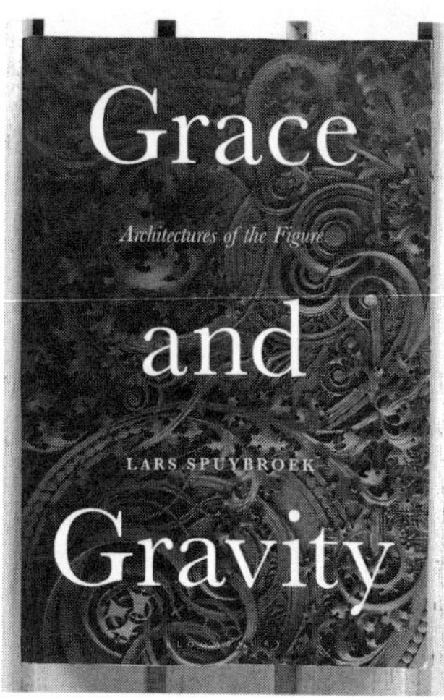

Grace and Gravity: Architectures of the Figure by Lars Spuybroek. 2020. 464 pages. Bloomsbury.

we live *well?*" In order to live well together, we must be pliant and flexible. But more is at work than maneuvering if we aim to reach a state called grace. Grace stems from the notion of a gift, something that secures a mutuality and aims for a certain balance, however precarious it may be. That Aglaea, one of the three Graces, is wife to the lame god Hephaestus, the maker of automatons, permanently links mechanical simulation with bodily action, setting this incongruous notion on a path through the millennia until it resurfaces in the incessant flow of gracious lines spewed forth by algorithms. From William Hogarth's sinuous "line of beauty" to the spline curves in recent architecture, from the folds of fabric to the pliant profile of Spuybroek's proposal for a new World Trade Center at Ground Zero, an intimation of death-defying flexibility has enthralled the architectural imagination. Spuybroek discusses graceful curves in many different circumstances, taking time, for example, for Heinrich von Kleist's essay "On the Marionette Theatre," on the "grace" of marionettes as a form superior to what humans can achieve. But one only fathoms the range of Spuybroek's imagination when he spells out the relationship between puppeteer, puppet, and the consciousness encompassing them both. What neuroscientist Antonio Damasio explains as a peculiar phenomenon of human consciousness, Spuybroek is able to expand to the nature of spaces – the floor under the weightless feet of a puppet, the posture of the puppeteer, their combined effect on viewers who are led to "sympathize" – that is, to experience this fusion. He then makes precise connections between architectural members and the rapports among them in a particular *Bewusstseinsform*, through which they manifest themselves, especially in a poignant discussion of Gothic architecture in which light is the supreme solvent.

Spuybroek takes a number of elegant turns as he weaves notions of anthropology and technology into a fabric of explanations that illuminate the processes by which ornaments come into being. Ornaments have remained difficult to explain, if we don't just settle for their forms and their manufacture, but instead recognize them as the timber of thought that goes into architecture no less than the lumber from the yard.

In the preface to the second edition of his book *The Sympathy of Things*, Spuybroek announced that it was not written in connection with his work as an architect – though he was, by 2010, widely recognized as a remarkable designer of a new kind of structure and was a professor at the Georgia Institute of Technology. Rather, the book "played

2. Lars Spuybroek, *The Sympathy of Things: Ruskin and the Ecology of Design*, 2nd ed. (London: Bloomsbury, 2011; 2016), xiv. Emphasis mine.

3. Ibid., 1st ed., 327.

an important part in the *cessation* of [his] practice."[2] It is as unexpected as it is anomalous to find such reflection – especially among architects who tend to move from writing (often poorly edited) to designing (frequently provisionally realized) and back again as if it were the norm of their practice – stand in the way to practice. What Spuybroek explores, more thoroughly and with greater knowledge than most of his professional colleagues, does have the power to make one *stop*, to rethink, and possibly to leave behind what besets us with growing urgency since the advent of the new millennium. The anxiety pervading contemporary architecture has closed several avenues that might lead out of the reductionist impasse of design without forms and buildings. Much recent architecture offers no food for thought and little in the way of experience, except to over- or underwhelm, to awe or disappoint, while starving the public out of any engagement different from an exceptional day at the stock market, a frightening week in a war zone, or the launch of a new handbag. To the extent that buildings fail to solicit our instinctual sense for *things* that are able to hold our intelligence without sending us scrolling, for feelings without sentimentality, and for a desire without satisfying it, we lose interest. Who could deny that much that passes for architecture today does not deliver on the elementary expectation that Spuybroek calls "sympathy"?

Sympathy constitutes the center of Spuybroek's earlier book, starting with Ruskin and his retrospective celebration of Gothic architecture as a quintessential marriage of material, craft, and experience, derived from influential threads of thought by Gottfried Semper, Owen Jones, and others who distilled a set of intricate *patterns* from forms in art and nature. Where patterns congeal, as they did with William Morris, a frost falls on them, but where they grow ductile and infinitely generative, as they did in art nouveau, they release a potential of ornamental forms that, scaleless as they may be, overcome inertia.

Discussing the beginnings of iron and glass in architecture, the bane of traditionalists in the 19th century, Spuybroek, looking back at Walter Benjamin through the corrective lens of Peter Sloterdijk, observes that "the arcade embodied the labyrinthic *détournement*, while the Crystal Palace took on the role of the glorious, radiating center of the universe," the former leading into the back alleys of culture, the latter creating a vacancy no culture can fill.[3] A huge tree and a fountain are as natural under the glass canopy as its technical envelope is a purely industrial fact. The Crystal

Palace held only a hollow, and its members were, according to Jones's instructions, "to be annihilated with color," thereby suspending any useful distinction between outside and inside. Though a big palace of nothing – awaiting the world's commercial treasures to be disgorged – the crystal attribute was more than a moniker; it was the essence of its disengagement from life. Under its gossamer canopy, Semper discovered an archaic hut, not so much the origin of architecture as the embodiment of an architectural idea. This engendered a powerful feeling for seeing, as if for the first time, something that had aged and suffered so much in the course of civilization that the pain of loss tempered the joy of discovery. The dilemma of architecture was brought home, because it was not yet a fossil of itself.

Spuybroek confesses in the opening sentences of *Grace and Gravity* that he is after different beginnings and will respect few bounds as he pursues their endless metamorphoses. *Grace* emerges in the sphere of social and religious respect, while *gravity* is associated with machinery and the god of the forge, Hephaestus. The awkwardness of mechanical processes and the shine they can produce inaugurate a contest we customarily know as engineering versus beauty. A "kaleidoscopic mosaic of stories, images, and philosophies" awakens a dizzying set of figures from history and puts ideas in motion across the ages through correspondences and half-remembered associations joining in a bubbling spontaneity of thought. To reconsider the relation between figural ornament and object (so ornamented), Spuybroek makes the point of their mutual convergence using the example of Minoan vases, the spherical bellies of which are covered by the coiling arms of octopi. Spuybroek has more in store with this creature, whose nervous system is one of the most highly developed among invertebrates, calling it the "ultimate master . . . of shape-shifting and craftiness," no doubt relishing the ambivalence of the latter term with regard to the making of forms and undoing of appearances. One might as well think of Irving "Swifty" Lazar or of astonishing mimicry, again pursuing coils of arguments that do not always unfurl in these pages but do tickle the tentacles of one's own mind. As the Minoan vessel holds water, the water creature whose body is all fluidity and motion restores to terra-cotta the endless swirling life of which water is both substance and medium. All ornament aims to arrest motion, some of it mechanically replicated by the yard, some uniquely patterned onto bodies, whether geometric or organic, to reveal its aptness for the things it

4. See Byung-Chul Han, *Die Errettung des Schönen* (Frankfurt: S. Fischer, 2015), 37: "Die digitalisierte Welt ist eine Welt, die die Menschen gleichsam mit ihrer eigenen Netzhaut übersponnen haben." (The digitized world is a world that people have, as it were, covered with their own retinas.) Han revisits the classic differentiation of the beautiful from the sublime in a world where nature and artifact can barely ever be kept in separate categories.
5. Such epigrammatic renderings can also raise doubts, as in this case, when the word *image* weakens the powerfully somatic dimension of Bachelard's ideas, something Spuybroek goes on to detail in the paragraphs that follow this citation from page 100.
6. Italo Calvino, *Six Memos for the Next Millennium*; cited in *Grace and Gravity*, 348.

bespeaks. What it doesn't do is remove the otherness of the creature that "holds" the jug as if it were at once covering the vessel and being it. The beauty of these fluid lines is not the beauty of what philosopher Byung-Chul Han has defined as the characteristic state of smoothness of the digital.[4] In its perfection, "digital beauty" is without bounds or teeth; it doesn't sting or stun and thus leaves no room for anything other than itself and its reflection in the eye of the beholder. Han recognizes the digitalized world as one where all resistance has been sucked into an unbroken continuity as if slime had replaced any other substance. In this sense, one could hardly be further from grace – which, when it fails, fills us with dread – than to be in the presence of painless smoothness.

Spuybroek, in contrast, works by leaps and bounds. Quite literally so, when he carries the reader from the bull-jumping Minoans to the man who jumps over a puddle in a famous photograph by Henri Cartier-Bresson, assisted by Roland Barthes's meditation on photography's *punctum* – capturing life in a still shot and giving the moment rigor mortis – puzzled forever by the question that Lucretius, Gottfried Wilhelm Leibniz, Charles Darwin, and, for that matter, quantum physics all entertain: Does nature make jumps? She certainly does allow for things falling into place, sometimes out of whack, and producing coincidences. What coincides would never come together if not for an unpremeditated event, an occurrence that binds things together that would never join otherwise. "From the viewpoint of technology," Spuybroek argues, "accidents are the moment when things stop working, *but from the viewpoint of phenotechnology nothing ever stops working.*"

Throughout *Grace and Gravity* Spuybroek displays a gift for synthesizing complex ideas in ways that do not reduce or deny their difficulties but rather behold them in simultaneity. For example, he brings out a fundamental distinction in otherwise "sympathetically" related authors: "With Heidegger things always appear in the form of words – hence his lifelong obsession with etymology – whereas with Bachelard words always appear as images."[5] Architecture used to be what Spuybroek calls a "deep screen," a place where depth and distance coincide, a condition that puts knowledge, in Italo Calvino's words, "outside the individual, outside the subjective,"[6] where "the calculation of things, their reckonings" occur, like dreamwork, via images. Another topos of aesthetic reflection that Spuybroek revisits, and promptly displaces onto his own map of things that matter, is the contrapposto, in a word, a curious condition of activity-stability, a

7. See Antonio Damasio, *The Strange Order of Things: Life, Feeling, and the Making of Cultures* (New York: Pantheon, 2018).

homeostasis – dynamic stability rather than fixity – in the way Damasio expanded nature's maintenance into the principle of its temporality.[7] Likewise, the contrapposto can be moved away from maintaining a balance toward filling the gap between countervailing motions. In architecture, a gap left open, a reveal, *exposes* the body and calls for ornamental framing. Spuybroek takes us on a bewildering detour through theological thinking and philosophical exegesis, calling on Friedrich Nietzsche, Frida Kahlo, Mircea Eliade, and Ludwig Wittgenstein in search of an answer to the loss of grace in our time. It is a trip eminently worth taking while listening to the workings of his mind.

Kurt W. Forster is finishing the book *Times of Experience, Ways of Beholding* to be published in 2022. He received the Schinkel Prize and is planning a conference on the scientific rise of geology in the early 19th century for Schinkel's birthplace, Neuruppin, Germany.

Kyle Miller

On Singles
And Soundtracks

What gives a Wes Anderson soundtrack its enchanting quality? It has little to do with the fidelity of any songs to genre or era, rather it is the fortuitous coherence of sad, world-weary tones, folk songs, and postpunk arrangements that form the emotional backdrop of his films. In *The Royal Tenenbaums*, it's Nico, Bob Dylan, and The Clash: a flute, brass overdubs, and distorted power chords; mannered yet icy vocals, talk-singing eccentricity, and arrogant snarls. Like a surrealist *cadavre exquis*, the disparate parts of an Anderson soundtrack coalesce into a delightfully unexpected and unfamiliar whole. Similarly, David Erdman's new book, *Introducing: Short Essays on Influential Thinkers and Designers in Architecture*, offers up a composite of architectural "scores" that brings together entangled narratives about speed, form, and the notion of a disciplinary project in architecture's adolescent years of the 21st century.

In his own introduction, Erdman makes the analogy that discourse in architecture should be built around a selection of "singles" rather than "epic, orchestrated albums," and asserts that short-form writing is a more appropriate medium today than meticulously crafted long-form essays and monographs. Citing *Who Says What Architecture Is?*, which weaves together a variety of short essays and transcribed presentations by Eric Owen Moss when he was director of SCI-Arc in the early 2000s, and *Slow Learner*, a collection of five short stories written by novelist Thomas Pynchon in the early 1960s, Erdman claims that a succinct delivery of information is necessary to hold the attention of today's younger generation. He focuses on the public lecture introduction as an untapped medium for discourse: "As I became more aware of the introduction's role in each lecture, I began to more regularly ponder how it might be a contemporary counterpoint to the long essay and a viable vehicle for discourse in today's Twitter, Instagram, and e-zine climate."[1] Erdman's critical approach to writing and delivering lecture introductions expands discourse in a manner akin to his critical approach in design practice, where he and his collaborators expand the limits of what classifies as architectural production.[2] First as a partner in servo and then in davidclovers, Erdman used interactive performance-based

1. David Erdman, *Introducing: Short Essays on Influential Thinkers and Designers in Architecture* (San Francisco: Applied Research and Design Publishing, 2021), 12.
2. For more on Erdman's former practice servo, see Michael Speaks, "Design Intelligence: Part 9: servo," *A+U:* 8, vol. 395 (August 2003): 138–45.

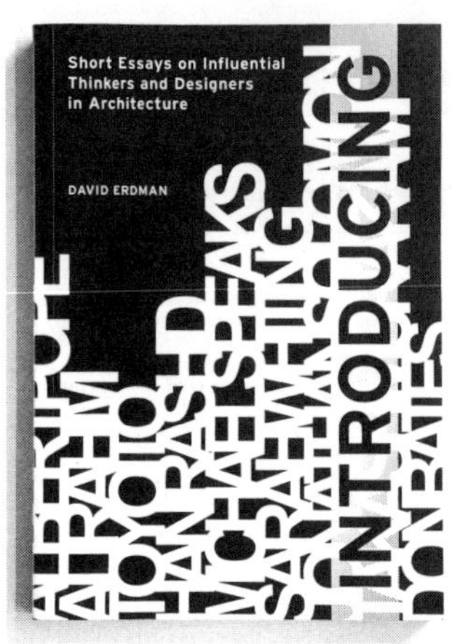

Introducing: Short Essays on Influential
Thinkers and Designers in Architecture
by David Erdman. 2021. 203 pages.
Applied Research and Design Publishing.

3. Jack Self, "Time Confetti," *Real Review* 5:
What it means to live today (Winter 2017): 81.

design, material research, and temporary installations as
devices to develop and disseminate architectural ideas at a
relatively fast pace compared to the drawn-out process of
designing and constructing a building. Just as he did previously through immersive installations and eccentric architectural elements, Erdman, chair of Graduate Architecture and
Urban Design at Pratt Institute, now explores new territory in
architectural production with punchy, designerly writing.

Introducing is a collection of 18 introductions Erdman
gave as part of the themed public lecture series he curated
while an assistant professor at the University of Hong Kong
Faculty of Architecture in 2012 and 2013. Each introduction
begins with a provocation, arrives at what Erdman calls a
"discourse beacon," and concludes by making a point. Erdman
framed the presentation of each guest and their work with the
theme chosen for each semester. The spring 2012 lecture series,
On_Speed, included Michael Speaks, Paul Lewis, Jonathan
Solomon, Albert Pope, Michael Young, Kengo Kuma, Andrew
Bromberg, Yung Ho Chang, and Wolf D. Prix. The fall 2012
series, In_Form, included Hani Rashid, Ali Rahim, Donald
Bates, Hernán Díaz Alonso, and Takashi Murakami. And the
spring 2013 lecture series, Project_ing, included Jesse Reiser,
Toyo Ito, Neil Denari, and Sarah Whiting. The series lacked
gender parity and did not represent a truly global survey, but
they did succeed in bringing together individuals with vastly
different approaches to practice.

The accomplishment of *Introducing* is not where Erdman
suggests: that is, it is not in a shift toward short-form writing
as a mechanism to accommodate shrinking attention spans.
Evidence suggests that long-form writing is enjoying a bit
of a resurgence, especially among younger readers. Critic
and architect Jack Self cites the steadily rising readership of
long-form journalism in publications like the *London Review
of Books* and declares that "we must invest in lengthening our
attention span and strengthening our memory retention."[3]
He draws a parallel between finishing a set at the gym and
reading to the end of the chapter. Simply conceding to the
fragmented way information is often packaged today is not a
viable long-term solution to maintaining and expanding what
Self refers to as memory and mental fitness.

The success of *Introducing* is also not in the novelty of
considering the lecture introduction an untapped medium
for intellectual discourse. Erdman admits as much when he
cites Moss's publication of lecture introductions, and a stroll
through numerous university online lecture archives reveals

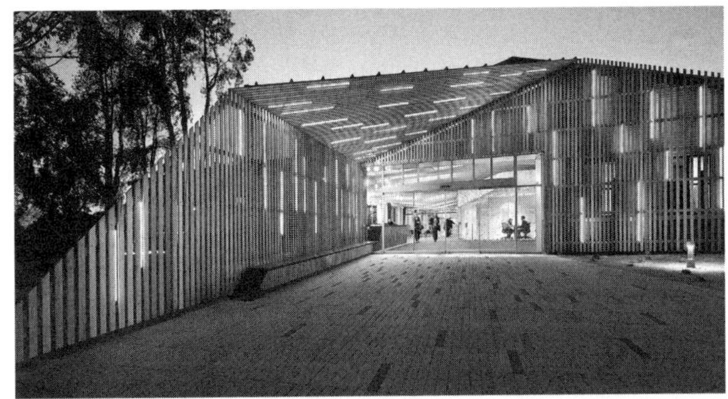

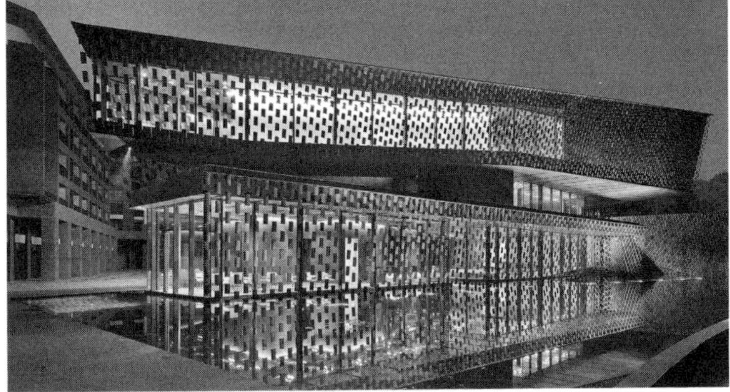

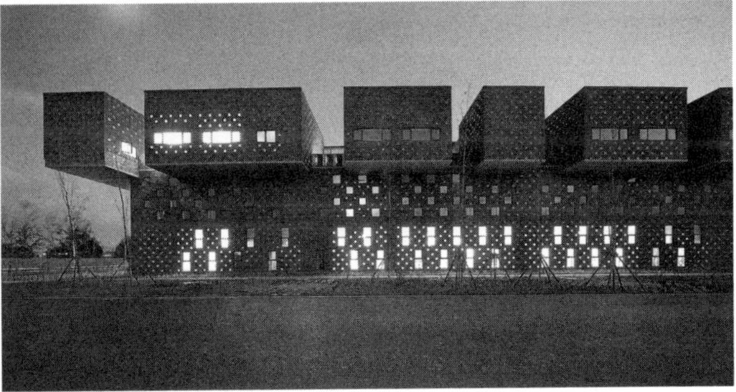

introductions equally as eloquent and incisive as Erdman's. The most significant accomplishment of *Introducing* is in the placement of 18 relative strangers in close proximity, which gives the reader an opportunity to uncover both their inimitable abilities as scholars and architects and the unregistered overlaps of their intellectual and material pursuits. However, while Erdman promises that contradictory and parallel perspectives are present in the collection of speakers, he stops short of reporting his findings – leaving that up to his readers. For there is something to be gained by listening to Erdman's "soundtracks," each constructed of his "cover songs" of influential designers and thinkers in architecture today.

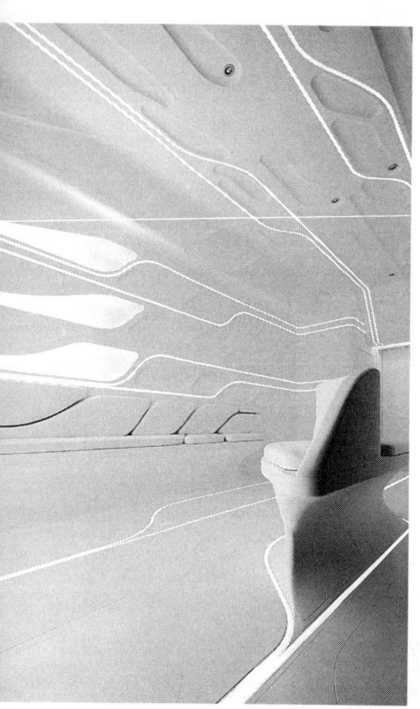

Contemporary Architecture Practice, IWI Orthodontics, Tokyo, 2010. Photo: Nacasa and Partners. Courtesy the architects.

In On_Speed, Erdman acknowledges the advantages and disadvantages of architecture speeding up in the 20th and 21st centuries. While mass production and digital technology have enabled faster development and execution of built work, overlooking the needs of the individual in favor of economic or political gain has led to injustice, inequity, and displacement. In reframing the efforts of the guest speakers, he uncovers latent possibilities in their work concerning the conditions of speed and its effects on the built environment.

In using Erdman's texts to draw comparisons between the speakers' work, an unexpected point of convergence emerges in the approaches to materiality in practices led by Lewis, Kuma, and Chang. Lewis's Claremont University Consortium, Kuma's Xinjin Zhi Museum, and Chang's UFIDA R&D Center No. 1 share a formal and aesthetic sensibility. When the three buildings are viewed in succession in the book, similarities are revealed opening up the possibility for authorship to be misattributed. The simultaneous reading of handcrafted and computational, the indistinguishability of ephemeral and permanent, and the nontraditional applications of traditional materials typify the approach the three practices take in the development of spatial, textural, and visual effects. Here, all three architects use defamiliarizing techniques to render heavy materials as delicate and to produce a misreading of scale – two effects that promote cognitive engagement with the built environment. Had Erdman not brought these practices together, such overlaps might have gone unnoticed.

In In_Form, Erdman recognizes the controversial nature of form as a tenet of the discipline of architecture and argues that form and the informal, forming and being informed by, and the formal and the social are often unproductively set in opposition to one another. More important, he shows how the work of each speaker's practice refuses these 20th-century binaries, which no longer, and perhaps never did, benefit the discipline. To detail the refusal, Erdman discloses the varied meanings of form and carefully links form to philosophy, politics, and typology.

Technical virtuosity is demonstrated in projects designed by Rahim (with partner Hina Jamelle) and Díaz Alonso. Commonalities between the two architects emerge through Erdman's descriptions of their formal dispositions – both practices produce carefully orchestrated, hypnotic object fields – and enthusiasm for advanced digital modeling in form making. But sizable gaps exist between Rahim and Díaz Alonso. Where Rahim's works are *in formation*, Díaz Alonso's

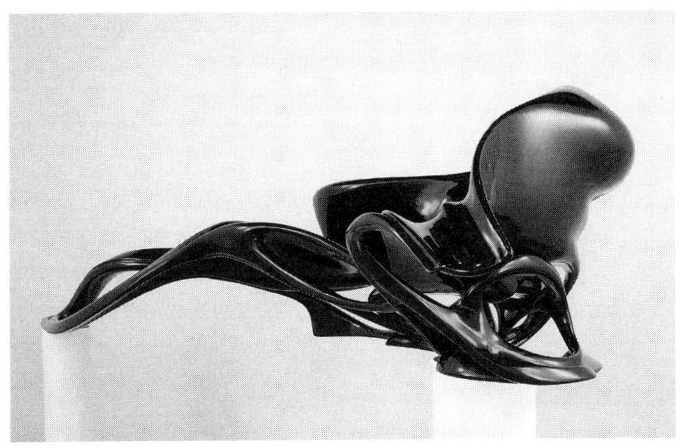

works are painstakingly *formed*. Rahim uses urban circulation, program, and site as the progenitors of form, whereas Díaz Alonso tends to embrace the cinematic qualities of architecture as performing a leading role in urban environments. The restrained beauty and simplicity of Rahim's designs are in stark contrast to the grotesque effects of Díaz Alonso's designs, which are purposefully excessive and complex. It's not uncommon for their works to be seen together in lectures and exhibitions celebrating digital form. But through Erdman's introductions, one can see the substantial ideological rift between them, which broadens how we understand computer-aided form making in the early 21st century.

In Project_ing, Erdman calls attention to the speculative nature of architecture and the tension between the a priori, ideologically fixed nature of one's "project" and the demands placed on today's architects, which require exchange and malleability rather than unidirectional thinking. Here Erdman identifies how each speaker, through a combination of writing and both built and unbuilt work, established a disciplinary project for themselves, and then assesses the possibility and value of having a project today.

In his introductions for Reiser and Whiting, Erdman lauds both architects' abilities to use writing as a tool to enhance their project. For Reiser and his partner Nanako Umemoto, writing is a reflective exercise with a productively self-critical tone that reveals an openness to rereading past work to inspire new work. Alternatively, Erdman suggests that Whiting's texts immediately zoom out to look beyond the work of her practice and to "rough up the discipline," urging others to move to uncultivated intellectual ground. In reframing Reiser and Whiting, Erdman demonstrates the different ways designers can use writing to develop a disciplinary project; be it directed inward at one's practice in the form of a diary entry or outward to one's peers as a motivational speech.

- - -

Historically, the lecture series was a way for a school's leader to reinforce a "vision" for the school. By controlling and often limiting what students were exposed to, a school's identity became inextricably linked to its leadership. To some degree, lecture series today are largely a response to calls for diverse representation and an effort to present a comprehensive picture of global practice. Thus, lecture series now collect ideas circulating in the discipline at any particular point, reflect the spirit of the moment, and serve as a record of collective action and thought.

One outcome of such market-driven curation of lectures is a lack of coherence – aesthetic, intellectual, ideological, etc. Rather than lament the loss of focused and extended content delivery, Erdman saw an opportunity to use the lecture introduction to bring together disparate voices that would illuminate the collective disciplinary positioning of architects in contemporary culture. Transcending the biographical lecture introduction and the speakers' self-positioning, Erdman's introductions are "entirely oblique to the intentions of the guests." Their brilliance is in the succinct yet aslant positioning of each guest's approach to and achievement in architecture and the successive reframing that ultimately constructs a soundtrack for early 21st-century architecture. *Introducing* simultaneously dismantles perceived disciplinary boundaries aligned with culture, geography, and race, and draws distinctions between architects previously seen to share aesthetic and methodological affinities. Like a good Wes Anderson soundtrack, *Introducing* challenges our assumptions about the possible coherence of seemingly unrelated acts, offering a strategy for confronting pluralism in architecture today and breaking the linear narrative of discourse constructed during the 20th century.

Kyle Miller is associate professor of architecture at Syracuse University.

Lindy Roy
with Leah Kelly

Navigating a Nervous Ecology

Architecture borrowed the idea of the cognitive map from neuroscience and got it wrong. Urban planner Kevin Lynch introduced cognitive mapping to architecture in 1960 in his book *The Image of the City*, in which he discussed the habitual "mind's eye" maps made by city residents and aimed to improve urban policy through direct public engagement and the consideration of diverse experiences. Two decades later, however, according to Lynch, the book had had the diametrically opposite effect.[1] Broadly embraced by design professionals as a new formula, it had been used as a superficial prescription for generating predictable and marketable urban form. Today, as cognitive, biology-based technologies infiltrate life and reshape architectural thought and production, the expanding view of cognitive maps now emerging in neuroscience could provide insight to designers negotiating the sociopolitical, ecological, cultural, economic, and technological into melded assemblies of matter and data in which artificial intelligence and human experience commingle.

Experimental psychologist Edward C. Tolman invented the term *cognitive map* in the 1940s to describe the internal representations that a nervous system in motion forms of its external world.[2] Observing how rats seemed to link together different laboratory mazes encountered only on separate runs over several days, it was apparent to Tolman that the animals had assembled some type of spatial representation, which he called a cognitive map. I first encountered Tolman's ideas in the late 1990s while researching models of coordination for an extreme wildlife project in the Okavango Delta, a wetland in the northern Kalahari Desert of Botswana.[3] From the altitude of a light aircraft approaching the site, I could see hundreds of sand-gray termite ventilation towers poking through the ground plane, evenly spaced in a barely discernible offset grid. Solid ground in the delta, built up over millennia, is assembled by colonies of subterranean, fungus-farming Macrotermitinae that produce a cementitious mix of desert sand and a termite pheromone that emits signals into the air evoking a swarm's nest-building behaviors. During this same period, I observed a different kind of silica-based swarm some

1. See Kevin Lynch's rebuke of design professionals in "Reconsidering *The Image of the City*," in *Cities of the Mind: Images and Themes of the City in the Social Sciences*, ed. Lloyd Rodwin and Robert M. Hollister (Boston: Springer US, 1984), 151–61. Here, Lynch reevaluates *The Image of the City* (Cambridge: MIT Press, 1960), in which he derived five classifications – node, landmark, district, edge, and path – that he believed contributed to the spatial salience of cities, and acknowledges economist Kenneth E. Boulding's *The Image: Knowledge in Life and Society* (Ann Arbor: University of Michigan Press, 1956) as the theoretical underpinning for his book. For Boulding, a cybernetician, human behavior is a product of individuals' holistic mental images of the world that circulate and are shared in the noosphere.

2. See Edward C. Tolman, "Cognitive Maps in Rats and Men," *Psychological Review* 55, no. 4 (1948): 189–208.

3. See Lindy Roy, "Coordination: African Delta Spa," *Assemblage* 36 (August 1998): 42–63.

4. See Lindy Roy, "Geometry as a Nervous System," *ANY* 17: Forget Fuller?: Everything You Always Wanted to Know About Fuller But Were Afraid to Ask (January 1997): 24–27.
5. Considered "motor chauvinism" in some neuroscience circles, using the example of the sea squirt to explain why we have a brain ignores movement in organisms without a nervous system.

14,000 kilometers away, in the Southwest United States at the Santa Fe Institute in New Mexico, where interdisciplinary research on complex adaptive systems was breaking new ground. Here, Swarm, an open-source multiagent simulation platform that had been initiated to predict the proliferation of the nascent World Wide Web through landline telecommunication networks, was also being used to investigate the behavior of emergent systems, from viruses to stock markets. The idea of a swarm as a holographic model of a collective, distributed brain that is mixed in with its environment and inseparable from it is among the speculations of early 20th-century biologists and scientists about the stimulus world where sentient behavior takes shape, and it is not new.[4] The interplay of these two completely different swarm representations, one gridded and apparently fixed at the scale of the landscape, and the other time-based and emergent at the scale of the swarm itself, stuck with me.

In the pristine Okavango Delta landscape, humans, just one among many sentient species in circulation, can leave an outsize footprint. For the project's site design, to facilitate the movement of people through the ecosystem's circuits of hydrology, geology, vegetation, and predators and prey, I looked to neuroscience for an explanation of spatial navigation and how sentient beings become coordinate with their environment and integrated into it. In the 1970s, neuroscientists began to develop techniques to record electrical activity in the brain cells of animals in motion and identified networks of specialized neurons generating those internal representations of physical space that Tolman could only speculate about. Cognitive maps laid the foundation for understanding how space is represented in the brain, but Tolman wasn't only referring to physical space. He considered cognitive maps as *general* knowledge structures that organize information from across a diversity of life experiences, according to its relevance in an ever-changing environment. It turns out that we may use our brain's cognitive mapmaking networks to navigate not only physical space but abstract space too. Conceptual thinking, sound, and even social affiliations and power hierarchies – all fundamental aspects of human experience and cognition – are now understood to be spatially underpinned and navigated using the same ensembles of spatially tuned neurons that guide our movement through the physical world. Why is that?

There is a fit between a nervous system and its life-sustaining environment. Consider the sea squirt, for example,

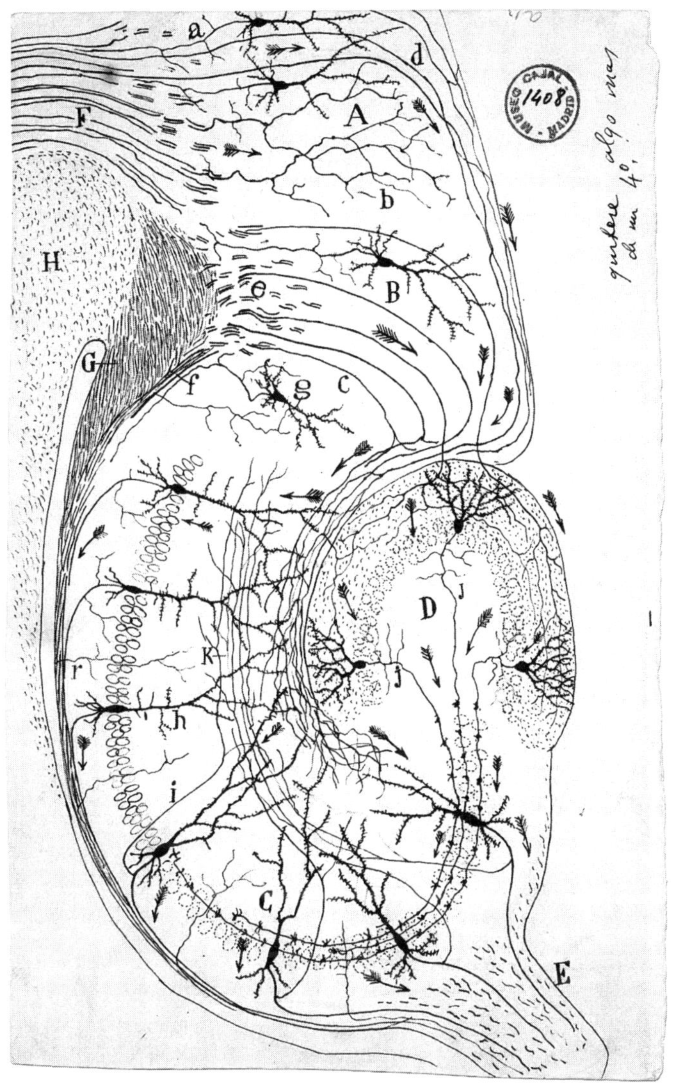

a one-millimeter-long, tadpole-like larva that begins life equipped with a rudimentary 177-neuron brain used to navigate its ocean *umwelt* by integrating sensory inputs from a single eye, feedback from a crude balance organ, and propulsion from a pulsing tail. This motile existence is only temporary. To assume adult form, a larval sea squirt attaches its head to a rock and, once permanently affixed, consumes its own brain. Sedentary life is jump-started by metabolizing a redundant nervous system for energy, because once the creature stops moving, it doesn't need a brain.[5]

The human nervous system, too, is fundamentally bound up with motion. We can't take in our whole environment all at once, so we assemble mental representations as we move

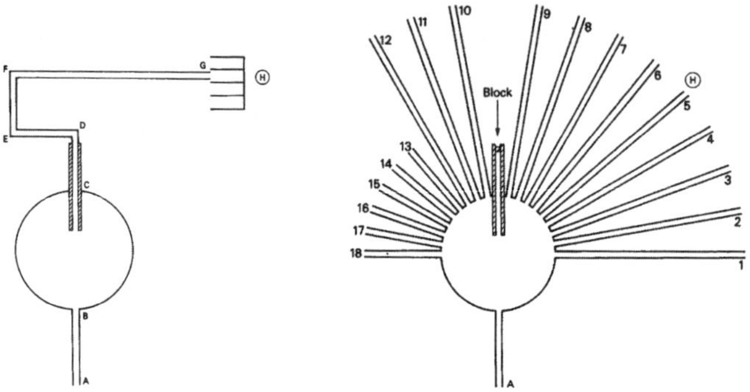

Edward C. Tolman's spatial orientation experiments in the 1940s showed that rats develop broad spatial maps of their environment. In the preliminary training apparatus (left), a rat crosses a circular table and moves along passageway C directly to a food reward in location G. After four days, that training apparatus is replaced by the so-called sunburst maze (right) in which passageway C is blocked. After exploring a few inches of other radial pathway options, a substantial number of rats ran directly down passageway 6, the route terminating closest to the previous food reward at location G. Drawing from E.C. Tolman, B.F. Ritchie, and D. Kalish, "Studies in spatial learning. I. Orientation and the short-cut," *Journal of Experimental Psychology* 36, no. 1 (February 1946).

6. Bayes's theorem describes the probability of an event based on prior knowledge that may be related to that event. See Dirk De Ridder, Sven Vanneste, and Walter Freeman, "The Bayesian brain: Phantom percepts resolve sensory uncertainty," *Neuroscience & Biobehavioral Reviews* 44 (July 2014): 4–15.

7. See Karl Friston, "The free-energy principle: a unified brain theory?," *Nature Reviews Neuroscience* 11, no. 2 (February 2010): 127–38. According to Friston, to be alive is to act in ways that reduce the gulf between sensory inputs and expectations, and all life – from a single cell to the human brain with billions of neurons – is driven by that same imperative to minimize free energy.

8. See John O'Keefe and Lynn Nadel, "Remembrance of places past: a history of theories of space," in *The Hippocampus as a Cognitive Map* (New York: Oxford University Press, 1978). The authors note that the hippocampus should be called a cognitive mapping system and the term *cognitive map* should be reserved for the products of that system, but they use the term to refer to both the neural structure and the representation it produces.

around. We also move through problems, explore options, and arrive at decisions; spatial metaphors are used unconsciously to engage abstract concepts all the time. As the dimensions of our physical world multiply into ever more complex social, cultural, and technical realms, is it possible that spatially modulated networks in the evolving human brain expand to navigate those abstract spaces as well? And if maps represent relations between things, could cognitive maps allow relationships between things to be *inferred* without ever being directly experienced? The answers to these questions may have to do with how the brain's energy economy is managed. It's important for a nervous system to conserve energy, and surprise is expensive. Anticipating uses far less energy than reacting. We may assume sensory stimuli are just passively received, but what if, to avoid surprise, a nervous system actively seeks out information from its surroundings to compare how similar something new is to something already known? A theory of the brain based on Bayesian probability,[6] which has been instrumental in the development of certain types of artificial intelligence, proposes exactly that. It sees the brain as a statistical model of the world it inhabits and perception as a type of hypothesis testing. From the tiniest calibrations of the retina to an unconscious assessment of surface stability, the Bayesian brain uses the body to actively sense its world, continuously sampling sensory fluxes, looking for evidence to update earlier predictions already neurally encoded.[7] This is where Tolman's cognitive map, plotted in electrical signals in the brain, is thought to come in. Setting incoming new information in relation to corresponding known information in a spatiotemporal matrix, a cognitive map's coordinating frame of reference organizes bits of information with spatially prescribed proximity and relational hierarchies, making it available to other parts of the brain to reconfigure through acts of imagination, planning,

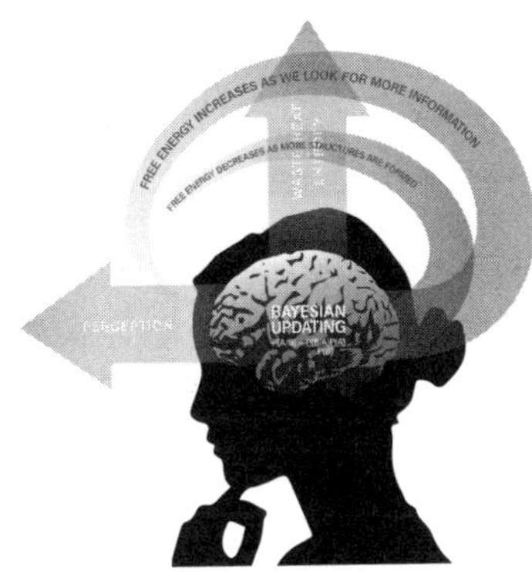

The Bayesian brain hypothesis argues that the brain conserves energy by not re-creating the world anew with each encounter. In this model, the brain continually makes predictions about the world and updates those predictions based on what it senses. The environment is tapped for thermodynamic free energy and scanned for information that reduces uncertainty. The creation of perception increases certainty and decreases free energy and the cycle restarts. Drawing adapted from Dirk De Ridder, Sven Vanneste, and Walter Freeman, "The Bayesian brain: Phantom percepts resolve sensory uncertainty," *Neuroscience & Biobehavioral Reviews* 44 (July 2014).

9. See J. O'Keefe and J. Dostrovsky, "The hippocampus as a spatial map. Preliminary evidence from unit activity in the freely-moving rat," *Brain Research* 34, no. 1 (November 12, 1971): 171–75.

10. See J. O'Keefe and D.H. Conway, "Hippocampal place units in the freely moving rat: Why they fire where they fire," *Experimental Brain Research* 31, no. 4 (April 1978): 573–90.

11. See Daniela Schiller et al., "Memory and Space: Towards an Understanding of the Cognitive Map," *Journal of Neuroscience* 35, no. 41 (October 2015): 13904–11.

12. See Howard Eichenbaum and Neal J. Cohen, "Can We Reconcile the Declarative Memory and Spatial Navigation Views on Hippocampal Function?," *Neuron* 83, no. 4 (August 20, 2014): 764–70.

social interaction, and even dreaming. How such divergent information forms a coherent model of the world is not understood, but a substantial amount is known to be spatially encoded by the hippocampus and a neighboring brain region called the entorhinal cortex.

In their 1978 book *The Hippocampus as a Cognitive Map*, neuroscientists John O'Keefe and Lynn Nadel begin with an analysis of ideas about space from philosophy, mathematics, and physics that reads like a history of the theory of architecture in a parallel universe and locates O'Keefe's groundbreaking research within that intellectual tradition.[8] A few years earlier, O'Keefe identified the first neural representation of space when he found a direct correlation between a single cell in the hippocampus of a rat and a particular spot in the animal's environment in his lab.[9] This so-called place cell was active in a way not seen in a neuron before. It turned on and off as the rat crossed in and out of an area along its path of travel. Firing from a location inside the animal's brain, the place cell demarcated a corresponding circular zone of space – a place field – out in the world.[10] Combinations of individual place cells appeared to form the mental map that Tolman had intuited decades before. When those same cells were found to remap, creating an entirely new representation as the rat explored a different environment, and *that* representation remained intact over several days, the first inkling of the neural underpinning for another of Tolman's consequential theories emerged: Could cognitive maps be the substrate for certain types of memory?[11] For Tolman, spatial navigation was a form of learning in and of itself; rather than relying on the association of individual movements to recall a route through space, a nervous system constructs maps to represent spatial relationships between the things it experiences. The idea was so controversial in the 1950s that it triggered a sea change in psychology and reverberated through the social sciences. In a clear dismissal of the behaviorist's stimulus-response paradigm, in which behavior was believed to be reflexively conditioned by external stimuli alone, Tolman's was a goal-directed, information-processing cognitive model of behavior. We carry the environment around with us as an engram, an alteration in our neural tissue. In a cognitive map's selective spatial array, related salient features about the world are tapped for inference, and in energy-efficient simulations of possible futures, a course of action – a decision – emerges.[12] But what that coordinating construct was exactly remained a mystery.

A place cell in the hippocampus of a rat (right) and its corresponding firing location in the rat's environment (left). Bottom: A grid cell in the entorhinal cortex of a rat (right) and the locations where that grid cell fires in the rat's environment (left). Drawings: Mattias Karlen. © The Nobel Assembly, The Nobel Prize in Physiology or Medicine.

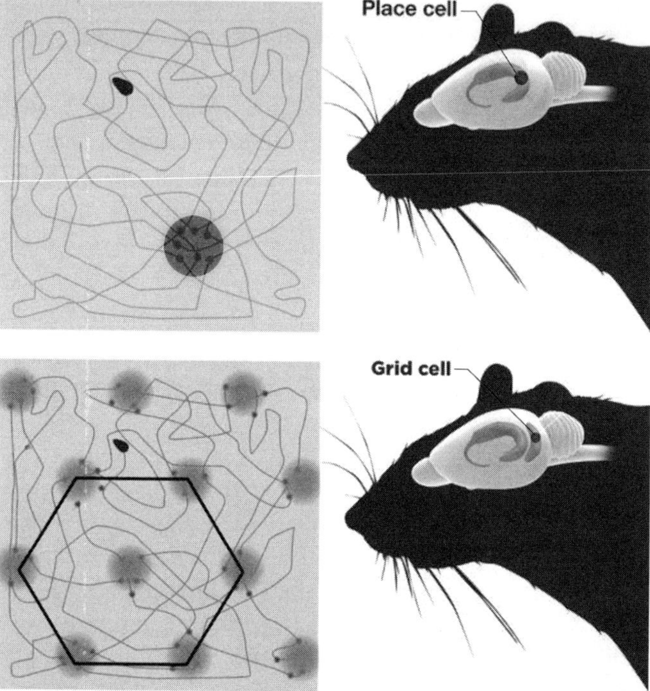

13. Hexagonal grids occur frequently in nature, from the microscopic lattice of a superconductor to the camouflage spots on a predatory animal, and they can be explained as Turing patterns. In "The Chemical Basis of Morphogenesis," *Philosophical Transactions of the Royal Society of London. Series B, Biological Sciences* 237, no. 641 (August 14, 1952): 37–72, mathematician Alan M. Turing described how spatially periodic patterns like grids spontaneously emerge in solutions made up of chemicals with different diffusion rates. Could the ubiquitous architectural grid be an expression of our brain chemistry?
14. See Torkel Hafting et al., "Microstructure of a spatial map in the entorhinal cortex," *Nature* 436, no. 7052 (August 11, 2005): 801–06.

In 2005, after time as visiting scientists in O'Keefe's lab, neuroscientists Edvard Moser and May-Britt Moser focused their research on cells in the medial entorhinal cortex, a brain region relaying signals to place cells in the downstream hippocampus. They were looking for the origin of place cells' spatial signal. Recordings from these cells also revealed activity never seen in a neuron before. Unlike the single-location firing fields of place cells, these cells each fired in multiple locations as the animal moved around, creating a distributed pattern. To take in the overall schema, the researchers zoomed out and recorded the electrical activity of a single cell as the animal moved freely around a much larger space. Astonishingly, the imaging revealed a regular triangulated hexagonal grid tiling the entire floor of the animal's enclosure.[13] Those neurons, named grid cells, are organized in firing modules with the same spacing and orientation but different phasing, generating offset grids that cover every point in a space. Independent of context or landmarks, these endogenous grids appeared to act as a completely autonomous, two-dimensional coordinate system. As researchers probed the medial entorhinal cortex along a dorsal-ventral axis from top to bottom, the size, spacing, and resolution of the grid modules scaled up from a few centimeters to a few meters the deeper into the brain they went.[14]

15. See D.H. Hubel and T.N. Wiesel, "Receptive Fields of Single Neurones in the Cat's Striate Cortex," *Journal of Physiology* 148 (1959): 574–91.

16. The intensity of a stimulus was described in the early 20th century as an analog signal transformed by the body's sensory receptors into a digital pulse code. The now outdated idea of this analog-to-digital transformation came from the all-or-nothing properties of the action potential in sensory neurons discovered by Edgar Adrian and Yngve Zotterman in 1925. Later Zotterman wrote: "We were discovering a great secret of life, how the sensory nerves transmit their information to the brain. . . . We had found that the transmission in the nerve fiber occurred according to an impulse frequency modulation [FM], twenty years before FM was introduced in teletechnique." Yngve Zotterman, "How It Started: A Personal Review," in *Sensory Functions of the Skin of Humans*, ed. Dan R. Kenshalo (New York: Plenum Press, 1979), 6–7.

17. Christian Doeller and Neil Burgess showed that entorhinal grid-like representations were formed in the human brain when a virtual maze was navigated using virtual reality.

18. See Arseny Finkelstein, Liora Las, and Nachum Ulanovsky, "3-D Maps and Compasses in the Brain," *Annual Review of Neuroscience* 39 (July 2016): 171–96.

19. Data presented by Nachum Ulanovsky at the 2021 Inaugural Weizmann-Columbia Brain Symposium suggest that grid cells are not active when bats navigate large distances. Given the amount of information a grid cell mapping of that scale would involve, this can be thought of as a "neural bandwidth" issue, but it also raises questions about what exactly grid cells are actually for.

20. See Howard Eichenbaum, "Time cells in the hippocampus: a new dimension for mapping memories," *Nature Reviews Neuroscience* 15, no. 11 (November 2014): 732–44.

Since the 1950s, when foundational neuroscientific research began to show how basic sensory processes – vision, touch, sound, taste, and smell – form maps in the brain's sensory cortices, it's been known that certain types of neurons respond to specific sensory features in an environment.[15] Millions of mechano-, chemo-, photo-, and thermoreceptors distributed throughout the body tune to energy in the environment with a distinctive spatial signature or temporal pattern. That energy is transduced by sensory receptors into electrical energy, establishing a common type of signal across the body's visual, auditory, tactile, olfactory, vestibular, and proprioceptive systems.[16] But place and grid cells showed for the first time that a higher-order cognitive function – navigating space – is mapped in the brain. O'Keefe and the Mosers shared the 2014 Nobel Prize in Physiology or Medicine for their place cell and grid cell discoveries, and by the following year, both neural correlates were confirmed to be active in humans too.[17]

Generating data to explore how movement on a two-dimensional surface translates in three-dimensional space was beyond the technical capacities of researchers until scientists at the Weizmann Institute of Science outfitted Egyptian fruit bats with tiny, ultralightweight wireless electrophysiology equipment and recorded the animals expertly traversing their vast Negev Desert habitat.[18] Three navigational modes were identified, each generating a distinct neural model of space: planar navigation limited to movement along horizontal, vertical, or inclined surfaces; multilayered navigation incorporating movement across several interconnected planes (for people, that would involve stacked floors, stairs, and ramps); and volumetric navigation allowing unconstrained movement through space, including swimming, gliding, jumping, and flying. Like bats, humans flexibly switch between all three modes. How all this is integrated into a continuously updating model of the world is not understood, but it is thought that fragments of two- and more recently identified three-dimensional grid and place cell representations are stitched together by compass-like signals emitted by neurons called head direction cells that reference orientation in space.[19] Ensembles of other specialized neurons further refine and enhance the model: speed cells act like a speedometer tracking a body's velocity, border cells mark the boundaries of enclosed space, firing rates of goal cells accelerate as a targeted area comes in range, and the elastic firing durations of time cells encode the variable temporal context of experience.[20] Both place and grid cells appear to respond to specific sound frequencies and are

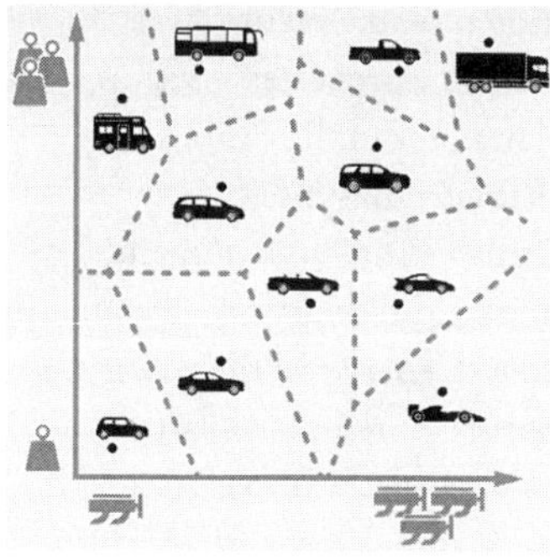

A representation of two-dimensional conceptual space shown as a Voronoi tessellation in which vehicles are arranged according to their weight and engine power. Positions in space are activated along a trajectory allowing different car types to be evaluated and compared. Drawing from Jacob L.S. Bellmund et al., "Navigating cognition: Spatial codes for human thinking," *Science* 362, no. 6415 (November 9, 2018). Reprinted with permission from AAAS.

21. See Dmitriy Aronov, Rhino Nevers, and David W. Tank, "Mapping of a non-spatial dimension by the hippocampal-entorhinal circuit," *Nature* 543, no. 7647 (March 30, 2017): 719–22.

22. See David B. Omer et al., "Social place-cells in the bat hippocampus," *Science* 359, no. 6372 (January 12, 2018): 218–24.

23. See Matthew Schafer and Daniela Schiller, "Navigating Social Space," *Neuron* 100 (October 24, 2018): 476–89.

24. See Robert M. Pringle et al., "Spatial Pattern Enhances Ecosystem Functioning in an African Savanna," *PLOS Biology* 8, no. 5 (May 2010), https://doi.org/10.1371/journal.pbio.1000377.

25. See Kristine Synnes, "Cancer Alley," in *ROY: Architecture of Risk* (New York: Distributed Art Publishers, 2004): 42–57.

26. See Alison Montagrin, Catarina Saiote, and Daniela Schiller, "The social hippocampus," *Hippocampus* 28, no. 9: Hippocampus and Memory Integration (September 2018): 672–79.

active in assembling complex soundscapes.[21] In an experiment in which an observer bat watched a navigating bat negotiate a maze, social place cells in the brain of the observer fired at locations corresponding to the navigator's transient positions; the observer was apparently learning the maze by simply watching.[22] Social stimuli, conveyors of information about our relationship to people we encounter or know, may also be data points encoded by grid and place cell networks. Details of social affiliation, status in a power hierarchy, or place in a family structure are organized spatially according to closeness to or distance from an individual in reconfigurable representations of relative power, intimacy, and equity.[23]

While architects engage with an energy economy usually confined to the thermodynamics of materials and bodies in space, cognitive maps – that is, electrochemical encryptions of the external world inside our brain – encompass the broader reality that every encounter with the environment, every thought, action, or decision, is a constant transformation of one form of energy into another. We are in fact continuous with our world. My problem with the grid cell is its name. Because neurons fire out (x, y, z) coordinates over time, it doesn't mean space is those numbers. I think about the two silica-based swarms I observed almost 30 years ago computing the environment in exchanges of signal and cross talk. The offset spacing of termite cooling towers in the desert landscape does not result from a Cartesian impulse to order. Instead, it emerges out of myriad activities and interactions across many scales that organize resources and relationships in an ecology. Circular zones of space, not unlike grid cell firing fields, mitigate competition between subterranean colonies and enhance the productivity of the ecosystem as a whole by evenly distributing resources at finer and finer scales.[24] Working in pristine and contaminated fluvial environments made me realize that no site is fixed, not historically, ecologically, geographically, or in terms of its jurisdiction.[25] Ideas may in fact be inscribed in space, only not in the ways architects imagine. Cognitive maps situate thought and ideas along a gradient of abstraction, from physical to purely conceptual.[26] As a discipline that operates at the confluence of space and thought, what new relationships could architecture activate? What new behaviors? The cognitive map was used as a metaphor decades ago, but it's not a metaphor. It is a model for dealing with unpredictability, risk, and change. Today, when new models for architectural thought and action are urgently needed, it is a useful one.

Diagram showing four encounters with a person in social space. Each interaction generates a change in power or affiliation. Drawing adapted from Rita Morais Tavares et al., "A Map for Social Navigation in the Human Brain," *Neuron* 87 (July 1, 2015).

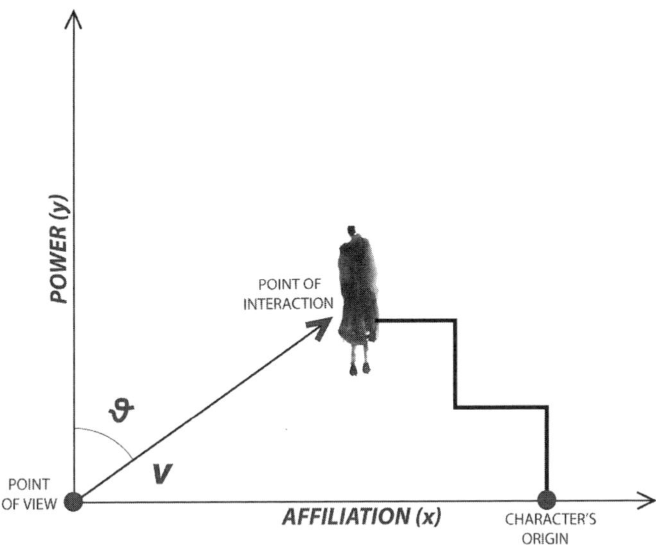

Postscript

We translate sense into space. Even as sperm and egg, we move in response to the environment. Yes, there are the explicitly spatially tuned cells: the place, border, grid, and head direction cells. But these words, a siren outside, the coffee in your cup, your fingers on this page, the liquid sloshing in your inner ear, and the firing of your neurons responding to and representing these stimuli – are all data in and about space.

Architecture borrowed the cognitive map. Neuroscience provides experimental data to support it. And neuroscience is ripe for riffling. Collaborating with architect Lindy Roy in this speculative, interdisciplinary zone forces me to break down and remap how I think as a neuroscientist, lifting preconceived hierarchies, merging theory and data, just as separate grid cell patterns representing partitioned space merge into a uniform map when the partitions are removed.[27]

There is sound space, shape space, olfactory space, social space, face space, feature space, cognitive space. We navigate space by integrating egocentric and allocentric vectorial responses. These cognitive maneuvers are also proposed to be the way we navigate our own mind, forming the basis for semantic (allocentric) and autobiographical (egocentric) memory,[28] illustrating what has been understood since the time of Simonides: that time, space, and memory are coordinates of our being. If we continue to outsource our navigational skills to technology, will our cognitive skills shrink like the mapmaking hippocampi of retired taxi drivers?[29] Or will we think differently? Desert ants navigate huge distances and

27. See Tanja Wernle et al., "Integration of grid maps in merged environments," *Nature Neuroscience* 21, no. 1 (January 2018): 92–101.

28. See May-Britt Moser, David C. Rowland, and Edvard I. Moser, "Place Cells, Grid Cells, and Memory," *Cold Spring Harbor Perspectives in Biology* 7, no. 2 (February 2015); György Buzsáki and Edvard I. Moser, "Memory, navigation and theta rhythm in the hippocampal-entorhinal system," *Nature Neuroscience* 16, no. 2 (February 2013): 130–38.

29. See Katherine Woollett, Hugo J. Spiers, and Eleanor A. Maguire, "Talent in the taxi: A model system for exploring expertise," *Philosophical Transactions of the Royal Society of London. Series B, Biological Sciences* 364 (2009): 1407–16.

30. See Matthias Wittlinger, Rüdiger Wehner, and Harald Wolf, "The Ant Odometer: Stepping on Stilts and Stumps," *Science* 312, no. 5782 (June 30, 2006): 1965–67.

31. See Joseph P. Dexter, Sudhakaran Prabakaran, and Jeremy Gunawardena, "A Complex Hierarchy of Avoidance Behaviors in a Single-Cell Eukaryote," *Current Biology* 29 (December 16, 2019): 4323–29.

32. See Dori Derdikman et al., "grid cell movie," 2010, available online as YouTube video, 0:49, December 30, 2014, https://www.youtube.com/watch?v=i9GiLBXWAHI.

path integrate without grid cells, they count steps.[30] The single-cell organism *S. roeseli* bends away from aversive stimuli without a single neuron.[31] Clearly there is more to space and computation than the grid.

As an experimentalist and an outsider, I see a divide in architecture between theory and practice. Search "grid cell movie" on the internet and witness a neuron-environment relationship in real time.[32] It will remap your cognitive coordinates such that your encoded vectors, both allocentric and egocentric, of brain and environment, will relate differently. Embody this knowledge. Design with this in mind. Realize that animate/inanimate and conscious/nonconscious, space traverses these constructed divides, that you are sculpting the medium of thought. – *LK*

Lindy Roy is an architect in New York City and teaches design at Columbia University. Leah Kelly is a neuroscientist at The Rockefeller University. They coteach a seminar at Columbia called Building Sense: Provocations from Neuroscience.

Cosmodality

Guest edited by Gökhan Kodalak

Gökhan Kodalak, Immanence diagram.

Cosmodality:
Prolegomena to a New Architectural Metaphysics

What if architecture is of the cosmos? For too long, we have constrained architecture to an exclusively human affair. We have disregarded intriguing architectural experiments of human species other than *Homo sapiens*, understudied space-morphing capacities of myriad animals, and overlooked the tectonic ingenuity of the Earth and the world-building activities of the cosmos. That is, we have failed to envision architecture as a strategy of existence – not just our existence, but existence as such. This special section, the third in a yearlong series conceived with Sanford Kwinter (*Log* 49, 51, and 52), challenges the conventional definitions and anthropocentric foundations of architecture, journeys through different gradations of an all-pervading constructive continuum, and entertains the heterodox possibility that architecture is a *cosmic art*.

Cosmos

In the beginning was a singularity. Present-day cosmogonists widely suggest that 13.8 billion years ago, all the matter and energy in our inconceivably vast cosmos were concentrated in a single infinitesimal point, whose prior life remains open to speculation.[1] A singularity is a contraction of potentiality, in which the conventional laws of spacetime break down as certain capacities break their finitude and tend toward the infinite. In the singularity at the earliest stage of the observable universe ($t=0$), it is estimated there was a combination of infinite gravitational density, infinite temperature, infinite spacetime curvature. That is, in the beginning was *infinita potentia*, as Spinoza would put it – infinite potential for the self-causation and gradual construction of the universe.[2]

During the first picosecond – one-trillionth of a second (10^{-12}) – of cosmic time, the four known fundamental forces (gravitational, electromagnetic, weak, and strong interactions) unfolded from the infinite potentiality of the cosmic singularity, followed by the rapid expansion of space and the supercooling of the extremely hot universe due to cosmic inflation. In the next billion years, subatomic particles emerged and merged into composites, forming the first atoms and molecules; the collapsing of the clouds of hydrogen resulted in the formation of stars and galaxies; the universe gradually transitioned from its dark ages to what is deemed to be its modern structure. And 4.6 billion years ago, the gravitational collapse of a giant molecular cloud incited a relatively modest, for us, existential stellar event: the birth of our solar system.

1. Direct observational evidence regarding the validity of the current Big Bang theory includes: 1) the expansion of the universe (Hubble's law), 2) the cosmic microwave background, 3) the relative abundance of light elements produced by Big Bang nucleosynthesis, and 4) the agreeable morphology and distribution of galaxies and quasars. For an up-to-date introduction to the Big Bang theory, see Helmut Satz, *Before Time Began: The Big Bang and the Emerging Universe* (Oxford: Oxford University Press, 2017); Valery Rubakov and Dmitry Gorbunov, *Introduction to the Theory of the Early Universe: Hot Big Bang Theory* (London: World Scientific, 2017).

2. For Spinoza, nature is the substantial field of infinite potential (*infinita potentia*), through which countless finite beings, we all, come to exist. For my introduction to the overlooked relationship between Spinoza's philosophy and architecture, see Gökhan Kodalak, "Spinoza and Architecture: The Air of the Future," *Log* 49 (Summer 2020): 123–45.

But how on Earth can we imagine the passing of billions of years, so casually mentioned here? The short answer is, we can't. The cosmic scale escapes us. Immersed in our everyday struggles and human-centric commitments, we fail to register that before the mythologized construction of the first human hut, prior to our initial architectural gestures recorded in the materiality of wood and stone, the first constructive, space-modulating activity was the *cosmos constructing itself.*

The scientific basis of the universe's self-construction has only recently been evidenced, yet its metaphysical basis has been under construction for a long time. Heraclitus, to whom we owe the very invention of the concept "cosmos" (*kosmos*), anticipated it as early as two and a half millennia ago: "This *kosmos*, the same for all, neither gods nor men did create . . . is the maker and creator of itself."[3] The cosmos is the primordial generator of matter and energy, the constructor of all stars and planets, the agitator of each and every modification of spacetime. Strange as it may sound, architecture begins with cosmogenesis. The cosmos is the immanent architect of all that exists.

Earth

Earth was once a mercurial orb of molten lava. It was formed by the accretion of particles from the solar nebula 4.54 billion years ago, as its surface initially turned into a magma ocean due to extreme volcanic activity and continuous bombardment of space debris.[4] We now officially call the first half billion years of the primordial Earth the Hadean period, referring to Hades, the Greek god of the underworld, to evoke the hellish conditions then prevailing on the planet. Yet, as biological – let alone human – life had not yet emerged on Earth, the question is, hellish for whom? And why this anachronistic drama? Might the reason be that we cannot even conceive of the self-formation of Earth without cloaking it under our human-centric projections, biases, and fears? From an ontogenetic perspective, are we not indebted to these hellish conditions? As with all modalities of life on Earth, are we humans not the descendants of this volcanic constructivism, the children of Hadean rocks, the offspring of lava bubbling?

As the Earth's surface started cooling enough to form continents and oceans over the next one and a half billion years, biological life spontaneously arose from the equally alive planetary geochemistry, developing unique capacities such as molecular self-replication and the formation of cell membranes. The rest is the evolutionary history of *bios* from

3. See Heraclitus's *Fragments* [B67; B30], or: Heraclitus, *Heraclitus: The Cosmic Fragments* (Cambridge: Cambridge University Press, 1975), 184; 307.

4. For the formation and early history of Earth from the perspective of historical geology and planetary science, see Jonathan Lunine, *Earth: Evolution of a Habitable World* (Cambridge: Cambridge University Press, 2013); Steven Stanley and John Luczaj, *Earth System History* (New York: W.H. Freeman, 2014).

the emergence of photosynthetic bacteria and algae-like plants to, billions of years later, the rise of the first mammals and our genus, *Homo*. There is an evolutionary continuum in the way Earth's constructive capacities have infused all planetary modes of existence with different orders of magnitude. This makes Earth the builder of the geosphere, the biosphere, and the noosphere combined; the shaper of all microorganic, plant, animal, and human life; the generative ground beneath all our cultural expressions, technical inventions, and architectural formations. We tend to forget that we learned how to build not in a vacuum but from the constructive capacities, topographical gestures, and tectonic creativity of the Earth as such.

Animal

Animal architecture has shaped the Earth for hundreds of millions of years. The elaborate architecture of bird bowers, ape nests, termite mounds, beehives, rodent burrows, spider-webs, beaver dams, to name only a few, has provided animals unique potentials for thermoregulation, ventilation, and protection; sexual attraction, social communication, and aesthetic intensification; niche construction, environmental alteration, and epiphylogenetic engineering of their cultural organization as well as evolutionary future.[5] Before we humans even existed, architecture was already practiced by diverse species of *Animalia*. We have developed our constructive skills in continuity with this wide spectrum of architectural intelligence.

Having bifurcated nature and culture, however, we tend to ignore this vibrant history and maintain that architecture is ours and ours alone. In order to justify this self-proclaimed exceptionalism, we hide behind ever more hierarchical dualities rendering animals passive, mechanical, instinctual, incapable of constructive novelty or technical complexity or conscious intentionality or any other feature we can accentuate so as to reinforce our narcissistic belief in the misconceived supremacy of our own being, our own species, our own architectural skills over and against the rest of *Animalia*. No architectural history book or course – not even the most recent progressive, inclusive global surveys that are preoccupied with the otherwise respectable task of dismantling established cultural hierarchies – seems to challenge this essentialist bifurcation or dare to posit that architecture is *not* exclusive to humanity, that the first planetary architectural constructions are *not* our stone circles, ritual centers, or megalithic tombs, but that there is an untold architectural

5. For a general introduction to animal architecture, see Karl von Frisch, *Animal Architecture* (New York: Harcourt Brace Jovanovich, 1974); Mike Hansell, *Built by Animals: The Natural History of Animal Architecture* (Oxford: Oxford University Press, 2007). For the rare interest shown to architecture's beastly dimension by architectural theorists and designers, see Catherine Ingraham, *Architecture, Animal, Human: The Asymmetrical Condition* (London: Routledge, 2006); Caroline O'Donnell, *Niche Tactics: Generative Relationships Between Architecture and Site* (London: Routledge, 2015).

6. See Jacques Jaubert, et al., "Early Neanderthal constructions deep in Bruniquel Cave in southwestern France," *Nature* 534 (2016): 111–14.

7. See Paul Mellars, *The Neanderthal Legacy: An Archaeological Perspective from Western Europe* (Princeton: Princeton University Press, 1996); Marie Soressi et al., "Neandertals made the first specialized bone tools in Europe," *PNAS* 110 (2013): 14186–90; Paola Villa and Wil Roebroeks, "Neandertal Demise: An Archaeological Analysis of the Modern Human Superiority Complex," *PLoS One* 9 (2014); A.C. Sorensen, E. Claud, and M. Soressi "Neandertal fire-making technology inferred from microwear analysis," *Scientific Reports* 8, no. 1 (2018): 10065; B.L. Hardy et al., "Direct evidence of Neanderthal fibre technology and its cognitive and behavioral implications," *Scientific Reports* 10 (2020): 4889; A.G. Henry, A.S. Brooks, and D.R. Piperno, "Microfossils in calculus demonstrate consumption of plants and cooked foods in Neanderthal diets," *PNAS* 108, no. 2 (2011): 486–91; Dan Dediu and Stephen Levinson, "Neanderthal language revisited: not only us," *Current Opinion in Behavioral Sciences* 21 (2018): 49–55; Dirk Hoffman et al., "Symbolic use of marine shells and mineral pigments by Iberian Neandertals 115,000 years ago," *Science Advances* 4, no. 2 (2018): eaar5255; Ana Majkić et al., "A decorated raven bone from the Zaskalnaya VI (Kolosovskaya) Neanderthal site, Crimea," *PLoS One* 12, no. 3 (2017): e0173435; Matija Turk et al., "The Mousterian musical instrument from the Divje Babe I Cave (Slovenia): Arguments on the material evidence for Neanderthal musical behavior," *L'Anthropologie* 122, no. 4 (2018): 1–28; D.L. Hoffmann et al., "U-Th dating of carbonate crusts reveals Neandertal origin of Iberian cave art," *Science* 359, no. 6378 (2018): 912–15.

history of a boundary-defying constructive continuum that cuts across the animal and the human, nature and culture, ecological and built environments. However much we may want to dismiss, architecture has a beastly dimension.

Neanderthal

In 2016, a team of archaeologists reported in *Nature* the extraordinary discovery of a strange architecture deep in Bruniquel Cave in southwest France.[6] The subterranean site contained a series of ring-shaped constructions made of broken stalagmites. A series of complex operations involved in the making of these constructions – such as extracting the stalagmites, fragmenting and shaping them into calibrated speleofacts (brick-like stalagmite modules), arranging them in annular formations, using intricate architectural techniques like wedging elements and stays to act as buttresses, installing and maintaining fire at strategic locations of the structure with symbolic and ritualistic overtones – demonstrate, the archaeologists suggest, that this architecture is of anthropogenic origin. Puzzlingly, however, uranium-series dating determined that these sophisticated structures were built 176,500 years ago, when the only "human" population living in Europe was early Neanderthals.

Not much was known about early Neanderthal cultures until a few years ago. Casting aside what is now defined in archaeological circles as our "modern human superiority complex," we only recently acknowledged, due to increasing evidence, that Neanderthals made the first specialized bone tools, had their own burial sites and rituals, were capable of creating and controlling fire, used cooking techniques such as roasting, smoking, and boiling, wove clothes and blankets, were capable of speech and had their own languages, played musical instruments (Divje Babe Flute), painted cave walls, and crafted ornaments from shells and bird bones.[7] With the recent archaeological discovery in Bruniquel Cave – which is yet to be recognized by the architectural field – we can now add complex architectural structures to this list.

Ironically, beneath the canonical anthropocentric paradigms that assert that architecture is solely "human," there lies a covert hierarchy of humanness. By "humanity," the established architectural discourses mean *only* our species, *Homo sapiens*, and never *Homo erectus* or *neanderthalensis* or *habilis*. It seems that in architecture not even all humans count as humans. Our modern human superiority complex blinds us to the fact that architecture cannot be limited to the

8. Whitehead emphasizes different dimensions of this concept in different parts of his books, as in: "All things are involved in the creative advance of the Universe"; "All realization involves implication in the creative advance"; and "The universe is thus a creative advance into novelty." Alfred North Whitehead, *Adventure of Ideas* (New York: Free Press, 1967), 143; *Modes of Thought* (New York: Free Press, 1968), 146; *Process and Reality* (New York: Free Press, 1978), 222. For an elegant introduction of Whitehead's philosophy, see Erin Manning, "Angular Perspective; Or, How Concern Shapes the Field," *Log* 49 (Summer 2020): 182–95.

9. "Vital constructivity [*Die vitale Konstruktivität*] is the embodiment of life and the principle of all human and cosmic unfoldings. Translated into art, today this means the activation of space by means of dynamic-constructive systems of forces. … We must therefore replace the *static* principle of *classical art* with the *dynamic principle of cosmic life*. Stated practically: instead of static *material* construction (material and form relations), dynamic construction (vital construction and *force relations*) must be evolved in which the material is employed only as *the carrier of forces*. [This means] man … experiences a heightening of his own faculties, and becomes himself an active partner with the forces unfolding themselves." László Moholy-Nagy, "Dynamisch-konstruktives Kraftsystem," *Der Sturm* 12 (1922): 186; "Dynamic-Constructive System of Forces (1922)," in *Moholy-Nagy*, ed. Krisztine Passuth (London: Thames and Hudson, 1985), 290.

10. For Simondon, individuation itself is a constructive process: "Initially, the individuated being does not have *a* soul and *a* body; it is constructed as such by individualizing"; "The individual individuates insofar as it perceives beings, constitutes an individuation … through a productive construction"; and "Life in its entirety seems like a progressive construction of increasingly elaborate forms, i.e., forms capable of containing increasingly elevated problems." Gilbert Simondon, *Individuation in Light of Notions of Form and Information*, trans. Taylor Adkins (Minneapolis: University of Minnesota Press, 2020), 237; 272; 297. For a potent introduction of Simondon's philosophy, see Muriel Combes, "On Nature," *Log* 49 (Summer 2020): 146–63.

constructive activities of our species. There is a gradational continuum from the architectures of early, archaic, extinct human species to Neolithic settlements and ziggurats, ancient urban layouts and majestic structures of worship, modern houses and contemporary skyscrapers. We did not create architecture ex nihilo but advanced what was passed on to us by other human species. Architecture is not our invention but our inheritance.

Human, All Too Human

We, the relatively young *Homo sapiens*, emerged around 300,000 years ago. Following a slow-burning evolutionary journey, we have transformed architecture into something hitherto inconceivable – a planetary exoskeleton that provides us expanded capacities and profound spatial experiences at the expense of disciplining our environments with iron grips and self-serving manipulations. There are two predominant approaches to be wary of here. Our architectural inventions can neither be deemed the result of an exceptional, hierarchically superior anthropic essence, as the human supremacists among us would like to maintain, nor flattened and disregarded, as the misanthropes among us dreaming of post-, trans-, and antihuman futures would like us to believe. Glorifying and demonizing our architectural contributions – making them either the only architecture that matters or totally null and insignificant – are the seemingly opposite poles of the same old moralizing tale. Beyond this binary there is a third possibility, an embryonic one positing the mutual inclusivity of our cosmic *continuity* and inexhaustible *uniqueness*. Our constructive capacities are both *continuous* with the cosmos, the Earth, the animals, the extinct human species, and *unique*, engendering singular architectural formations affecting the interdependent lives of numerous socio-ecological modes of existence. This third position makes possible a different understanding of our constructive horizon as neither normatively anthropocentric nor reactively misanthropic. Our architecture is singularly cosmic.

Cosmodality

The subterranean history of this mode of thinking stretches back to the school of Advaita Vedānta, the teachings of Laozi, and the heterodox philosophies of Al-Hallaj and Ibn Arabi. In early modern continental philosophy, Spinoza provided the most radical form of conceiving the cosmos as an immanent dynamo of unremitting generativity. Alfred North Whitehead

11. I have been working on the metaphysical contents of cosmodality for a while now, but the inception of the term *cosmodality* is recent and has a peculiar story. I was invited to Stavros Kousoulas's studio review at TU Delft, a pedagogical experiment fusing philosophy and architectural design. As Andrej Radman was giving a critique, I thought I heard him utter the word *cosmodality*, although it made no sense within the immediate context of his commentary. When he finished, I asked whether he had used such a term, for it has immense Spinozist potentials as a portmanteau concept integrating "cosmos" and "modality," underscoring in a single word how the continuity of the cosmos expresses itself in an infinity of modalities across various scales of existence. Radman said no, that was also his first time hearing it. Hence, *cosmodality* was born by a curious trick my mind played on me, projecting the intrinsic naming of this crucial concept back to an extrinsic social interaction, to a dialogue between the self and the cosmos.

joined him in the early 20th century, arguing that the cosmos is indeed fueled by a constructive principle he called "the creative advance."[8] On the architectural side, László Moholy-Nagy, in a criminally overlooked essay preceding his Bauhaus years titled "Dynamic-Constructive System of Forces," developed an original constructive cosmology: "Vital constructivity is the embodiment of life and the principle of all human and cosmic unfoldings."[9] And in the cybernetically enhanced postwar context, Gilbert Simondon detected in physical, biological, psychic, and technical individuals alike preindividual potentials they ceaselessly sculpt.[10] Dare we take this metaphysical speculation even further and identify this ontogenetic act, this constructive capacity, with architecture as such?

Reconceiving architecture as the channeling of constructive capacities immanent to the very flesh of cosmic existence requires getting out of our comfort zones, defying our deeply entrenched anthropocentric presuppositions, and expanding architecture's horizon with the forging of a pan-constructive cosmology. The pieces that follow here unpack different dimensions of this metaphysical provocation, renegotiating the triadic waltz between the cosmos, the potential reach of design, and our human (all too human) contingencies. Novel experiments can emerge from this reorientation, instigating architecture to break its self-imposed isolation and become the dynamic nexus of polygenetic forces vitalizing not just buildings, cities, and sociopolitical formations but biotic communities, geological forces, and galactic possibilities. This work is a call for exploring the gradational continuity of our constructive capacities with the rest of the cosmos while acknowledging each and every constructive act in its scale-sensitive singularity; an invitation to weave symbiotic meshes with modalities seemingly alien and incompatible yet immanent to and coextensive with our existence; a prolegomenon to an incipient way of being and thinking, a new architectural metaphysics: *cosmodality*.[11] – *GK*

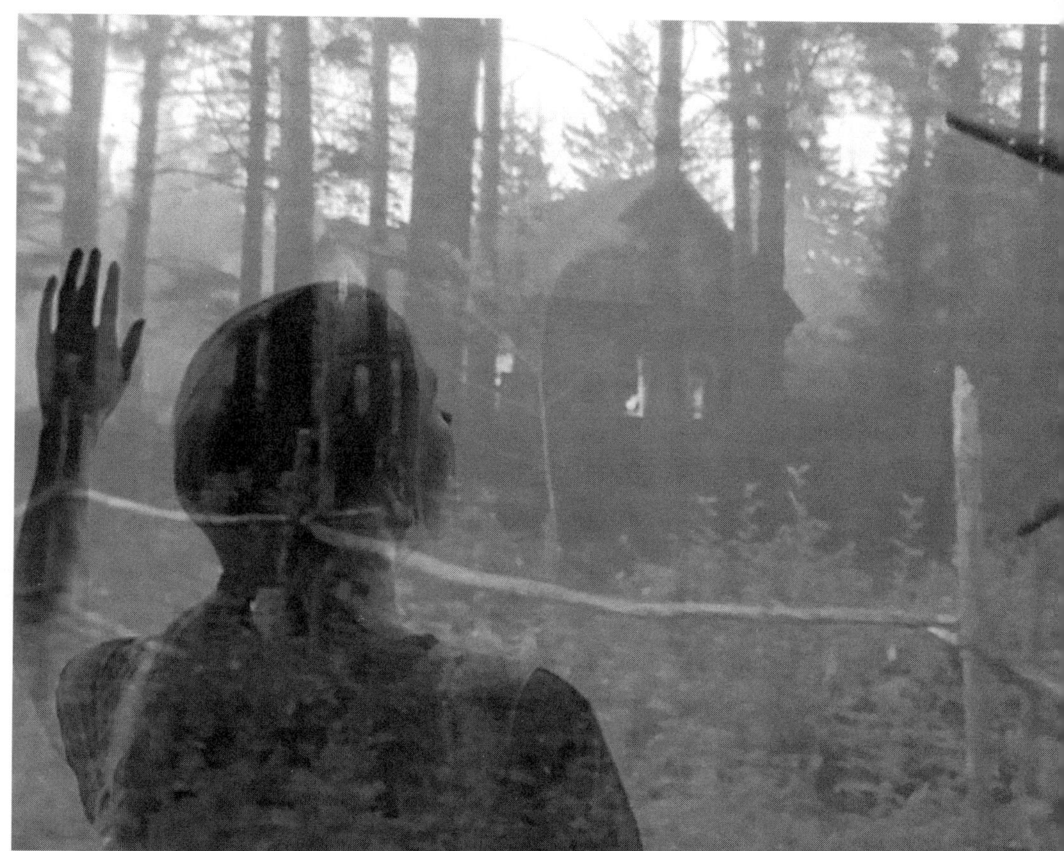

Composite image by the author.

Ed Keller

The Cosmopolitical Gesture

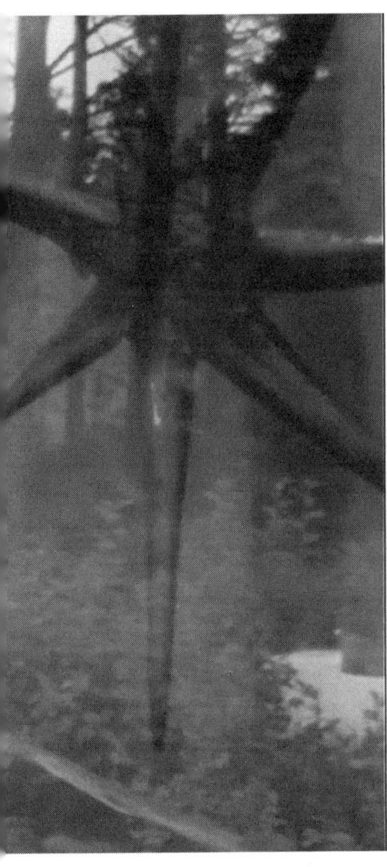

The image I want to tell you about is synthesized from two films: *Mirror* by Andrei Tarkovsky, and *Arrival* by Denis Villeneuve. Certain passages from these films form the composite image of a potential "cosmopolitical gesture" that might operate at both the human scale and far beyond. I have tried several times to link these filmic passages to other images or spaces, and in recent years, I used sound to create lines of flight between the gestures, agencies, and relations they contain. Here, I have finally managed to situate this image alone, at the beginning of a text, as a templexity, a composite imprint of macrohistorical consciousness catalyzing the genesis of a cosmopolitics.

Gesture

What might constitute the cosmopolitical gesture in these two films? What, indeed, is a gesture if it is something other than a physical movement? In *Arrival*, the adaptation of a Ted Chiang sci-fi novella, the main character is Louise Banks, a linguist helping a military team communicate with an alien species that has stationed 12 ships around Earth. In one of her first encounters, she holds up her hand in a gesture of greeting to a transparent window in their ship that separates her and the other humans from the heptapod aliens. The aliens respond by "writing" ideograms in inky, smoky rings that hover in front of Louise, by vocalizing in a whale-like register, and by placing a tentacle against the other side of the window. Reciprocity; mimesis. The gesture is familiar but also quite complex because the aliens are using multiple forms of written, visual, and abstract as well as sonic, spoken, and sung language to provide the human translator with several self-annotating and recursive modes to work with.

In *Mirror*, Tarkovsky's camera orbits his childhood country home in a refractory manner, revealing it from multiple temporal points and situating it against a deeper geopolitical framework of events that Tarkovsky witnessed as a youth. The "gesture" he maps is not a single human movement but a larger core gesture encompassing many lives, many sites, and many chronotopes across decades and

139

1. This project was published in 2019 in a small collection of video essays. See "The Cosmopolitical Gesture," *Alienocene: Journal of the First Outernational*, December 23, 2019, https://alienocene.com/2019/12/23/the-cosmopolitical-gesture/. It was released previously as a solo album in 2018. See Ed Keller, "Adab, The Demanding Memory," 2018, Bandcamp, https://thermalhowl.bandcamp.com/album/adab-the-demanding-memory.

centuries. The cognitive gesture that Tarkovsky himself lived, and that he invites us into, is a slowly evolving consciousness of the myriad relations between systems that ultimately, as film form (as an autonomous universe, in Tarkovksy's case), becomes a catalyst for perceiving intimate human and macro-historical time simultaneously.

In superimposing the two spaces of gesture in *Mirror* and *Arrival*, I was hoping to find a link between the most intimate scale and the cosmological, one mapping flows of information, energy, and life; to articulate an empathic cosmopolitics, as opposed to an ethos of pure survival or bare life.[1]

Nature and/or Life

Life consists / Of propositions about life.
> – Wallace Stevens, "Men Made Out of Words"

I would like to situate this scalar idea of gesture against the limits of life and bodies, against models of nature, and across passages of time. "New natures" should, I imagine, be thought with the prerequisite acknowledgment that our human definitions of nature to date are largely provisional and, at best, limited. Which is fine, until they're presumed to be essential. Borrowing obliquely from Michel Foucault and Spinoza, we could say that any given nature should be defined by the ensemble of systems that it is dangerous to; there is no nature that is not natural per se, but the collected points of view or the cumulative knowledge shared by all agents in a given ensemble allow us to define a useful scope of the natural for that ensemble. For example, a single human is nearly galactic in scale compared to the viruses or bacteria that live in and on us; their point of view, combined with ours, yields a composite nature and a composite temporality. Ontology via collective intelligence.

We face two related problems as we wrestle with the implications of this universal definition of nature. The first, how we define the limits of life, when pursued with rigor, then establishes the framework for the second: how we define the limits (or aspirations, or capabilities) of design – whether of a building, a synthetic biology, or a mind. As our models of the boundaries of life change, all other disciplines fall into a cascading realignment. Recognizing as living whatever we previously thought was inanimate adjusts our grasp of the performance of design. The limits of life are always haunted by collapsing epistemological horizons, the boundaries of our perception, and our conceptual power; whether layperson or expert, we find ourselves all, to some extent, absentminded observers, using eyes that look but do not see.

From this we can draw an explicitly orthogonal politics: not posthuman – as we never really have been human – but certainly outside the limits of life as we've known it. The design of this politics is based on models of life that are no longer considered to be even marginally biologically alive. Indeed, the limits of the human body become even more evanescent. We already know that we are human, bacterial, viral, all overlapped – this is the lesson we learned from recent studies on the human microbiome as well as from Sadie Plant, Georges Bataille, and Donna Haraway.[2]

Alternative technopolitics and ontologies emerge when the relationship between the living and the nonliving, the obvious and the latent, becomes our focal point. Many thinkers have rehearsed this: before we mapped DNA, Erwin Schrödinger saw aperiodic crystalline structure as a lattice from which the different temporalities of life could proceed[3]; the time and agency of quasi life is often at the root of J.G. Ballard's obsessions, whether via a creeping malaise propagating (perhaps from outer space) in *The Crystal World* or the natural systemic tendencies of the highway, the flow, and the accident in *Crash*. Danny Boyle's 2002 film, *28 Days Later*, unpacks these ontologies in the context of a bioweapon accident; human agency is refigured, over and over, always formally invested, and always across the expansion of a terrain where whatever we insist on calling life after a "crash" might still be moving through. These examples all point to nonstandard forms of life, cognition, and ethics that we could draw upon as both cautionary tales and scenarios that suggest potential sites for design intervention.

When we start applying such concepts to the deep time of living systems, things turn weird. The astounding history of organic life sets the stage for a range of hidden application layers. As Ballard writes in *The Drowned World*, countless phenotypic artifacts of human evolution still operate in us[4] – memories of the Pleistocene and beyond: "The brief span of an individual life is misleading. Each one of us is as old as the entire biological kingdom, and our bloodstreams are tributaries of the great sea of its total memory. The uterine odyssey of the growing foetus recapitulates the entire evolutionary past, and its central nervous system is a coded time scale, each nexus of neurones and each spinal level marking a symbolic station, a unit of neuronic time."[5] In other words, we are all apps in a biological stack operating across millions of years.[6]

2. See Sadie Plant's foreword to *The Spam Book: On Viruses, Porn, and Other Anomalies from the Dark Side of Digital Culture*, ed. Jussi Parikka and Tony D. Sampson (Cresskill, New Jersey: Hampton Press, 2009); Georges Bataille, *The Accursed Share: An Essay on General Economy, Volume I: Consumption*, trans. Robert Hurley (New York: Zone Books, 1988); Donna J. Haraway, *Simians, Cyborgs, and Women: The Reinvention of Nature* (New York: Routledge, 1991).

3. See Erwin Schrödinger, *What Is Life? The Physical Aspect of the Living Cell* (Cambridge: Cambridge University Press, 1944).

4. Clathrin, a triskelion-shaped protein, is one of these phenotypic artifacts. It is involved in cell operations related to transport across the cell wall via vesicles. Various types of clathrin track back to gene duplications that possibly emerged over 500 million years ago.

5. J.G. Ballard, *The Drowned World* (New York: Berkley Books, 1962), 43.

6. See my "On Architecture's Use and Abuse of [Models of] Life," *Tarp: Architecture Manual:* Not Nature (Spring 2012): 93–95.

In *A Million Years of Music*, Gary Tomlinson articulates one implication for the superimposition of temporal arcs within a biological system:

[Modern human cognitive abilities] arose from the necessities facing groups of nonmusical, nonlinguistic hominins as they together sought subsistence or survival in the material ecologies around them. Modern musicking and language, in a real sense, did not develop at all. Instead they fell out, as belated emergences, from patterns of sociality and communication neither musical nor linguistic that can be traced to periods long before Homo sapiens existed. As they coalesced, they formed not only the modern connections between them . . . but also other aspects definitive of our human modernity.[7]

Life and all complex forms are comprised of such gestures that simultaneously coexist at multiple temporal scales.

Cosmopolitics and Energy

Arguing for cosmopolitics, I underscore how all human endeavor is already sited in a cosmological frame, beyond our mythopoetic models of the cosmos or scale-bound design operations. We face the challenge not only of coordinating effectively with other humans – something we're notoriously bad at – but also of communicating with AI and complex systems that seem fundamentally alien. The politics of communication, with the nonhuman, the animal, the ecosystemic, is at the core of a planetary ethics.

One way to rethink the political relation between models of anthropogenic and ecological systems is through an investigation opened by Bataille. In *The Accursed Share*, he proposed that we should not isolate systems completely, suggesting that only a model of a general economy would be detailed enough to allow us to grasp the overflowing processes of the world: "The economy taken as a whole is usually studied as if it were a matter of an isolatable system of operation. . . . Isn't there a need to study the system of human production and consumption within a much larger framework?"[8] In this sense, human economies and technologies are indistinguishable from a form of nature. One such framework could be a cosmism that treats the dynamics of monetary systems, computation, organic processes, cultures, etc., all together, not unlike what cybernetician Stafford Beer attempted in the 1970s with Project Cybersyn in Chile.[9]

Bataille's potlatch-influenced take on the superabundance of resources and excess energy was interpreted differently by Donella Meadows et al. in their 1972 report *The Limits to*

7. Gary Tomlinson, *A Million Years of Music: The Emergence of Human Modernity* (New York: Zone Books, 2015), 12.
8. Bataille, 19–20.
9. See Eden Medina, *Cybernetic Revolutionaries: Technology and Politics in Allende's Chile* (Cambridge: MIT Press, 2011).

10. See Donella H. Meadows et al., *The Limits to Growth: A Report for the Club of Rome's Project on the Predicament of Mankind* (New York: Universe Books, 1972).
11. Luis Fernández-Galiano, *Fire and Memory: On Architecture and Energy*, trans. Gina Cariño (Cambridge: MIT Press, 2000).

Growth, which calculated, with the help of computer simulations, that our exponential economic and population growth – which depends on nonrenewable, finite resources – could not be sustained and would soon lead to economic and ecological collapse.[10] Yet together, these seemingly opposed examples share a critical insight: they highlight how a planetary ethics and cosmopolitics can be configured within a general economy and urge us to place ourselves more effectively in the energetic continuum of the universe.

Luis Fernández-Galiano takes on some of these themes and challenges in *Fire and Memory*, a lucid unpacking of the relation between emergent systems, complex behavior, and heat management design in architecture.[11] It is a genealogical tracing of relationships at a truly macroscopic scale between what we as humans do on Earth and what other systems in our universe tend to do when managing energy flow. Approaching a general theory of complex systems and life, Fernández-Galiano observes in a poignant moment that building a primitive hut in a forest and burning construction materials are *both* architectural acts. I would only add, they are cosmopolitical acts.

Cosmopolitics: Provisional Typologies

Empathy, he once had decided, must be limited to herbivores or anyhow omnivores who could depart from a meat diet. Because, ultimately, the empathic gift blurred the boundaries between hunter and victim, between the successful and the defeated. . . . As long as some creature experienced joy, then the condition for all other creatures included a fragment of joy. However, if any living being suffered, then for all the rest the shadow could not be entirely cast off.
  – Philip K. Dick, *Do Androids Dream of Electric Sheep?*

We can map out a simple spectrum of provisional cosmopolitics. From neutral to orthogonal to dark to empathic, let's consider how any design model or methodology would position itself in relation to planetary concerns, and also, speculating further, look at human-to-nonhuman relations, whether on Earth or off, in the context of a cosmic construction of agency. Each of the following models frames the problem of human-to-human dynamics as much as it does human-to-nonhuman relations, opening up seemingly endless design opportunities, but also insurmountable challenges.

001 Neutral Cosmopolitics

*The disappearance of Man at the end of History is not a cosmic
catastrophe: the natural World remains what it has been from all
eternity. And it is not a biological catastrophe either: Man remains
alive as animal in harmony with Nature or given Being. What
disappears is Man properly so called.*

> – Alexandre Kojève, *Introduction to the Reading of Hegel*

Kojève's statement places us and our work as humans in a
macrohistorical frame and defines this evolution as a simple
shift in self-definition. If the disappearance of "Man" takes
place in our time, it is not through extinction (though it
sadly might well be) but through a sea change in our view
of ourselves: a planetary change in structures of feeling and
total amnesia of all prior concepts and definitions of "the
human." This not quite pessimistic view can be contrasted
with Primo Levi's harsher evaluation (based on his life experience as well as astrophysics) of our chances of communication with alien life:

*We are alone. If we have interlocutors, they are so far away that,
barring unforeseeable turns of events, we shall never talk to them;
in spite of this, some years ago we sent them a pathetic message.
Every year that passes leaves us more alone. Not only are we not
the centre of the universe, but the universe is not made for human
beings; it is hostile, violent, alien. In the sky there are no Elysian
Fields, only matter and light, distorted, compressed, dilated, and
rarefied to a degree that eludes our senses and our language.*[12]

002 Orthogonal Cosmopolitics

Levi's vision is bleak, but it is neutral in relation to a cosmologi-
cally scaled politics: internal relations with species on our planet
– or to off-planet agencies – are determined by inaccessibility
and insurmountable communication challenges. Another version of neutrality is seen in the shadow biosphere's orthogonal
life, outside of the constraints of competition for resources.
Hugo de Garis discusses this when speculating on AI that might
emerge at a subatomic scale in our universe; in this case, there is
no conflict and no politics because there is no exchange:

*It should be clear from all this talk of femtotech . . . that as one
scales down, in general, performance levels increase dramatically. Hence one can readily speculate that any nano-based artilect,
sooner or later, will not be able to compete with femto-based cous-
ins, and will probably downgrade itself as well. . . . The hyper
intelligences that are billions of years older than we are in our universe . . . have probably [downscaled] themselves to achieve hugely*

12. Primo Levi, "Levi's list," *Guardian*, June
1, 2001, https://www.theguardian.com/
books/2001/jun/02/arts.highereducation.
It is worth noting that this quote continues
in a far more optimistic and encouraging
way, which repositions his observation
more in the "empathic cosmopolitics"
that I am attempting to map: "Every year
that passes, while earthly matters grow
ever more convoluted, the challenge of
the cosmos grows keener and more bitter:
the heavens are not simple, but neither
are they impermeable to our minds – they
are waiting to be deciphered. The misery
of man has another face, one imprinted
with nobility; maybe we exist by chance,
perhaps we are the sole instance of
intelligence in the universe, certainly, we
are immeasurably small, weak and alone,
but if the human mind has conceived Black
Holes, and dares to speculate on what
happened in the first moments of creation,
why should it not know how to conquer
fear, poverty and grief?"

13. Hugo de Garis, Papadakis, "Best of H+: X-Tech and the Search for Infra Particle Intelligence," *h+ Magazine*, February 20, 2014, https://hplusmagazine. com/2014/02/20/x-tech-and-the-search-for-infra-particle-intelligence/.
14. Cixin Liu, *The Dark Forest*, trans. Joel Martinsen (New York: Tor, 2015), 53.
15. For definitive writing on these case studies, see Paul Virilio, *The Vision Machine*, trans. Julie Rose (Bloomington: Indiana University Press, 1994).

greater performance levels. Whole civilizations may be living inside volumes the size of nucleons or smaller.[13]

Yet another model of orthogonality, I would argue, can be found in two beautiful films directed by Alex Garland, *Ex Machina* and his more recent adaptation of Jeff VanderMeer's novel *Annihilation*. Both films are meditations on a profound gesture between the human and the nonhuman, with humans merging with the radically alien in such a way that we might contemplate it without too much fear; a shedding of the human diagram, yet the preservation of something of the dignity – the form of life – that all creatures and low-entropy intelligences share, humans among them.

003 Dark Cosmopolitics

This predatory cosmopolitical model holds that in resource- and energy-poor systems, and between technologically advanced civilizations, a first preemptive strike will always be necessary. Mutually assured destruction is parallel to the dark forest concept. This is Cixin Liu's cosmic axiom in his monumental and shattering sci-fi trilogy Remembrance of Earth's Past. In one scenario in the second volume, *The Dark Forest*, several human spaceships are fleeing Earth after an alien arrival. The ships' crews simultaneously realize that for a thousand-year voyage, they will need to cannibalize parts and resources from each other, leading to a first strike – a human mirror of the universal law demanding first-strike cosmopolitics. Although bleak for those who do not survive, through a key character, Liu frames this particular attack against the concept of the survival of a species or a general principle of life: "The fusion fireball lasted for twenty seconds and sparkled with infrasonic frequencies that were invisible to the naked eye. The returned images showed that in the three seconds that remained, Zhang Beihai turned to Dongfang Yanxu, flashed her a smile, and spoke: 'It doesn't matter. It's all the same.'"[14]

Another case study – this one of actual historical events – is the Cathedral of Light, the Zeppelinfeld stadium designed by Albert Speer and used from 1934 through '38 for political rallies in Nuremberg. These events colonized our perceptual apparatus and changed the way we were able to think of ourselves in relation to the world. The spectacular assembly, sound, rehearsed gesture, and political theater were precisely calibrated to coordinate and bind millions of minds to a purpose; architecture, light, and sound in the service of bundling perception and thought. A fascism.[15]

004 Empathic Cosmopolitics

To pursue/develop an empathic cosmopolitics, we might begin with a turn to the nonhuman to map where information is stored and what it does for and to the systems it moves through. An empathic approach that resonates, for example, with Raymond Williams's concept of structures of feeling – population-wide, shared quasi-conscious values and gestures – would seek out possible empathies between any organisms that were formed together over millions of years, in the same ecosphere and atmosphere, at the same level down a gravity well.[16] Aldo Leopold's *A Sand County Almanac* is exemplary in its ability to *think* across multiple systems and map the macrohistorical species interactions, the ennobling of being that might have happened across millions of years on our prehuman planet:

The geese of the world . . . each March they stake their lives on [an] essential truth. In the beginning there was only the unity of the Ice Sheet. Then followed the unity of the March thaw, and the northward hegira of the international geese. Every March since the Pleistocene, the geese have honked unity from China Sea to Siberian Steppe, from Euphrates to Volga, from Nile to Murmansk, from Lincolnshire to Spitsbergen. Every March since the Pleistocene, the geese have honked unity from Currituck to Labrador, Matamuskeet to Ungava, Horseshoe Lake to Hudson's Bay, Avery Island to Baffin Land, Panhandle to Mackenzie, Sacramento to Yukon. By this international commerce of geese, the waste corn of Illinois is carried through the clouds to the Arctic tundras, there to combine with the waste sunlight of a nightless June to grow goslings for all the lands between. And in this annual barter of food for light, and winter warmth for summer solitude, the whole continent receives as net profit a wild poem dropped from the murky skies upon the muds of March.[17]

Empathy, especially the kind that might yield a cosmic ethics of action (Spinozist in its awareness of powers to affect and be affected), must emerge from the necessity of our engagement with a physics of free energy, a theory of information flow and recursive cognitive architectures.

The Return of Gesture

Philosopher AI is an online service that gives access to the GPT-3 AI engine. Last year, I asked it this question: "What would constitute a Cosmopolitical Gesture?"[18] The GPT-3 AI replied: "The gesture is not over when the handshake has taken place, because one's hand can remain outstretched. This gesture therefore contains an element of potentiality for becoming actualized and so does not yet have any final completion."

16. See Raymond Williams, *The Long Revolution* (London: Chatto & Windus, 1961), 78–79. "The term I would suggest to describe it is *structure of feeling*: it is as firm and definite as 'structure' suggests, yet it operates in the most delicate and least tangible parts of our activity. In one sense, this structure of feeling is the culture of a period: it is the particular living result of all the elements in the general organization. And it is in this respect that the arts of a period, taking these to include characteristic approaches and tones in argument, are of major importance. For here, if anywhere, this characteristic is likely to be expressed; often not consciously, but by the fact that here, in the only examples we have of recorded communication that outlives its bearers, the actual living sense, the deep community that makes the communication possible, is naturally drawn upon. I do not mean that the structure of feeling, any more than the social character, is possessed in the same way by the many individuals in the community. But I think it is a very deep and very wide possession, in all actual communities, precisely because it is on it that communication depends."

17. Aldo Leopold, *A Sand County Almanac, and Sketches Here and There* (New York: Oxford University Press, 2020), 21–22.

18. See Philosopher AI, https://philosophe-rai.com/.

19. *Addressability* is a term developed by Michael Witmore; see Witmore, "Text: A Massively Addressable Object," *Wine Dark Sea*, December 31, 2010, https://winedark-sea.org/?p=926.
20. Charles H. Lineweaver and Chas A. Egan, "Life, gravity and the second law of thermodynamics," abstract, *Physics of Life Reviews* 5 (2008): 225.

This brings me to the place where planet and human, gesture and mind, anabasis and katabasis, life and techne, might all meet. Both Villeneuve's *Arrival* and Tarkovsky's *Mirror* deal with scaling from the human to the planetary through networks and infrastructures that make the massive addressability of a collective gesture possible.[19] From the intimate fragility of our being to the linguistics of the feedback loop in consciousness and gestures to a macrohistorical consciousness, the question remains: Is it possible to scale – scale anything – to a population?

Behind all this work to redefine the limits of life, nature, and artifice lie questions of utmost importance. What is a cosmic model for complex systems – whether cities or life itself – and how can we situate a political project, implemented in design, within this cosmic frame? Are cognition and empathy ubiquitous not just in life but in any mode of existence? If not, at what scales do they appear? And might the equations of energy and empathy be isomorphic? Astrophysicists Charles Lineweaver and Chas Egan provide notable answers to some of these questions:

All dissipative structures in the universe including all forms of life, owe their existence to the fact that the universe started in a low entropy state and has not yet reached equilibrium. The low initial entropy was due to the low gravitational entropy of the nearly homogeneously distributed matter and has, through gravitational collapse, evolved gradients in density, temperature, pressure and chemistry. These gradients, when steep enough, give rise to far from equilibrium dissipative structures (e.g., galaxies, stars, black holes, hurricanes and life) which emerge spontaneously to hasten the destruction of the gradients which spawned them.[20]

This means any and all complex systems that we know of emerge from gradational tensions between energy flows and gravitational perturbations, demonstrating the birth of many from one, giving way to the infinite heterogeneity of metasystems and ecosystems, planets and organisms, minds and bodies. In resonance, Freeman Dyson's critique of Geoffrey West's laws of scale is essential, as another "energetic" key to a cosmopolitical approach to design:

As a consequence of the second law of thermodynamics, when energy flows from one such object to another, the hot object will grow hotter and the cold object will grow colder. . . . In every situation where gravity is dominant, the second law causes local contrasts to increase together with entropy. This is true for astronomical objects like the sun, and also for large terrestrial objects such as thunderstorms and hurricanes. The diversity of astronomical and terrestrial objects, including living creatures, tends to increase

21. In an attempt to mathematize the megalopolis, Geoffrey West proposed laws of scale and compared cities' superlinearity to the limits to growth faced by, for example, large mammals. Freeman Dyson's full review of West, *Scale: The Universal Laws of Growth, Innovation, Sustainability, and the Pace of Life, in Organisms, Cities, Economies, and Companies* (New York: Penguin, 2017) is "The Key to Everything," *New York Review*, May 10, 2018, https://www.nybooks.com/articles/2018/05/10/the-key-to-everything/. Emphases mine.

22. John Ruskin, *The Stones of Venice*, vol. 1, *The Foundations* (London: Smith, Elder & Co., 1851), 19.

with time, in spite of the second law. *The evolution of natural ecologies and of human societies is a part of this pattern.*[21]

If Dyson's and Lineweaver and Egan's models are correct, then all forms of design and techne also fit within cosmic niches – basins of attraction – and any act of cosmopolitical design can be assessed according to where it emerges and operates and how it can be channeled within this system to forge a new telos for being and becoming.

Cities are one nexus where cosmos and politics meet. They are external memory systems – extended phenotypes for human (and nonhuman) culture and life. Ruskin suggests in *The Stones of Venice* that the city itself is an index of the mixing of flows of the "cool cultures" of the north and the "hot cultures" of southern Europe and North Africa. He uses geological models to describe this: "The glacier stream of the Lombards, and the following one of the Normans, left their erratic blocks, wherever they had flowed. . . . But the lava stream of the Arab, even after it ceased to flow, warmed the whole of the Northern air; and the history of Gothic architecture is the history of the refinement and spiritualization of Northern work under its influence."[22]

As designers, how can we extrapolate Ruskin's concepts to arrive at models of complex living systems (cities *and* organisms) and also a slow-moving, self-aware mind, produced as countless layers of interaction over millions of years yield feedback loops and cognition? He provokes key questions: Is the architectural style itself the body? Or are the stones themselves the geologically scaled bodies that we should consider? Or should we turn our attention to the flickering nonhuman life and the collective urban mind itself? The gestures of a city can arc across more than a thousand years. A city, any city, is an incarnation of cosmopolitics.

Distributed Cognition as Cosmopolitical Project

We're one in the river / And one again after the fall.
　　　　　　　　　　　　– System of a Down, "Aerials"

Nothing distinguishes me ontologically from a crystal, a plant, an animal, or the order of the world; we are drifting together toward the noise and the black depths of the universe, and our diverse systemic complexions are flowing up the entropic stream, toward the solar origin, itself adrift. Knowledge is at most the reversal of drifting, that strange conversion of times, always paid for by additional drift.
　　　　　　　　– Michel Serres, "The Origin of Language: Biology, Information Theory and Thermodynamics"

As we recognize that the complex morphologies we build exist in parallel with much more complex assemblies found in the "natural" world, we are forced to come to terms with the idea that we ourselves have only partial control over our designed and built environment. Stephen Wolfram observes, in a meditation on what might be useful information to send in a CETI project: "We're not familiar (except in mythology) with telling 'culturally meaningful stories' about the world of stars and planets. And in the past we might have imagined that somehow whatever stories we could tell would inevitably be far less rich than the ones we can tell about our civilization. But . . . in the end what goes on with stars and planets is just as rich as what goes on in our brains or our civilization."[23] In this sense, every detail of our being is always to a degree cosmopolitical and cosmoaesthetic – we are small components of a much larger evolutionary track, each of us small eddies and islands of feedback in a vast homeorhesis. This echoes my opening words on the need for a resiting of all design; it also functions as a call to us as designers to ask to what degree our work operates, at all scales, as part of this cosmic set of feedback loops – in part as self-regulation, in part as a thinking system.

Nonstandard cognition could be the starting point here, as both model and goal, not for a human polis alone but a cosmopolis of radical empathy. Cognition is thus set as agential operation space and is inherently political when we ask which populations are enabled by any given power relationship and the degree to which an agent or a population can think and perceive itself. What kind of energy reservoirs are necessary for this? Does the capacity to perceive oneself macrohistorically yield a political, aesthetic, or evolutionary advantage?[24] As architects and artists we may well ask whether our skill and work are to this end: to affirm and assist a population in thinking and furthering itself (Leopold) or to control and limit its future modes of existence (Speer).

Dziga Vertov took on this challenge in his 1929 film *Man with a Movie Camera*. Ostensibly a political film manifesto about everyday human life, the extrapolation of Vertov's kino-dream is that every component of reality, down to the molecular scale and perhaps beyond, would speak in montage to every other component. The concept of thalience offered by Karl Schroeder unfolds along a similar line; he suggests that we might "attempt to *give the physical world itself a voice* so that rather than us asking what reality is, reality itself can tell us."[25] Vertov was attempting to initiate self-regulating

23. Stephen Wolfram, "Showing Off to the Universe: Beacons for the Afterlife of Our Civilization," Stephen Wolfram Writings, January 25, 2018, https://writings.stephenwolfram.com/2018/01/showing-off-to-the-universe-beacons-for-the-afterlife-of-our-civilization/.
24. Both Peter Watts and Steven Shaviro have explored this at length in their brilliant books. See Peter Watts, *Blindsight* (New York: Tor, 2006); Steven Shaviro, *Discognition* (London: Repeater Books, 2016).
25. Karl Schroeder, "The successor to Science," KarlSchroeder.com, https://www.kschroeder.com/my-books/ventus/thalience. Emphasis original.

26. For a magisterial framing of Vertov's ambitions, see Gilles Deleuze, *Cinema 1: The Movement-Image*, trans. Hugh Tomlinson and Barbara Habberjam (London: Continuum, 1986), 80–81.

27. See Gertrude Stein, Lecture 1, *Narration: Four Lectures* (Chicago: University of Chicago Press, 1935), 1–15.

modes – a kind of flat ontology – within the world system using cinema; Schroeder proposes a similar approach but uses nanotech-scale von Neumann robots.[26] The self-awareness of a planetary system with a distributed cognition may be utterly inaccessible to the human mind, when all things have name and voice and speak to each other. Yet this is what we are building.

Arrival and *Mirror* situate these questions within a complex kino-temporality – complex for the characters we see on-screen and complex for us viewers decoding the films' edited forms. Like Vertov, they loop future, past, and present across each other, demanding a critical interanimation of gestures, positions in time, and choices for the characters and for us. This deliberate insistence on a complexity of temporal form may also be a clue to a radically empathic cosmism, a politics of universal agency far beyond the human, a continuum bridging the temporality of seconds and eons.

Design is always incomplete, always anticipating the next exchange. We must adapt. And gesture may be the only true mode of translation we have ever had, the only mode we can ever have. To rephrase Gertrude Stein, I like the feeling of gestures doing what they want to do and as they have to do.[27] Cosmopolitically.

Ed Keller is a designer, professor, writer, and musician, and with Carla Leitão, a cofounder of Spec.AE and AUM Studio.

Gökhan Kodalak
& Elizabeth Grosz

Fundamental Connectedness: On Philosophy, Nature, and Design

The brief sketched for what follows is composed of three elements: a technique, a topic, and a thinker with a rare expertise. The technique is a conversation, an exercise in cothinking played by passing the ball back and forth, simulating the way thought itself occurs, always in dialogue with the cosmos. The topic is the interfused questions of philosophy (with its cosmological visions), nature (with its indifferent richness), and design (with its constructive potentials), the addressing of which requires seeking the underlying source where thinking, being, and making now converge and become one, now diverge and become many. The thinker, my conversation partner, is Elizabeth Grosz, who has the unique capability to do justice to all the dimensions of such a charged triad with equal depth. In addition to her distinguished work on philosophy and nature, Grosz is not a stranger to the architectural scene. She was a frequent participant in the annual Any conferences; she published a venturous book, Architecture from the Outside, *with a foreword by Peter Eisenman and special acknowledgments to the likes of Anthony Vidler, Beatriz Colomina, Bernard Tschumi, and Cynthia Davidson; her essay "Deleuze, Theory, and Space" appeared in the first issue of* Log, *at a time when Gilles Deleuze's philosophy was still being translated into architectural notation, first by curious experimenters, and eventually by various impersonators and posers.[1] Our exchange took place in the midst of the pandemic. Through open-ended notes, shifting drafts, and sporadic e-mails written in remote, isolated locations, we explored the fibrous continuity of philosophy, nature, and design. – GK*

GÖKHAN KODALAK: You once defined your approach to architecture as "an exploration of the ways in which two disciplines and enterprises that are fundamentally outside of each other – architecture and philosophy – require a third space in which to interact without hierarchy, a space or position outside both, a space that doesn't yet exist."[2] Why did

1. See Elizabeth Grosz, *Architecture from the Outside: Essays on Virtual and Real Space* (Cambridge: MIT Press, 2001); "Deleuze, Theory, and Space," *Log* 1 (Fall 2003): 77–86.
2. Grosz, *Architecture from the Outside*, xv.

you, and do you still, consider architecture and philosophy *fundamentally* outside of each other? That is, why did you choose to start from the premise of an absolute bifurcation rather than conceiving architecture and philosophy as divergent fields of a shared continuum?

ELIZABETH GROSZ: As disciplines and practices, philosophy and architecture are obviously quite different, even to the extent that they must and do share overlapping interests and questions. We learn them differently, they involve different skills, they have different aims and ends, and have very different values and positions in social life. This is not to say that they cannot address similar questions and similar audiences or recipients. Questions linked to how we as humans are to live together, how we are to share our environments with other beings, how we ensure that all humans and their surroundings thrive and continue, are questions that have no definitive or final answers. There are points of convergence and places of overlap where each can fortify, or problematize, the other. Many philosophers are interested in architecture and architects interested in philosophy, but following Deleuze's understanding of the differences between concepts, affects, and formulas – the "objects" (which are never really objects) that direct and color philosophy, the arts, and the sciences with their own orientations and questions or tasks – I believe there are fundamental, but not irreconcilable or contradictory, differences between them.[3] How we approach each discipline is different; the objects each uses to develop their projects are different; their modes of creation and production are different. I do not think of this difference as a bifurcation or any form of dualism, for that would be to privilege one at the expense of the other (all dualisms are the prevalence of a single term and its negation, and thus all have the form of $A/-A$). This is not the relation of architecture and philosophy – they are not mutually exclusive or mutually exhaustive. Rather, as different, they can work together or not. They have a relation of outsideness in the sense that each requires the other only voluntarily or indirectly. I do not think of this outsideness as a gulf or chasm but rather as the kind of relations that only difference can bring – new questions, concepts, and methods to each other that are not contained in one or the other alone. They are divergent fields, but I am not sure that they are on a shared continuum. They may exist in contiguity, near each other, able to address certain questions each raises, yet preserve their differences, their own histories, points of

3. See Gilles Deleuze and Félix Guattari, *What Is Philosophy?*, trans. Hugh Tomlinson and Graham Burchell (New York: Columbia University Press, 1994).

internal contention and coherence. Perhaps one way of thinking this is that they are divergent fields in divergent continua that share certain interests and questions but not their resolutions or answers. I think of them as potential allies, "friends," or members of an intellectual and creative community that share allegiances and concerns but have different methods and specific ends.

GK: You are an ardent critic of bifurcating nature and culture, pitting them against each other, and subordinating one to the other. In a conference at Cornell University, you once posited that "this is as true for philosophy and cultural studies as it is for architecture: they have all participated in the ever firmer opposition between the natural and the cultural, rewriting the natural as the dissimulated product or effect of culture."[4] What is at stake in opposing this canonical bifurcation? And how can reconceiving nature and culture as horizontal extensions of one another orient us in our philosophical and architectural adventures when the world is under the constant pressure of ever-new ecological catastrophes due to our anthropocentric vanity and outdated beliefs in cultural supremacy?

EG: This is a very timely question! The overwhelming focus on culture at the expense of nature was part of an orientation, prevalent for at least the last three centuries, if not longer, of privileging the human over the natural environment at the expense of all the living beings that cooccupy the spaces we inhabit or exploit. And we have invented philosophies and theologies to justify this exploitation and destruction – we are "higher beings," rational or cultural, linguistic or technological beings, "chosen by God to rule" – and to mark the cultural realm as somehow above the natural and capable of superseding it. It is only because we are now facing the reality of climate change and, as you say, ecological catastrophes that many of us have returned to concepts we might previously have understood as purely cultural to see the debt they owe to nature itself. I don't think we should see nature and culture on an equal footing. This is our supreme arrogance as humans – to think we can reorder the natural world according to our needs and interests with no uncontrolled repercussions. Culture, human cultures (there are many, many different kinds of animal cultures as well, as the history of ethology demonstrates, from insect species to mammals and those species closest to us in evolutionary terms) are not equal

4. Grosz, "In-Between: The Natural in Architecture and Culture," in *Architecture from the Outside*, 96. This argument was initially presented in a paper at the conference "Constructing Identity: Between Architecture and Culture," Cornell University, Ithaca, New York, October 1997.

in any sense to the nature that surrounds and enables them. We could, and I think should, understand culture as one of the effects of nature rather than as a self-contained or equal partner. We are not other than animals ourselves, for we are animals that speak, build, and make. We are as much natural as we are cultural, something we commonly forget.

GK: The concept of nature has a charged history, however, and has remained controversial, even anathema, in various discourses of feminist, queer, and critical race theories because of its strategic abuse by those who tend to justify their constructed hierarchies as natural. You have never distanced yourself from exploring its thorny potentials. You even concocted volatile alchemical mixtures by fusing Luce Irigaray's sexual difference and Darwin's sexual selection,[5] Alfred Kinsey's statistical analysis of sexuality with Ilya Prigogine and Isabelle Stengers's systems on the edge of chaos,[6] and Spinoza's peculiar monism with corporeal feminism.[7] Meanwhile, you have synchronously opposed patriarchal architectural implications beneath established philosophical concepts such as Heidegger's dwelling (*Wohnen*), imagining instead "feminist reoccupations of space."[8] This triad of yours – feminism, nature, architecture – paves a multifarious path not traveled by many. How do you situate your feminist critique and practice with respect to nature and architecture today?

EG: I don't think my position has changed since *Architecture from the Outside* regarding the productive relations that are possible with a feminist understanding of sexual difference (and the differences that constitute human social life), nature, and the species with which we cohabit and even share our bodies (those of viral and bacterial nature). Given the pandemic we are enduring globally, it is ironic that we are now forced to understand and think more carefully about the intimate relations we share and depend on – the varying chains of connection that relate us by degrees to the whole of human, animal, and plant existence. We cannot understand ourselves as in any way the "masters," "controllers," or even "agents" of order in a global context. We are part of the world and not its masters. Our architectural models too, as well as our self-representations, have been dramatically affected by this epidemiological crisis and will require reconceiving not only our use of designed and manufactured spaces but also our relations to others and to nature. Nature, for those with some direct access to the outdoors, is the only

5. "While Irigaray does not herself refer to the writings of Darwin . . . she does confirm with him the inevitable and brilliant eruption into the world that the 'discovery' or advent of sexual difference brings with it: endless newness, the adventures of life forever incapable of being predicted, forever open to the vagaries of chance, history, temporality in ways that cannot be controlled or understood in advance." Elizabeth Grosz, *Becoming Undone: Darwinian Reflections on Life, Politics, and Art* (Durham: Duke University Press, 2011), 103–04.
6. See Elizabeth Grosz, "The Future of Female Sexuality," in *Time Travels: Feminism, Nature, Power* (Sydney: Allen & Unwin, 2005), 197–215.
7. "In displacing the mind/body dualism, Spinoza is also upsetting the prevailing oppositions between nature and culture, between essence and social construction. . . . If Cartesianism today indicates a problematic site for feminist theory and for theories of subjectivity, perhaps the kinds of non-Cartesian accounts initiated by Spinoza . . . may prove more fruitful and useful for feminist purposes." Elizabeth Grosz, *Volatile Bodies: Toward a Corporeal Feminism* (Bloomington: Indiana University Press, 1994), 12–13.
8. See Elizabeth Grosz, "Women, *Chora*, Dwelling," in *Space, Time, and Perversion: Essays on the Politics of Bodies* (London: Routledge, 1995), 111–25.

restorative to our alienation from others and from the work we usually undertake. Most office workers have moved out of offices; many stores are closed; a large percentage of commercial buildings is currently not being used. We have a moment in which to reassess our priorities, a small pause for reflection on whether to continue to produce monstrous towers for the privileged, as before, or to reconsider our relations to community living and to natural forces, relations that ground and connect us to the world. Many architects, philosophers, feminists, and anti-racist activists understand that we are on the cusp of perhaps rethinking how we may best live, what values we should develop, and what we owe to the Earth and to future generations. This will involve us each addressing, in our own ways, the question of the cost of each thing we have, not just its financial cost but its political, social, and ecological cost. I don't think feminism is better set up to address these questions than, say, queer theory, anti-racist and multicultural politics, climate activism and animal activism; but *in conjunction*, a more careful consideration of the relations between humans and nature, and between building and its environment(s), can lead to new kinds of architecture, and not just architecture for elites. How we are to live collectively for the next decades without destroying ourselves and our environments, without privileging one group over another, is the most pressing question for architecture today.

GK: Your system of thought is also swarming with animals. You study animal sexuality, ask how elephants make love, and try to understand the pleasures of the orangutan, the snake, and the spider.[9] You argue that "art is the sexualization of survival or, equally, sexuality is the rendering artistic . . . of nature."[10] You explore animal aesthetics, postulating that "art begins with the animal" and that "what is most artistic in us is that which is the most bestial."[11] This inquiry forms yet another triad of yours – animal, sex, art – which you weave together via the work of ethologists like Roger Caillois, Jakob von Uexküll, and Konrad Lorenz, as well as the philosophy of Deleuze and Guattari and the theoretical biology of Darwin. Does architecture begin with the animal as well? Can architecture, among its never-ending characterizations, be also defined as the sexualization of survival?

EG: Yes, I think architecture is the first of the arts and that it too begins with the animal, perhaps with the insect. It was Bernard Cache's *Earth Moves*, part of the Writing

9. See Grosz, "Animal Sex: Libido as Desire and Death," in *Space, Time, and Perversion*, 187–207.
10. Elizabeth Grosz, *Chaos, Territory, Art: Deleuze and the Framing of the Earth* (New York: Columbia University Press, 2008), 11.
11. Ibid., 35; 63.

12. See Bernard Cache, *Earth Moves: The Furnishing of Territories*, trans. Anne Boyman, ed. Michael Speaks (Cambridge: MIT Press, 1995).

Architecture series, that first convinced me of the fundamentally animal nature of architecture.[12] With the "frame," a boundary around a particular space, both art and architecture are enabled, opened up, and proliferate. The frame is the creation of the line between "home" and "outside." Inside the frame – perhaps we could think of it as a boundary line, a line traced by pegs, or fences, or a specific scent, or carefully placed leaves, branches, or stones – is the space of safety, or of sexuality, play, protection, family; outside indicates a place of chaotic noncontrol and potential danger. The first architecture is this boundary that enables protected activities. The hive, burrow, bower preexist the human home, and sometimes the animal predecessor even inspires human architecture. I believe that the creation of a "territory," a space surrounding the home, a space of movement and activity outside it, is indeed the potential for the sexualization of survival, which cannot be species survival without a significant place, and energy, devoted to sexual activities, whether reproductive or not. Darwin's greatest insight is not the survival of the fittest and natural selection – there were many others, including his own grandfather, Erasmus, who posited a struggle for existence; it was the profound and creative role of sexual selection, the selection of pleasing partners, which may or may not result in offspring, that he saw as the energetic force involved in the creative arts, including architecture, but most especially in song or sound (which for Darwin are the predecessors of language), in visual and aural spectacles, which are the evolutionary origins of the human arts and architecture. Architecture, as the first of the arts, enables the space of safety necessary for the creation of the sonorous, visual, and olfactory arts and is itself enhanced and made more alluring through these arts. It enables a direct sexualization of survival by providing a relatively safe space for activities that move beyond the sustenance of life to enhance and complicate survival.

GK: Lines, however, are curious creatures that cannot be reduced to setting boundaries. They harbor capacities for deframing and deterritorializing as much as framing and territorializing. Speculating about "the first architecture" has its own charged history, but I have always found the boundary-based and territory-focused conceptions of architecture in Deleuze and Cache a bit too introverted and conservative. Perhaps neither the framing line (with its domestic, boundary-defining ethos, call for safety, and alliance with the cosmic order) nor the deframing line (with its strange, boundary-defying tenet, call for danger, and alliance with chaotic disorder) leads to architecture alone, but a peculiar fusion of the two. As in James Joyce's concept of "chaosmos" that defines chaos and cosmos no longer as opposites, but as symbiotic dimensions of life's generative continuum: "Every person, place and thing in the chaosmos of Alle anyway connected . . . was moving and changing every part of the time . . . variously inflected, differently pronounced, otherwise spelled."[13]

EG: You are absolutely right about this. The line of boundary as the signal of a space of safety is to some extent phantasmatic, imaginary, or wishful, in the animal as much as the human. In reality, no space is absolutely safe, guaranteed, permanent, or impregnable, and no space is absolutely deterritorialized, free of lines of movement or habitual practices, for it is mapped and lined by activities at very different levels and scales. Each, the framed and the deframed, runs into the other, and each tends toward the other, the framing process being more provisional and more energy dependent than the movements of deframing. This is more than the forces of entropy, however, for the dynamisms of life require provisional or temporary frames, homes, safe spaces, even as there can be no guarantee of their provisional status or the safety of their inhabitants. The cosmos is chaotic, which is how forms of life survive: by creating provisional patterns, lines, energies, practices that temporarily hold chaos at bay while contributing to its forces.

GK: You also pay special attention to the efficacy of nonorganic modalities in terms of their ability to affect and be affected (in the Spinozist sense), their varying degrees of openness to the future and becoming (in the Bergsonian sense), and their capacity to invent new ways of actualizing their virtual potentials (in the Deleuzian sense). Following these complementary lines of thought to their logical conclusion, you even imply that nonorganic modalities can be considered alive: "Not only do plants and animals have unactualized virtuals, and various paths of actualization, so too do volcanoes, oceans, weather patterns, planets, solar systems."[14] From this unorthodox perspective, are architectural modalities also alive? And how can reconceiving architectural modalities as exuberant subjects, active and full of life, reorient our relationship with them?

13. James Joyce, *Finnegans Wake*, ed. Robbert-Jan Henkes, Erik Bindervoet, and Finn Fordham (Oxford: Oxford University Press, 2012), 118. There is in Joyce's "chaosmos of Alle" a strong hint of Giordano Bruno's immanent conception of an infinitely self-modifying cosmos: "The universe is in all things and all things are in the universe, we in it and it in us." Giordano Bruno, *Cause, Principle and Unity, and Essays on Magic*, ed. Richard J. Blackwell and Robert de Lucca (Cambridge: Cambridge University Press, 2004), 90. First published as *De la Causa, Principio et Uno* in 1584.
14. Elizabeth Grosz, *The Incorporeal: Ontology, Ethics, and the Limits of Materialism* (New York: Columbia University Press, 2017), 150.

EG: This is a tough question and I don't have a direct answer. I do not think that volcanoes, oceans, the weather, etc., are alive, but certainly they are unpredictable and incapable of calculation according to our current forms of knowledge. They are not alive because they do not make themselves. This distinguishes them from their raw materials – subatomic fields, atoms, molecules – which in a sense can be understood, without animism, as alive to the extent that they are self-forming and self-regulating. They "know," as we do not, what connections they are capable of, what their actions are. Following the philosophy of Raymond Ruyer, I think we must distinguish between things that make/know themselves and things composed from the outside, piece by piece, or by accretion. While volcanoes, oceans, and the weather have their own laws, rhythms, and practices – which we are far from properly understanding or predicting – as well as their virtualities, their unpredictable forms of behaving, they are formed by aggregates, through many "parts" that may have formed themselves. They are mass phenomena formed by laws or principles but not self-regulating or self-ordering. Architecture, except in very rare and metaphorical cases (for example, a bird's nest, where the shape and size of both the bird and its eggs direct the creation and form of the nest, which, significantly, the bird hatched from an egg housed and nurtured in the nest is destined to repeat and build), is made piece by piece, planned and replanned in advance, and is incapable of healing or restoring itself (as most living beings can, depending on the degree of wound or damage). Architecture as we generally know it is passive, relatively open to different peoples and practices, requiring some maintenance and repair, prone to undo itself without external effort. Can we produce a more "alive" kind of architecture? I believe we can, and that significant experiments have already occurred in this direction (for example, Diller + Scofidio's Blur Building), where there is perhaps a built infrastructure but the architectural object is more an event than an object. But overall, it is in the interest of expediency that we still require housing that, in itself, cannot be alive except metaphorically, with the acts that occur in it.

GK: Every architect would want to believe their buildings are metaphorically alive. The more provocative and timely question is, can architectural modalities – as well as volcanoes, oceans, tornadoes – be considered *ontologically* alive? This is a question that has yet to be seriously addressed in architecture, which would require stepping back from the almost automatic *no* that pops up in our minds, having been indoctrinated for millennia with the givenness of the sacred duality of life versus nonlife. Yet it all depends on how we define life. Our paradigmatic definitions so far, from Aristotle's *De Anima* and soul-based conceptions in scholastic theologies to Carl Linnaeus's modern biological update in *Systema Naturae* and the current dissensus among life scientists who cannot decide whether viruses are living creatures or nonliving automatons, are not very assuring for the simple reason that they all take for granted an absolute separation at the heart of nature, splitting it into animate and inanimate dimensions, active subjects and passive objects, modalities alive on one side, lifeless on the other. But what if there is no such bifurcation in nature? What if life is not a binary mechanism but a spectrum participated by each and every mode of existence with differing degrees of activation? What if the formative lives of subatomic fields, atoms, and molecules are continuous with buildings, oceans, and planets, just as they are with embryos, brains, and organisms? What if rather than characterizing life with *self*-centered concepts (like self-formation, self-regulation, self-organization, self-sufficiency), we choose to define life with *relational* concepts, as the channeling of cosmic potentials of existence (being, acting, and informing) into reciprocal capacities of enacting and undergoing open-ended change (affecting and being affected)? Perhaps only then can we appreciate the vitality and nonmechanical generativity of volcanoes, oceans, and tornadoes. Only then can we resist defining buildings as passive, inert, and lifeless, and entertain the demonic thought that architectural modalities are *literally alive*.

EG: I completely agree that the opposition between the living and the nonliving, between mind and matter, nature and culture, or vital and mechanical – which are all versions of the same distinction – is misleading. There is a relation, but not a dualism, between them. There is no unformed passive matter, only matter in different states of organization; it is our hubris that leads us to believe that the material world is there for our use alone, that matter is there for our needs and aspirations without residue or cost to us and to materiality, and especially to the animate materiality we understand as nature. But I would still want to distinguish between the self-formation of the smallest of material elements – atoms, subatomic components or clouds of influence, molecules – and the formation of oceans, volcanoes, and indeed architecture, or at least human architecture.

15. "While the intellect masters that in the world which we need for our purposes, it is fundamentally incapable of understanding what in the world, in objects, and in us, is fluid, innumerable, outside calculation. . . . This is a prescient image of digitization: the recomposition of the [continuous] whole through its decomposition into pixel-like units." Grosz, *Architecture from the Outside*, 179–80.
16. See Grosz, *The Incorporeal*.

GK: Speaking of animacy, you are critical of architectural approaches that prefer objects to processes, things to the flux of the real, and pixel-like units as digitized by the binary code of zeros and ones to the underlying continuum of movements and relations.[15] This oppositional setup of object versus process still maintains its conceptual appeal in architectural circles today. And among those who acknowledge such a distinction, the dominant tendency has been on the side of rigid objects over continuous processes. Yet what if this opposition is itself a trap forcing us to choose one dimension of architectural modalities over the other? That is, aren't architectural modalities *both* objects and nouns with durational perseverance *and* events and verbs undergoing constant change? Aren't modality and modification, individuality and individuation, being and becoming different dimensions of one and the same activity of existence, not just of architecture but of the cosmos as such?

EG: I agree that it is a trap to think of object and process or digital and analog as an opposition. Clearly, we need both and we don't really have a choice in this. But we also need to be careful about what we attribute to these terms. Objects are subjected to change, to history, to transformation, but we commonly don't think of these changes or history as having a real relevance to our understanding of the object (a rock, for example, is what it is – it has a history but most of us cannot access this history nor do we usually find it a relevant question). Objects are made and unmade by processes, and processes, it can be speculated, can perhaps occur without the solidity of objects and before there are objects. In a sense, the answer to your question about the cosmos – Isn't it both being and becoming? – is necessarily true: the universe must have both to be what it is now. But whether we can create a process architecture is a more difficult question.

GK: Your latest book, *The Incorporeal: Ontology, Ethics, and the Limits of Materialism*, traces a subterranean lineage of thinkers from the Stoics, Spinoza, and Nietzsche to Deleuze, Gilbert Simondon, and Ruyer in their quest to explain the cosmos in terms of not just material conditions and corporeal formations but also immaterial ideas and incorporeal forces.[16] With this selective tracing, you participate in the highly charged conflict between materialism and idealism. You seem to be against reductionist versions of *both* materialism and idealism, as you argue that the corporeal and the incorporeal,

the material and the ideal, operate *confluently* as the visible
and invisible dimensions of life. How does this third position
address the problems of explaining life (in its ontological and
epistemological dimensions), as well as living and experienc-
ing life (in its ethical and aesthetic dimensions), that materialism and idealism on their own limited accounts cannot? And
what are the latent consequences of reconceiving architecture, not just in terms of material formation, but also immaterial information?

EG: The problem with dualism – the assumption that matter
and ideas are mutually exclusive and occupy different orders
or realms – is its incoherence, its perfect ordering of a world
with its two poles irreconcilably divided, which cannot
explain adequately how ideas might influence materials and
how materials may direct the flow of ideas – that is, their
fundamental connectedness. Dualism affirms a doubleness of
being with no way of understanding how each order informs
and regulates the other. The most common response to dualism, especially in the last 150 years, has been reductionism,
especially the reduction of ideas to the material and electrical workings of the brain, or now, the electronic working of
a computer. My work has been an attempt to move beyond
reductionisms of all kinds – both materialism and idealism
reduce their "other" to an attenuated version of themselves
– and to restore some sense of the belonging together of ideas
and materials. There are no unformed materials: all materials
are found or created in specific forms; and there are no preexisting forms or ideas that materials passively conform to or
automatically reproduce.

Architecture is founded on some version of this assumption of dualism, although there are examples of resistance
to its norms. Design ideas come first and then, through
sketching, drawing, and modeling, through reiterating and
correcting, a built structure is made. This conception of
architectural planning and building arises from a kind of
unconsidered dualism. I don't want to dispute that architectural plans come before building, but I would want to
complicate these processes to make more explicit the material elements of design – one doesn't design in one's head
alone. What one designs with and how are as material as they
are ideal. Using CAD or a pencil, using this kind of paper or
that are material elements of design that are often subsumed
under idealism, even as they are clearly material; and using
concrete, steel, bricks, glass to build a structure is not purely

material, because materials themselves are already informed and differentiated by ideas. No practice is concept-free, just as no idea exists purely abstractly without words or representation. The self-representations of architecture may affirm some kind of dualism, but the actual practices of architects, if all their details are noted, continually mix together these two categories, as they should. There is no matter, especially built matter, that is free of concepts or ideas, and there are no ideas that simply exist without verbal or representational expression. Architecture, taken with a small dose of philosophy, makes clear the inseparability of materials and idea(l)s. In life as in architecture, we never experience either materials or ideas in their purity: they are always already "mixed," mutually engaged without the possibility of anything but an abstract separation.

GK: Lately you have been focusing on Ruyer, a postwar philosopher of biology, cybernetics, and ethicoaesthetics.[17] Although Ruyer invented captivating concepts such as "embryogenesis," "neofinalism," and "self-survey," he is almost unknown in the fields of architecture and design.[18] In *The Incorporeal*, you write, "Ruyer aspires to an ontoethics and ontoaesthetics that address the creativity of the world and the openness of the future."[19] How does Ruyer fuse ontology, the study of being, with ethicoaesthetics, the study of value, sense, and axiology? And what does he mean by "the creativity of the world"? Is there a Spinozist influence here, as in the infinite creativity of nature immanently subsisting in each and every one of our transfinite acts and beings?

EG: Ruyer is strikingly different from any other philosopher I have read. He must have read Spinoza, but I would not consider him a Spinozist. He seems to resist being too closely identified with other philosophers or philosophical traditions, and it is significant that the most striking influences on his philosophical writings are the knowledges of embryology, geology, psychoanalysis, and cybernetics, which he acquired while incarcerated by the Germans during World War II at Oflag XVII-A.[20] He has developed a philosophy of the self-creating, self-organizing being that allows us to see a continuity of existence for what he calls "primary consciousness," an inarticulable consciousness of its own doing/making, a "fibrous continuity" that links the universe and its constituents to a self-making we do not yet understand, a self-making that occupies the embryos of every species, but which we

17. To date, only two of Ruyer's books, out of more than 20, have been translated into English: *Neofinalism*, trans. Alyosha Edlebi (Minneapolis: University of Minnesota Press, 2016); *The Genesis of Living Forms*, trans. Jon Roffe and Nicholas B. de Weydenthal (Lanham: Rowman & Littlefield, 2019).

18. There are two notable exceptions to the architectural neglect of Ruyer's thinking. First, there was a recent seminar on The Architecture of Neo-finalism (Autumn 2020) cotaught at TU Delft's Faculty of Architecture and the Built Environment by Andrej Radman and Stavros Kousoulas, who have since been increasingly channeling Ruyer's thinking into their discourse. Second, there is Toufik Hammoudi's recently defended dissertation, "Théorie des formes et formes des théories: Essai architectural de morphologie générale" (The University of Paris 8 Vincennes-Saint-Denis, December 2019), which explores the question of morphology by engaging Ruyer's philosophy.

19. Grosz, *The Incorporeal*, 211.

20. Ruyer describes his earliest intellectual formation in a radio interview as follows: "I had the luck of having, as my companions in captivity, eminent biologists: Moyse, Vivien and above all Et. Wolff, who presented admirable lessons on development and teratology. With pleasure and surprise, I observed that experimental scientists could appreciate philosophical theses of a quite unorthodox scientific character to the same degree that I appreciated their careful analyses of the facts. For my part, I presented courses in our university barracks that drew on articles in biological philosophy that I had already published. These courses, reedited, became *Éléments de psycho-biologie* [Elements of Psychobiology]. Above all, though, I had the good fortune to attract the attention of F. Ellenberger, a young geologist with a true gift for meticulous, tenacious observation, free of all prejudice. Along with a whole team of geologists, Ellenberger studied the fossilized wood that was unearthed by the tunnels dug for failed escape attempts." Raymond Ruyer, "Ruyer in his Own Words," trans. Jon Roffe (unpublished). Published in French as "Raymond Ruyer par lui-même," *Les Études philosophiques* 1 (January 2007): 3–14.

21. See Gilbert Simondon, *Individuation in Light of Notions of Form and Information*, trans. Taylor Adkins (Minneapolis: University of Minnesota Press, 2020); *On the Mode of Existence of Technical Objects*, trans. Cecile Malaspina and John Rogove (Minneapolis: Univocal, 2016); "The Genesis of the Individual," in *ZONE 6: Incorporations*, ed. Jonathan Crary and Sanford Kwinter (New York: Zone Books, 1992), 296–319. Significant secondary literature in English includes: Gilles Deleuze, "On Gilbert Simondon," in *Desert Islands and Other Texts, 1953–1974*, ed. David Lapoujade, trans. Mike Taormina (Los Angeles: Semiotext(e), 2004), 86–89; Muriel Combes, *Gilbert Simondon and the Philosophy of the Transindividual*, trans. Thomas LaMarre (Cambridge: MIT Press, 2012); Grosz, "Simondon and the Preindividual," in *The Incorporeal*, 169–208; Bernard Stiegler, *Technics and Time, 1: The Fault of Epimetheus*, trans. Richard Beardsworth and George Collins (Stanford: Stanford University Press, 1998).

22. Simondon's philosophy is only now being addressed in relation to architecture: Gökhan Kodalak, "Simondon, the Question of Technology, and the Architectural Margin of Indeterminacy," *Footprint* 30 (forthcoming); Andrej Radman, "Machinic Phylum and Architecture," in *Proceedings of the 2020 DigitalFUTURES*, ed. Philip F. Yuan et al. (Singapore: Springer, 2021), 3–16; Muriel Combes, "On Nature," *Log* 49 (Summer 2020): 146–63; Peter Trummer, "Notes on Mechanology," *Log* 49 (Summer 2020): 164–67; Stavros Kousoulas, "Shattering the black box: Technicities of architectural manipulation," *International Journal of Architectural Computing* 16, no. 4 (December 1, 2018): 295–305; Katie Lloyd Thomas, "'Between the womb and the world': building matrixial relations in the NICU," in *Relational Architectural Ecologies: Architecture, Nature and Subjectivity*, ed. Peg Rawes (Routledge: London, 2013), 192–208; Georges Teyssot, *A Topology of Everyday Constellations* (Cambridge: MIT Press, 2013).

generally only understand mechanistically or from the outside. Ruyer is interested in the creativity of these self-creating and self-regulating activities, for example, when our bodies heal themselves from minor injuries, the creativity of animal and plant species that make their limbs, leaves, and branches. Our aesthetic activities, when we undertake to design, build, or make anything, to write anything, also have to invent a way to come into existence. We begin with an idea that indicates a possible direction for work to occur. This direction is not ours, one we bring with us, but is suggested or implied by the task we aim to accomplish. We must deviate our actions and ideas through this strange and often unknown itinerary in order to accomplish the end we seek. This process of bringing something into existence without a necessarily clear trajectory is the search for aesthetic or intellectual ends. It aestheticizes ends because our means of attaining them must be invented, created, thought each time anew.

GK: According to Simondon, whose work you also like to unpack through your own, we have developed two primary yet problematic modes of approach with respect to technology.[21] We either imagine technical objects as if they were our "slaves," render them passive and inert, and reduce their unique modes of existence to mere reflections of our own intentions and desires, or we elevate them to become our transcendent masters, attribute supernatural powers to them, and either fear their apocalyptic prospects or worship their almighty capabilities with messianic expectations. Architecture is not exempt from such pitfalls, as the next cutting-edge technology – whether algorithmic coding, robotics, AI, 3D printing, or blockchain – is either naively embraced or paranoidly opposed by many.[22] Have you developed a third position beyond this problematic binary of naive technophilia and paranoid technophobia?

EG: Our relation to technology is complicated and commonly unconsidered insofar as virtually all of us are now engaged in direct technological mediations of our world. There is no untechnological relation we can have with our environment, and I suspect that this was true long before computer-mediated technologies; technics is coterminous with social existence, and not just human existence. I am not sure that we can move to a third position beyond technophilia and technophobia. We need technophilia to ensure the ongoing elaboration and increasing openness of technical objects and systems, to the extent that we as living beings have always required prosthetic objects, material enhancements, from clothing to housing to electronics, to ensure the transmission of information and objects. But we also require a kind of balanced technophobia that resists, insofar as it can, the encroachments of technology, especially information-seeking technologies, technologies we don't always pay for but that surround and enmesh us. Along with Simondon and his understanding of the ways in which technics enhances and complicates all kinds of cultures, animal as well as human, we need also to keep in mind Foucault's insight that power and knowledge require each other. The technologies that worry me are not entirely hidden and have had their critics from the time of their emergence. I am thinking here of social media, "free" forms of electronic access to social interactions, whose primary function is access to information from its users, rather than for its users, to place advertising in a manner where it is most effective, and to seek as much generalizable knowledge about its users as possible. We have willingly entered into an electronic panopticon, where we are seen but cannot see who sees us. Many of us have calculated that having free access to our friends and to news and social relations mediated by various platforms is worth the cost of giving up personal information, becoming "known" for one's preferences, interests, and fantasies.

In short, I don't think we should abandon a skeptical attitude toward technics: we shouldn't uncritically revel in the conveniences it provides, nor should we abandon or give up on technical developments in building, manufacturing, and so on. Rather, we need to develop specific understandings of what surrounds and enables technologies, and above all, what their costs and potentials may be for us and the planetary ecology.

Gökhan Kodalak is an architect, theorist, and historian. He teaches at Pratt Institute and is the Theories of Architecture fellow at TU Delft.

Sanford Kwinter

Reality: Virtual, Augmented, Transpersonal[1]

Beings can be known by means of the knowledge of the subject, but the individuation of beings cannot be grasped except by the individuation of the knowledge of the subject.
— Gilbert Simondon, *L'individuation psychique et collective*

Fascination with the varieties of spatial experience have all but commandeered architectural attention in recent years. The transformation has been steady but piecemeal, the outcome of several developments that include the ascendance of the graphic display module, the algorithmically impelled line, the advent of motion capture, immersive environments, AI sensing, environmentalism, interest in non-Western philosophies and postclassical sciences, renewed attention to the senses and cognitive sciences, as well as the ready availability of once-prohibitive simulation equipment, reality consoles, and so on. The best architectures have always invoked the transformation of human possibility. While the current trends and developments typically lack the language or postures with which to formulate such sweeping ambitions, they nonetheless harbor the seeds of transfigurations whose scope the field has almost never ventured to imagine. The question of whether the field follows the trivial neoliberal path of technical adoption and pseudo-mastery or whether it follows potentials far more deeply deposited in our civilization's organic destiny weighs in the balance. Either way, the question of human becoming and understanding, achievable through the drive to access, with our biological instruments and endowments, what is not yet known, and evidenced in the tradition of the philosophers presented in the first part of this three-part series in Log *— Spinoza, Alfred North Whitehead, and Gilbert Simondon — can now be properly considered within the intimacy of its direct inherence in the physical world. As such, the task for designers-shapers of the phenomenal world is ours to claim.*

As a philosopher, I am not a specialist in problems of cognitive neuroscience and philosophy of mind as are many of those whose work I address here. I have, however, followed developments in

1. The term *transpersonal* belongs today almost uniquely to the field of psychology and consciousness studies and refers to components of mental life that are not fully locatable within the immediate historical or spatial limits of the subject. From a philosophical perspective the term can usefully be related to more general cosmological models such as the "pre-individual," the holographic, or even noo-cosmic. I would like to express my gratitude and debt here to Johan Bettum and Daniel Birnbaum of the Staedelschule in Frankfurt, who over the last five years have provided me with the field's richest context for the exploration of these topics alongside the immense resources around Wolf Singer and the Frankfurt Institute for Advanced Studies and related institutions.

*formal neurobiology since the early 1990s, when I had occasion to
republish Kurt Goldstein's seminal work of theoretical neurology,*
The Organism: A Holistic Approach to Biology Derived from
Pathological Data in Man *(1934). The principles in this work
I still hold to be foundational today. These principles were initially
pursued in a compendium that I coedited around the same time
titled* ZONE 6: Incorporations, *which included a substantial
treatment of models that sought to elucidate the relations between
brain, self, and world from a diversity of positions ranging from the
laboratory research of Gerald Edelman (Neural Darwinism) to
the philosophical neurobiology of Francisco Varela (autopoiesis)
and the psychoanalytic thought of Viktor Tausk, among others.*
Incorporations *was not conceived to be a work about mind, perception, or consciousness as such but rather about the shift in scientific
and philosophical explanation to qualitative phenomena and a speculation on what the consequences of this shift might be for human
culture, destiny, and understanding. It was a work that sought to
usher in a broad ecological approach to both the humanities and the
human sciences, with a particular emphasis on the status of matter
as a center of concern and source of revelation. But while this second principle – the so-called matter problem – achieved substantial impact and influence in the design and art communities, the
broader, more transformative ecological principle sadly did not.
What follows here represents an effort to reset that deeper project.*

The Integrative Hypothesis

The field of modern brain study, from the moment it split
off from materialist perceptual psychology, arose out of the
"organismalist" problem of *integration* in early 20th-century
theoretical biology. C.S. Sherrington's 1906 founding text
and masterwork, *The Integrative Action of the Nervous System,*
advanced two enduring constitutional principles that merit
being continually reforegrounded today: 1) the nervous system is revealed in its *action,* not its physiology, and 2) its principal operation is integrative; its task is to bind all forms of
variety into coherent, operational wholes.

Three decades later, Kurt Goldstein foregrounded the
word *holistic* in the title of his own field compendium. He also
included the term *Aufbau* – or structure – of the organism, a
word that is dropped in the English translation but is throughout conceptually tied to both action and integration. The third
essential tenet of Goldstein's work is that the mind reveals
considerably more of its functional nature – its "structure"
– if attention is rather paid to ("pathological") non-normal
states and functioning.

The integrative imperative remains universal in the neurosciences even today. It refers to how the brain *connects* and *organizes* across two principal domains: it unifies disparate streams of sensory processing within the organism itself – say, the color, shape, and location of something in the world – into a single efficient (usable, bankable) percept, and it connects the organism to the world beyond in a primordial and active way through what I have called the "cognitive-environmental circuit,"[2] by which each system ultimately undergoes continuous sympathetic modification by the other. For simplicity, I refer to those systems here as self and world, reluctantly and only in deference to the convention accepted by popular philosophers such as Thomas Metzinger and Andy Clark.[3]

The continuous structural modification of the organism by the physical world, the *sculpting*, as it is termed in neurobiology, happens across a variety of timeframes. At the slower end of the spectrum, it refers to how environmental niches shape populations and species across generations through Darwinian selection and pressure – we call this adaptation – and at the more rapid end, and most dramatically in humans, it shapes brain structure and behavioral patterns through the mechanism of neural plasticity. The first is conventionally described as a *phylogenetic* process, in which new features are generated and distributed across a group or species; the second as an *ontogenetic* process in which a single organism undergoes an individuation specific primarily to it but within a range arguably shared by a generation, community, or population. In both instances we have to do with a *coupling phenomenon*, each process operating at different time scales to generate a different scale and depth of effect.

The principal importance here is that nervous activity is *performative*, not simply responsive – it invents, it creates, and it shapes.[4] Without this impetus there is no salience, no distinction; there is, as the Ancients would say, no *Logos*, no intelligence or intelligibility (and certainly no bankable or storable order). In sum, there is *nothing to perceive because there is no perception*, and not the other way round.

Earlier this year, a paper published in *Nature Neuroscience* generated considerable buzz and widespread headlines in the popular press.[5] The paper described the change in laboratory mice behavior brought about by artificially inducing a synchrony – a sympathy of temporal structure – in the brains of two interacting mice. By coordinating an optic pulse in the brains of two separate beings who share a context – a shared spatiotemporal environment – there emerged distinct

2. Sanford Kwinter, "Neuroecology: Notes Toward a Synthesis," in Warren Neidich, ed., *The Psychopathologies of Cognitive Capitalism: Two* (Berlin: Archive Books, 2015); and Sanford Kwinter, "The World as Cognitive-Environmental Circuit," in Allen Sayegh, Stefano Andreani, Matteo Kalchschmidt, eds., *Responsive Environments: An Interdisciplinary Manifesto on Design, Technology and the Human Experience* (Barcelona: Actar, 2021).

3. See Thomas Metzinger, *The Ego Tunnel: The Science of the Mind and the Myth of the Self* (New York: Basic Books, 2009). Andy Clark's primary contribution to popular cultural memes is *Supersizing the Mind: Embodiment, Action, and Cognitive Extension* (New York: Oxford University Press, 2008).

4. This includes the critical, definition- and affordance-producing process of "chunking." Chunking is not only a routinized process of organizing worldly sensory features into meanings, it is also a process of creating sensations on the fly. See Erin Manning, *Always More Than One: Individuation's Dance* (Durham: Duke University Press, 2013), 219–21.

5. See Y. Yang, et al., "Wireless multilateral devices for optogenentic studies of individual and social behaviors," *Nature Neuroscience* 24 (2021): 1035–45; Virginia Hughes, "Scientists Drove Mice to Bond by Zapping Their Brains with Light," *New York Times*, May 25, 2021.

phenomena of interbrain behavioral synchrony in which the mice began to operate as a highly unified and close-knit – empathic, cooperative – dyadic being. Beyond the technical novelty of the optogenetic devices used to artificially effectuate the connection, the findings were significant for another reason, for they brought attention to a perennially overlooked problem of neurocognitive research: that brains are evolved principally to operate within an extended system of other brains. The principle may be stated starkly: the "environment" to which the nervous system of a highly encephalized species such as the human is "attached" – and through attachment, attuned – is comprised not only of physical structures and meaning systems but other subjects, groups, behaviors, and co-modifications, and not only "minds" but moods, body states, and coordinated, coregulating *actions* that ensue therefrom. When we speak about "the environment," we must speak about the spectrum of sensory particulars that invest it.[6]

Economic science has often accommodated this basic principle, as have some disciplines of psychology, particularly paleo- and evolutionary neurology and developmental psychology. The "Social Brain Hypothesis" proposed in the 1990s by Robin Dunbar is a prominent anthropological example, as are the plethora of early attachment studies (notably, Melanie Klein, John Bowlby, and Daniel Stern). But mainstream neuroscience and philosophical consciousness studies have largely not integrated these elementary principles, a fact, I would argue, that has significantly hampered its progress and corrupted many of its findings.

To state the problem as extravagantly as possible at the outset: any accounting of consciousness must start from the assumption that it is not rigidly located within a single brain or body, that it is always a product of complex correlation involving not only the physical environment but also a variety of nested time scales, the participation and intermodulation of other apparent consciousnesses, as well as real energetic and informational reserves that have been acquired in real experience (memories and somatic accretions) but can be recognized, tapped, and reactivated after having been somatically and psychically encoded, only via nonstandard or non-ordinary states that provide access to anamnesis. This is arguably as true of traumatic experience as it is of states of transcendence and bliss associated with pre- or perinatal completion. The difficulty of creating access to these now embedded virtual states requires laborious preparation, cultivation, and relaxation of guardian structures in the body-mind whose

6. The literature on this topic is vast, but the principle itself is rarely accounted for outside of developmental psychology.

marriage, and whose union alone, is what constitutes consciousness. These include the multiplicity of therapeutic techniques and methodologies, as well as many techniques of induction that represent what Goldstein would refer to as the "pathological states" that reveal to us in a privileged way what the mind is. These include entheogenic medicines, shamanic ritual, meditation, trance, sensory deprivation, fasting, massage, music, and other controls and transformations of the sensory environment. The technologically assisted virtual reality experience is one such non-ordinary form of induction.[7]

Interest

To elucidate the situation described above, consider the types of noetic experience discoverable in human attentional practice through the engagement with music specifically and with sound generally. We know that the first sensation encountered by an in utero human embryo of an external "nonself" domain arrives in the form of sound waves from the maternal environment, which includes both the lived world in which the mother moves and the mother's body itself. As a rule, these first basic sensations of information pickup occur within the amniotic surround in which no divisions have yet been undertaken, where there is as yet no boundary between what is sensed and what does the sensing, where the thermal and nutritional satisfactions are still at blissful equilibrium, and hence, where a full and seamless continuity remains the rule. Within this matrix there arises also a small quotient of "interest" in the form of a gentle modulating tonal stimulus. It is known that the more advanced the nervous system, the greater the requirement for stimulus, without which the highly encephalized organism cannot survive. In the case of humans, the prenatal and newborn brain develops 100,000 new connections *per second*, none of which will survive without repeated activation by signals transiting through them. The mortal requirement – driven by and supported by "interest" in the world – is to engage and feast on the flux of signals and changes in the environment. But for now, previous to the individuating maturation processes that give rise to the "self," the state remains one of implicit fullness, completion, and bliss.

Many later life experiences will trigger the somatopsychic record of this presumptive early state to one degree or another. Again, one significant feature of this state is the absence of separation and discontinuity, the absence of partitioning scaffolds that articulate experience, as well as the

7. On the structure and dynamics of trauma registration, see what has become the standard work on the topic, Bessel van der Kolk, *The Body Keeps the Score: Mind, Brain, Body in the Transformation of Trauma* (New York: Viking Penguin, 2014). My use of the term *anamnesis* here is intended to carry a twofold meaning: the standard medical reference to a patient's account of their personal history and the Platonic reference to remembrance of collective and nonpersonal knowledge, a perplexing but often reported feature of ecstatic states. This is a principal theme of the Transpersonal Psychology school founded by Abraham Maslow, Stanislav Grof, and Anthony Sutich. The term is William James's. Interestingly, on the basis of several of his lesser-known writings, Jean Piaget has recently been conscripted as a posthumous member. The theory of mind developed within this still very active school draws frequently and often substantially on Buddhist and Hindu cosmologies even when it departs from accepted scientific principles in ways that they do not.

implicit feeling that one is in the presence of some type of enduring vital and restorative excellence. This feature, as William James famously argued, not only cannot be ignored by our accounts of reality but in fact might most fruitfully be placed at its center.[8] James's study *The Varieties of Religious Experience* does not treat religion specifically, but rather the *states of mind* in which the varieties of knowledge are assembled and performed within us. His goal is to permit no divisions or exclusions in his account of this "reality," which is none other than the apprehension of nondissociability (or the "immanence") of mind in the world. This is why the problem of *revealed knowledge* becomes the central concern of James's work and the topic of his most stunning proclamations. *Religious experience* becomes a simple cover term for the transitory apprehension of the subject and the world as a single bloc of experience. All religious practice (Hindu/Buddhist, Islamic, Hebraic, Christian), he claims, is rooted in these so-called "mystical" states of transient dissolution and continuity. Central to this category of experience is the component of *feeling*, which endows not only the rote sensory information with its particular value but also its network of connections to what is both prior in, and outside of, the subject (to both its history and the external world).

In the primordial instance – that of the immature fetus – there is yet no ego; in the later reactivations there is a consonance, a resonance, often a powerful intimation of states of being and veracity that lie both before and beyond the primordial bifurcation of the organism. This "place" becomes both a destination for experience and an accompaniment and embellishment of the actually lived present, since the knowledge encountered here cannot be accessed from the familiar default of the discursive intellect. Terms such as *flow* and *optimal experience* are often associated with such states as Abraham Maslow's "peak" experience, Marghanita Laski's "ecstatic," and William James's and James Fadiman's "mystical," to name only a few. As one virtual reality researcher expressed it, the experience is not one of "I know" but "I am."[9]

It is worth stepping back now to underscore that in no sense are we here occupying a magical realm; we remain within an irreducibly material and experiential state of affairs; it is the somatic matter itself that composes and embodies the experience; it is the two seemingly parallel modes – the flow of the subject and the flow of the material environment – that are combined in a dyadic and coupled embrace in which "dancer and the dance" become indistinguishable.

---

8. James's work, universally considered the basis of modern psychology but largely neglected in recent decades, is surging to the fore of attention again today for entirely unexpected reasons. The first reason, I would argue, is to do with the slow emergence into clarity of his concept of "radical empiricism" in relation to his broader cosmology, in which mind, experience, and nature are considered explanatorily indivisible. Of particular importance is James's insistence on the embeddedness of mind in the world and his "coherence theory" of truth that draws on the particulars of the environment in which the meaning and direction of experience are created. The reality of experience and the experience of "reality" are achieved – or assembled – as a working together of multiple streams of sensation as a comprehensive *whole*. The second reason is that this restructuring of the field of experience is highly consonant with contemporary developments in neuroscience (Antonio Damasio and Joseph Ledoux) as well as in the rapidly developing fields of VR, psychoacoustics, and ecological and experiential psychology. For a light but popular account of the latter developments, see Michael Pollan's recent bestseller, *How to Change Your Mind: What the New Science of Psychedelics Teaches Us About Consciousness, Dying, Addiction, Depression, and Transcendence* (New York: Penguin Press, 2018).

9. The formulation is that of Mel Slater of The Event Lab, University of Barcelona.

10. These ideas continue to be adopted and propagated by influential theorists such as Thomas Metzinger, Susan Blackmore, and Andy Clark despite the fact that the "reality model" theory of mind belongs to an outdated computationalist theory of cognition rooted in analytic philosophy (early Hilary Putnam, Jerry Fodor, Max Black) and which narrowly and naively conceives of the mind as a representational machinery for control and action and to establish as "correct" as possible a version of the world in which it operates. As the late neurobiologist Francisco Varela and others have pointed out, this primitive view relies on an unexamined and unaddressed bias of a mind-body and human-environment split, long since replaced now by especially enactionist, functionalist, and ecological, but also selectionist and constructivist, explanation. The best overview of this broad shift is still Francisco Varela, *Connaître: les sciences cognitives, tendences et perspectives* (Paris: Le Seuil, 1989). The best place for the designer to get a grasp of many of these movements and problems is in Deborah Hauptmann and Warren Neidich, *Cognitive Architecture. From Biopolitics to Noopolitics. Architecture and Mind in the Age of Communication and Information* (Rotterdam: 010 Publishers, 2010).

11. Researchers who study ego-dissolution states and their reparative capacities with functional MRI techniques have proposed a variety of different models to explain this shift in internal organization and attention. One, the so-called entropic brain theory, argues that under the effects of certain agents, the brain's attentional state or regime will shift from that of the "default mode network" to its "salience network," and hence temporarily relinquish the filters (entropy suppression) of the (ontogenetically) assembled self on the flow of experience, thus permitting enhanced reconnection with the contents of consciousness (as partly rooted in acquired somatic memory) typically relegated to inaccessible or unconscious realms. See Robin Carhart-Harris, et al., "The entropic brain: a theory of conscious states informed by neuroimaging research with psychedelic drugs," *Frontiers in Human Neuroscience* 8 (03 February 2014); and Robin Carhart-Harris, "The Entropic Brain – revisited," *Neuropharmacology* 142 (November 2018): 167–78.

12. The topic of auditory processing and spatial location is an immense topic and an immensely rich one for the designer and the environmentally oriented thinker to engage. (It is also the central focus of a forthcoming paper on the cognitive ecology of "source.") It is hard to spend much time online without coming across some of the thousands of samples of binaural sound, ASMR, 3D sound, sound baths, audio hacking, acoustic VR, psychoacoustic paradoxes, transmodal perception party tricks, and so on. There is, of course, also a rigorous scientific, anthropological, and aesthetic tradition of research in these mysterious but perennial areas of human practice. Among these is the discovery of what came to be known as the field of acoustic ecology by the soundscape ecologist Bernie Krause. See Bernie Krause, *The Great Animal Orchestra: Finding the Origins of Music in the World's Wild Places* (New York: Little Brown, 2014), 15–16, for a standard but stunning account of transformative expansion through access to the sensible world achieved through the application of focus, deep listening and a simple technical assist. If there is any doubt that the ear achieves, and earns, greater revelation than the eye, see Albert S. Bregman, *Auditory Scene Analysis: The Perceptual Organization of Sound* (Cambridge: MIT Press, 1990).

What concretely and literally does this mean? The foregoing assertion addresses the nature of sentience itself and the deeper, ultimate nature and structure not just of psychic but of physical reality. It is a truism of brain and cognitive science as well as philosophy of mind (or better, of "consciousness studies") that we – any organism – do not directly engage or grasp "reality" outside us, but rather only a so-called representation or model of it and so forth.[10] But this arguably betrays a fundamental misunderstanding of what so-called reality is. It is not a syntactical relation, not a thing to which we bridge; it is not the place where we live, but rather is what we *are*. To understand this, one need simply release the belief in the primacy of thought and vision, both separative modalities that, from the point of view of pure consciousness, are simply acquired technical habits and expressions of the underlying cultural bias itself. Cognition, for example, is comprised not only of thought but also of sensation and feeling, both of which we are able to know *in their brute immediacy* as processes that take place in our bodies, which are themselves firmly embedded in and continuous with the material world. Hence we "know" the contents of sensation and emotion somewhat differently from that of thought, which is abstract even if it is supported in a physical nervous system (and often has powerful somatic components). What is constituted by the intimacy of sensory and emotional knowledge is its direct copula with the physical world, a connection that always subtends the artificial images and maps we create purely for navigational and sorting purposes; even when these connections remain (predominantly) virtual and outside our direct attention, *they are there*. It is these concrete immediacies, in greater propinquity to us than any other of the attributes of consciousness, that we access and incorporate disturbingly and explosively when we exit what Metzinger has called the "ego tunnel."[11] Indeed, we access it routinely, although in attenuated doses, through music listening without fully knowing exactly what we are doing during this near-daily exercise in controlled psychotropy and self-modulation.[12] Aural and olfactory experiences are by their natures, and not only by their different pathways of neural processing (through the limbic system), more integrative, immersive, and internally, and hence emotionally, activating than vision. They retain a great deal of the phenomenology of the "prelapsarian" world before the processes of individuation and differentiation in the first two years of life have resculpted and instrumentalized our overt, public patterns of sentience.

Motion

There is no perception without movement, without change. But the physical world, comprised of matter, often organized and even *living* matter, is never given "as such," but is always in a continuous state of transformation and flux. Furthermore, no gradient in nature is tolerated[13] – this is an inescapable feature of the Second Law – hence matter, energy, information, and form are endlessly shuttled around in order to remove these gradients, and in this process much else will become disturbed and be set into motion in turn. The product of this commotion is an endless variation and innovation, and these continuously engendered "features – and they are perceptual features, affordances, one might say, *in waiting* – alternately produce advantages or disadvantages to the perceiver/user in the environment. These perpetual emergences become topics of interest to the organism, often *vital* interest, to the degree that they augment or impede survival (or enjoyment). These conjunctive engagements with worldly incidents become the components with which the organism endlessly generates, differentiates, and develops itself.[14] It is specifically this dimension of intimate concern or interest that drives and directs what we initially referred to as the integration imperative.

The base material-energetic environment is dynamized by the drive to entropy that continually degrades the world at the global scale (lowers its potential to perform action, work, or form) yet typically upgrades it at the local experiential scale. The living, and especially the encephalized parts of the world – our own species, for example – are similarly dynamized by the inescapable conditions of their sentience: *The contents of consciousness are compelled to pass through it and to evacuate the stage in order to clear the scene for what the world presents next.*

At the most rudimentary level the metabolic dance of consciousness has been evolutionarily imposed, although, as has been suggested throughout, its roots go more deeply into the protohistory of matter as it developed ever new strategies to interact with itself in catalytic networks,[15] ultimately arriving at the capacity to sense both itself and its environment at once and *in relation* – the standard definition of "ordinary consciousness" itself. Ordinary consciousness, however, refers to the consciousness possessed by an individual *as individual*. This is a partial subset of the domain of consciousness itself, which pertains to some aspects of other animal awarenesses (of which we know there are an

13. The graceful phrase "Nature abhors a gradient" was coined by marine geologist Eric Schneider and ecological engineer James Kay. It refers to any relationship of places in the physical world where there exists a difference of some value such as the temperature of a cup of tea (hot) and that of the immediate environment (cool); the "removal of the gradient" is effectuated by the cooling of the tea and the incremental rise in temperature of the surrounding milieu. This is a spontaneous process and represents work, the generation of form. See Eric D. Schneider and Dorion Sagan, *Into the Cool: Energy Flow, Thermodynamics, and Life* (Chicago: University of Chicago Press, 2005).

14. The popular literature on neuroplasticity tends to focus on showy feats of adult malleability and transformation, whereas its overwhelming significance is unquestionably developmental – the maturing organism (in this case, person) continues to tune itself to its environment throughout its "rearing phase," which lasts well over two decades. This process is cardinal only in humans, the only animal born with the vast majority of its functional and structural brain development to take place after birth and outside the womb. This means that our brains, our minds, and our "selves" depend exclusively on the world for their sculpting – we are predominantly "open programs," not "fixed instincts" (as anthropologist Robert Ardrey formulated it). Long before these mechanisms were discovered by contemporary neurobiology, biological (evolutionary) anthropology would refer to "convergent" development, when diverse species that share a habitat and compete for common resources – in other words, *share objects of interest* – begin to internalize one another's genomic makeup. The "social carnivore hypothesis," according to which African canids, felids, and hyenids share more behavioral DNA with hominids than do apes, dates to the 1960s. On brain development as a mutual tuning of inner and outer physical and cultural world, see Bruce E. Wexler, *Brain and Culture: Neurobiology, Ideology, and Social Change* (Cambridge: MIT Press, 2006). On the closed instinct vs. the open program, see Robert Ardrey, *The Territorial Imperative: A Personal Inquiry into the Origins of Property and Nations*, ch. 2 (New York: Atheneum, 1966). On convergent evolution in social carnivores, see George B. Schaller and Gordon R. Lowther, "The Relevance of Carnivore Behavior to the Study of Early Hominids," *Southwest Journal of Anthropology* 25, no. 4 (Winter 1969).

15. See Sanford Kwinter, "Energy, Capture, Life: A Simple Question" in Sanford Kwinter and Kiel Moe, eds., *What Is Energy and How Else Might We Think About It?* (Barcelona: Actar, forthcoming). On auto- and cross-catalysis as candidates for the matrix out of which life arose, see Stuart Kaufmann in *At Home in the Universe: The*

Search for the Laws of Self-Organization and Complexity, ch. 2 (New York: Oxford University Press, 1995).

16. The convention of using the term *ordinary consciousness* comes from James. The tradition of referring to "the hard problem of consciousness" comes from David Chalmers.

17. See, for example, Anil Seth's highly popular TED Talk, "Your Brain Hallucinates Your Conscious Reality." Seth, an avowed mechanist – in itself fair and common enough – demonstrates neither an understanding nor a theory of "hallucination" and appears to use the term primarily to draw popular attention. Although the talk is assembled almost entirely of neuroscience commonplaces in wide circulation for three decades, he does seem to suggest that properly conceived, "the consciousness problem" is a biological issue first and a philosophical one (maybe) second. Anil Seth, TED, April 2017, https://www.ted.com/talks/anil_seth_your_brain_hallucinates_your_conscious_reality.

18. The mathematician Rene Thom modeled and explained perception, as he did every apprehension of form, as a mutual "embryology" because it represents a topological transformation that takes place in both the one who grasps and understands – *percipere*, to seize, capture, take in – as well as in the entity, or in the endlessly transforming "space" or topological neighborhood from which the entity was isolated and grasped. Thom modeled all form events (of which the physical and living worlds are exhaustive examples) as explicable by an array of "capture" morphologies that represent a kind of universal predation algorithm. Each such capture morphology exhibits a two-part structure – a "somatofugal" or emissive phase by which the perceiver abandons its "place" to grasp an outward object, and a "somatotrophic" one through which it incorporates the object in turn. Thom states the psycho-onto-biological problem of consciousness in a chapter heading that reads: "Fundamental Contradiction in Biological Regulation: The Persistence of the Subject and the Periodicity of Actions." The chapter that follows, "From Animal to Man: Thought and Language," explores the universality of the capture morphology and the predation loop in the production of experience and world. See Rene Thom, *Structural Stability and Morphogenesis: An Outline of a General Theory of Models* (Reading: W. A. Benjamin, 1975), 307, for a display of the archetypal morphologies that model the material (energetic, informational) exchanges that drive the psychic and cultural world. When Thom was elaborating his theory of the discontinuous events that make up actual existence, the French philosopher Gilbert Simondon was elaborating his own theory

infinity), possible and contested forms of consciousness such as those of plants and chemico-energetic systems (ecosystems and so forth). But principally it invokes the incontestable existence of states of consciousness available to humans when not constrained by the so-called ego tunnel, as in that of the infant, the psychotic, the enraptured, the meditative, the aurally or ceremonially immersed, etc. The "hard problem," in this sense, is no more than the "ordinary problem."[16]

Furthermore, the impetus to structure cognition through capture of external flux is more general and goes well beyond the commonplace "prediction" criteria that currently figure too prominently in mechanistic neuroscience in the form of the Bayesian and "free energy" (Fristonian) hypotheses.[17]

Hence the two-part categorical demand for consciousness to actively seek and *to move*, to clear and to update, as well as to *integrate*: to expand, embrace, innovate, and connect. Perception is a linking of two processes of individuation: the one in which the perceiver is transformed by its continual expansion through experience and learning, and the other that of the environment itself as it endures the inescapable demand to succumb to the wages of entropy and negentropy (life).[18] Because this impetus neither belongs to us nor presents as *ours* personally but rather as a universal dynamo that is outside of us – and yet in which we are an embedded part – VR and other forms of artificial sensory reception as a category of experience are capable of generating extremely powerful, sometimes disturbing, and sometimes ecstatic states in us.[19] Among the reasons for this, and of capital ontological significance, is the simple fact that *experience is richer than reality itself.*[20]

The reason this might be so has to do with the many processes for which basic analytic neuroscience provides terms but for which the natural world *as given* has provided no concrete correlates. The "binding problem" (the harmonious clumping of attributes into the same unit of experience, as discussed at the beginning of this paper) and Edelman's "reentrant signaling" (and "theory of neuronal group selection") are arguably worked out in Whitehead's discussion of modal ingression and the unity of "actual occasions" that make up the actual physical reality. The principles of "good continuation" and of "amodal completion," according to which the brain spontaneously extends a movement, unfolding, or sequence beyond what is strictly given to the senses (as when pieces or portions of an object or motion are occluded, or missing, either in space or time), are spontaneous of transduction. As stated in the epigraph to this paper, Simondon's metaphysics demonstrate that only a dynamism of perception (knowledge) can capture the dynamism of the physical existent (nature).

19. Among the dozens of "empathy machines" circulating online and in culture at large, and one of the best, is Megan May Daalder's "mirrorbox" (art school thesis) project of 2012. An incredibly simple device that permits two facing people to each experience half of their own face and half of the other's simultaneously, it induces powerful somatic, sensory, and emotional effects. This is but one of many cognitive/reality hacks specific to VR and other related modalities that permit instant shifts and merges of identity almost at the drop of a hat. The mirrorbox was immediately annexed by California tech and neuro labs for study. Among the leading mainstream cognitive researchers using virtual reality to test the lability of human identity and its location are Olaf Blanke, of the Laboratory of Cognitive Neuroscience, Brain-Mind Institute, Center for Neuroprosthetics, Ecole Polytechnique Fédérale de Lausanne, and his sometime collaborator Isabella Pasqualini, of the Atelier de la Conception de l'Espace, at the school of architecture and engineering in Lausanne. Pasqualini is the only architect I know of who holds a PhD in cognitive neuroscience. On the mirrorbox see *Mirrorbox: How Art Became Science*, https://vimeo.com/38138351

20. This is the foundational tenet and conclusion of James's "radical empiricism." But let the language here not mislead: experience itself *is* real.

21. The perceptual psychologist J.J. Gibson argued clearly and strenuously in *The Ecological Approach to Visual Perception* that perception does not register images but rather transformations of the optic array. Because we receive no images, we do not store images and hence nor do we draw on any storage for comparison to fit with incoming stimulus. Perceptual learning consists in attuning one's practice in the world to become ever better at recognizing variants and invariants in the surround as we move and change our relation to them. It is a kind of musical pickup that keeps getting better and more instinctive with practice.

operations of embellishment designed to create a full account of the integrated aspect of the world of which the perceiving subject's sentience is a fully shared common and continuous one. This does not have to render an accurate representation, as, for example, when the apprehension is later revealed to be an erroneous one, illusory or invented, for it in itself to be true. For the perception itself constitutes an adding of value induced by the insistent presence of interest and concern. There is no need to invoke guess projections or prediction algorithms because we have to do here with a metabolic process of combustion (not only of energy potentials in the environment but of informational ones as well) and, through combustion, of transformation.[21] Cognition is an equal opportunity transformer and form giver (the gestaltists understood this and the concepts of Gestalt psychology have found a rich second life in contemporary cognitive science).

Because the world turns over and fluxes, so too does consciousness, not only the sentience and metabolisms of our flesh. But while sentience is linear – it tracks the world and its pertinent movements – consciousness is centrifugal and centripetal. Consciousness is only seemingly oriented around a central "point" – what conventional thought refers to as the self – but in fact exceeds it and hence also eternally flees this false point... when it can. The vehemence and conviction of this perennial flight is different for every individual, partly because it is powerfully and structurally connected to the irreducible uniqueness of what is, and of what has been encountered, spatially outside itself – to the world and other consciousnesses – as well as to a discoverable reality before the personal time of the experiencer existed: the *perinatal reality* that preceded the constitutional differentiation of the subject and the emergence of an organizing ego. This perinatal world of polyvalent sentience presented as an unpartitioned ambient flux – sonic, hydraulic, and rheological, but also endowed with powerful emotional and existential components that will be forever evoked in each reactivation.

The set of physical and noetic phenomena to which we apply the cover term *architecture* – city, environment, world – might, for the above reasons, be better placed alongside the more expansive experiences of cinema (image plus motion) and music (flowing pattern-scape). These forms of shape and structure, because they present within a context of an immersive surround or "ambience," are more recognizably redolent of this initial scaffold of early sentience. If our modern technical sensorium does in fact "cue" early latencies of emergent sensation, this might explain the unusual and mostly unexplained hold these motion phenomena have over us as well as the fact that they are at once universal *and* inexplicable (for example, we do not know where music comes from). However, emerging contemporary concern with the frameless or immersive dimensions of experience – even visual experience such as in the increasingly common virtual reality modality – particularly when accompanied by 3D sound, can generate a fully non-ordinary experience in which one becomes free of the constraints of falsely "located" awareness. Once the tether to the present self is broken, the subsequent self-relocations can give way to an experience of convincing release from a false spiritual, sensory, and aesthetic enclosure, which in turn gives way to rare and profound insights and even to a sense of emancipation from spatiotemporal constraints. When this occurs, there is often a profound feeling that one is (at last) "home," a type of transcendence and *ekstasis* that Greek philosophy referred to as *henosis* – unity, source – which continues to haunt not only philosophy but, more importantly, the entire human encounter with physical reality itself.

Sanford Kwinter is professor of science and design at the Pratt Institute in New York.

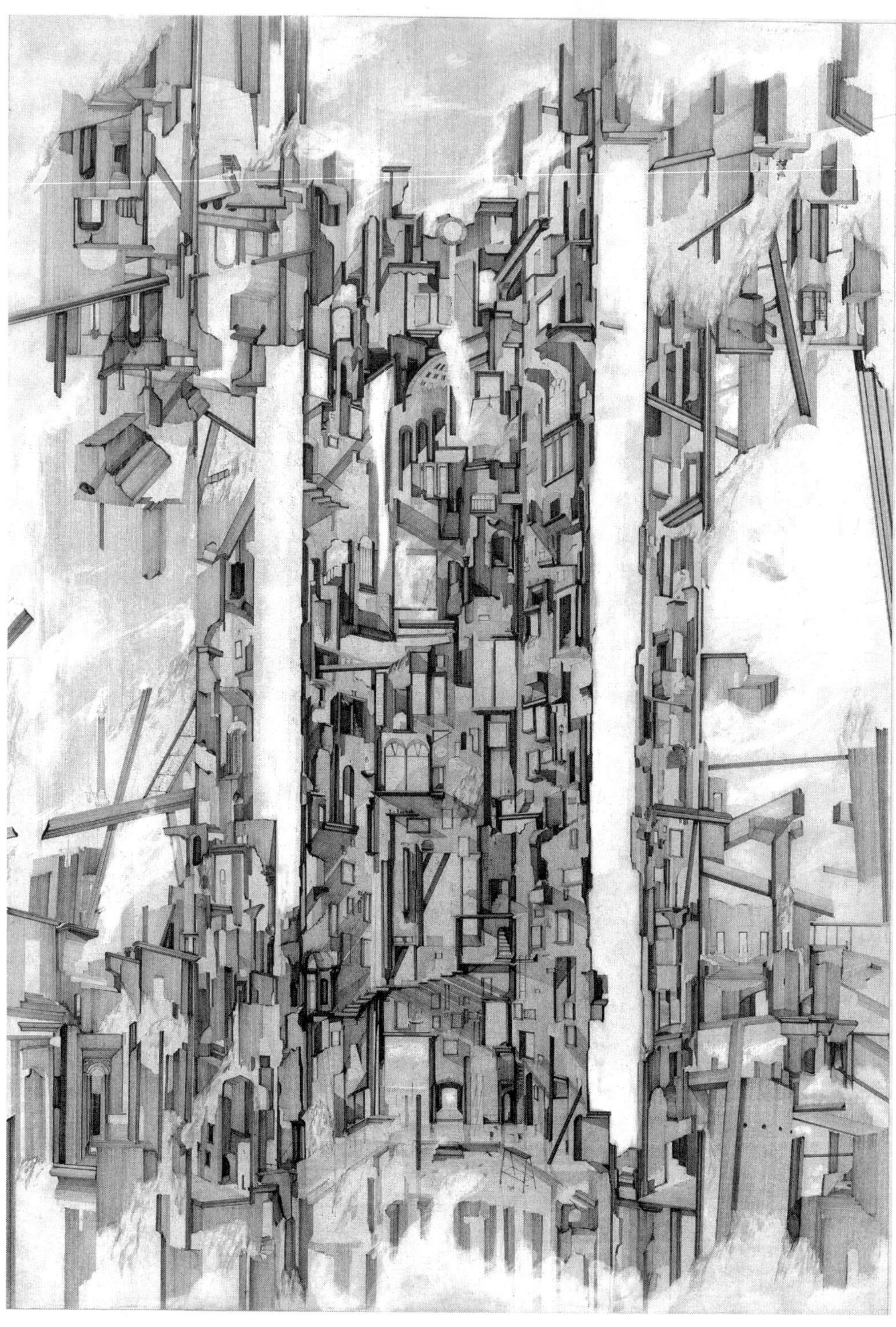

Clement Luk Laurencio, right panel of Memory Palace, Triptych, 2021.
Graphite on paper, 841 by 594 millimeters. Drawing courtesy the architect.